Advice to Young Men

Advice to Young Men

and (incidentally) to

Young Women

in the Middle and Higher Ranks of Life
in a series of Letters addressed to
a Youth, a Bachelor, a Lover, a Husband,
a Father, and a Citizen or a Subject

BY

WILLIAM COBBETT

With a Preface by George Spater

Oxford New York Toronto Melbourne
OXFORD UNIVERSITY PRESS
1980

Oxford University Press, Walton Street, Oxford OX2 6DP

OXFORD LONDON GLASGOW
NEW YORK TORONTO MELBOURNE WELLINGTON
KUALA LUMPUR SINGAPORE JAKARTA HONG KONG TOKYO
DELHI BOMBAY CALCUTTA MADRAS KARACHI
NAIROBI DAR ES SALAAM CAPE TOWN

First edition published 1830
First published as an Oxford University Press paperback 1980
at the suggestion of Jeanne MacKenzie
and simultaneously in a hardback edition

British Library Cataloguing in Publication Data
Cobbett, William
Advice to young men.
1. Conduct of life
I. Title
828'.6'08   BJ1661   80-40083
ISBN 0-19-212212-6
ISBN 0-19-281297-1 Pbk

Printed in Great Britain by
Cox & Wyman Ltd, Reading

CONTENTS

PREFACE

George Spater

WILLIAM COBBETT'S *Advice to Young Men and (incidentally) to Young Women* is his prescription for those who wish to live happy lives. 'Happiness ought to be your great object', Cobbett says almost at the outset, and the words 'happy' and 'happiness' appear throughout the book.

A modern-day reader may find much of it quaint, representing, as it does, the middle class *mores* of a hundred and fifty years ago when women were still regarded, and still wished to be regarded, with reverence, and when their place was still in the home. Quaint also may appear such concepts as patriotism, domestic servants, female chastity and buying goods for cash rather than on credit. Thus *Advice to Young Men* can be read as an interesting historical document, a picture of a society that has passed into oblivion. But beneath its quaintness are some messages of current value. Human nature has, presumably, changed less than social custom, and Cobbett talks about ageless problems that affect the ability of people to live together happily: such subjects as fidelity and jealousy, frowns and loving-kindness. 'Give me the smiling virtues', Cobbett wrote in another place, and it is the smiling virtues that dominate *Advice to Young Men*. The reader who looks for guidance in those areas of living where the fewest practical signposts exist, can find it in this book.

Then there is the literary quality of the work. Cobbett's style was described two hundred years before his time by Montaigne:

The speech that I like is simple and natural speech, the same on paper as on the lips: a succulent, nervous, short, and concise manner of speaking, not dainty and nicely combed so much as vehement and brisk ... difficult rather than tedious, free from affectation, loose, irregular, and bold; every piece to form a body in itself; not in the manner of the professor, the preaching friar or the pleading advocate, but rather soldier-like ...

And Cobbett, a soldier for eight years, was simple, vehement, brisk and bold in his writing. Lord Holland wrote: 'His style was plain and masculine. His perspicuity in statement unrivalled.' Southey said 'there never was a better or more forcible writer'. Spencer Walpole called Cobbett 'the comet of the literary hemisphere, dazzling the world with his brilliancy, perplexing it with his eccentricity, and alarming it with his apparent inflammability'. Cobbett's accounts of learning grammar in an army barracks (p. 47); or the selection of the girl he wanted to marry (pp. 104–6); or the near-betrayal of the girl he had selected (pp. 142–50); or his warding off barking dogs on a hot night in Philadelphia (pp. 160–1), display some of the talents which brought him the widest readership, during his day, of any journalist on either side of the Atlantic. In Britain, according to the rival *Edinburgh Review*, Cobbett had more influence than all the rest of the journalists put together. The scientist and theologian, Joseph Priestley, writing from America, to which he had migrated at the end of the eighteenth century, declared that Cobbett was 'by far the most popular writer in this country'.

Finally, one may read *Advice to Young Men* to see the flashes of superior understanding that character- ized much of this self-educated man's writings. These flashes appear more frequently in his political articles than in this type of homely treatise, but can be found here, mingled with many quirky ideas, in his thoughts on the education of children (pp. 266– 309); on literary fashion (pp. 80–6); and on the study of a country's history (pp. 77–80), from which the following excerpts are taken:

To read of the battles which it has fought, and of the intrigues by which one king or one minister has suc- ceeded another, is very little more profitable than the reading of a romance . . . To come at the true history of a country, you must read its laws: you must read books treating of its usages and customs in former times; and you must particularly inform yourself as to prices of labour and of food.

The author of *Advice to Young Men* was born in 1763, three years after George III came to the throne. Thus he lived, as did George III, through the American revolution, the French revolution, the Napoleonic wars, the British–American war of 1812, and the beginnings of the industrial revolution. George III died in 1820 after a reign of sixty years, for the last ten of which he was incapable of function- ing as monarch. Cobbett died in 1835, living long enough to suffer through the debaucheries of George IV while prince regent and king, but not quite long enough to see the throne occupied by Queen Victoria, who became an exemplar of the precepts expressed by Cobbett in *Advice to Young Men*, which was published in book form in 1830 when the future queen was eleven years old.

Cobbett's father was a yeoman farmer and the owner of a public house in Farnham, Surrey, where Cobbett was born and grew up as a farm boy with virtually no schooling. In 1784, after brief experience as a solicitor's clerk in London, Cobbett joined the army: His Majesty's 54th (or West Norfolk) Regiment of Foot. He rose rapidly from private to corporal, from corporal to sergeant and from sergeant to sergeant-major, serving most of his eight years in New Brunswick where he met his future wife, Anne Reid, the thirteen-year-old daughter of a sergeant in the artillery. When Cobbett returned to England in 1791 to marry Anne, he secured his discharge from the army (enlistment in those days was for life), and immediately brought charges against his superior officers for peculation.

He then discovered that the exposure of corruption among officers was not welcomed by the army hierarchy and, seeing the jeopardy to his former colleagues whom he intended to call as witnesses but who were still within reach of the army's cat-o'-nine-tails, Cobbett fled to France with his bride before the case came to trial. There Cobbett spent several months improving his French, which he had taught himself out of books. The massacre of the Swiss Guard at the Tuileries in August 1792, and the resulting turmoil throughout France, sent Cobbett and his wife on to America. First in Wilmington, and then in Philadelphia, the capital of the new republic, Cobbett taught English to *émigrés* fleeing from the revolution in mainland France and the French West Indies. War between France and Britain had broken out in 1793, and Cobbett, as 'Peter Porcupine', soon became a leading pamphleteer, taking the side of his homeland in opposition to the pro-French sentiment of most Americans, who could hardly forget Britain as the enemy and France as the friend during their war for independence. By 1797 Cobbett was publishing a newspaper, *Porcupine's Gazette*, which shortly attained the largest circulation of any in America. It was a supporter of the federalists under president Washington, and a fierce baiter of the democrats. This led to a series of lawsuits for libel, in one of which Cobbett was assessed ruinous damages in the amount of five thousand dollars. Several months later, in mid-1800, Cobbett with his wife and two small children returned to England. There he was received with open arms by the government for the distinguished service he had voluntarily rendered his country while in America. In 1802 Cobbett began the publication of a weekly paper, the *Political Register*, which was continued until his death in 1835. The *Political Register* was, at first, a supporter of the government, but as Cobbett learned more about the corrupt workings of the political system of the times, became increasingly an enemy of the establishment, an opponent of every type of injustice, a defender of the poor people of England, and the champion of parliamentary reform. In 1810 Cobbett was sentenced to two years in Newgate and fined a thousand pounds for an article condemning the flogging of English militiamen at Ely, under the bayonets of German mercenaries. The jail sentence, which took Cobbett away from a rural life on his farm at Botley, in Hampshire, was a torment to him and wrought an alteration in his character. He had become harder, more irritable, and more determined than ever to bring about change in the corrupt political system. The economic disruption and agitation for reform that followed the end of the Napoleonic wars in 1815 caused a frightened government under the leadership of Lord Liverpool to take severely repressive measures. When the habeas corpus act was suspended in 1817 Cobbett slipped away to America, where he lived for two years on Long Island, twenty miles from New York City. He was a welcomed visitor this time, since he alone, among English journalists, had openly opposed the war between Britain and America that lasted from 1812 to 1814.

In 1819 Cobbett returned again to England, bringing with him the bones of Thomas Paine, which he had removed from an unconsecrated grave in New Rochelle, a suburb of New York City. From 1819 on, Cobbett continued his battle for a broader electoral franchise and a more reasonable distribution of parliamentary representation. He had time, too, to take on all sorts of other activities for what he thought were good causes. In 1820 he supported the indiscreet Queen Caroline against her selfish and dissolute husband, George IV. From 1821 to 1826 he made occasional trips about England on horseback, recording his observations on the scenery, the crops, the people, and the thoughts they evoked regarding the politics of the period. These first appeared in the *Political Register*, and were later made into the book for which Cobbett is now best known, *Rural Rides*, which has been in print almost continuously in the hundred and fifty years since the date of publication. In 1829 Cobbett was finally successful in his long campaign for the removal of most of the disabilities imposed by law on Roman Catholics. *Advice to Young Men* was written in 1829–30, originally appearing in fourteen monthly parts at sixpence per copy. All his life Cobbett had been under the misapprehension that he had been born in 1766, instead of 1763, so that his age, whenever it is given in the book, is understated by three years. Thus when he married he was 29, eleven years older than his bride. The book, typical of all Cobbett's writings, tells us much about himself and, in this case, about his wife and the bringing up of their seven children.

The nineteenth century produced a number of books on how to lead a good and happy life, but *Advice to Young Men* is the only one that has survived. The present edition is the seventh since 1900. Although Cobbett continued to write until his death, *Advice to Young Men* was the last of his great works.

Two further personal triumphs still lay ahead. In 1831 he successfully defended himself against an action brought by the attorney general for seditious libel. And in the following year, after the passage of the first reform act, he was returned to parliament for Oldham in Lancashire. Cobbett was then 69 (he thought himself 66), and no longer the vigorous fighter of his youth. He was not well, either in body or mind. The late hours demanded by the House of Commons provided the finishing touch and, although it was not observed by many of his contemporaries or admitted by himself, he suffered a serious breakdown. He struggled on for several years, quarrelling with his family, writing and speaking with none of his old effectiveness, but refusing to quit, still forcing himself to produce the weekly article for the *Political Register*, until the big man – the lover of everything that represented Old England – was brought down like a great English oak. On 18 June 1835 at his farm at Ash, Surrey, only a few miles from his birthplace, Cobbett died, lonely and penniless. He was 72 years old.

The obituary in *The Times*, after stating that Cobbett was 'in some respects a more extraordinary Englishman than any other of his time', added that he had been 'by far the most voluminous writer that has lived for centuries'. And it is doubtful whether any one since has produced a larger body of work. Selections from his writings that appeared in America between 1794 and 1800, plus some related comments penned after Cobbett's return to England, constitute twelve bound volumes. For the period

1802–35 there were eighty-eight large volumes of the *Political Register*. Many articles from the *Political Register* were republished as books, in addition to the famed *Rural Rides*. Other volumes written by Cobbett that appeared first in pamphlet or book form, rather than in his weekly paper, include:

A Year's Residence in the United States (1818)
A Grammar of the English Language (1818)
Cottage Economy (1821)
The American Gardener (1821)
A French Grammar (1824)
A History of the Protestant Reformation (1824–6)
A Treatise on Cobbett's Corn (1828)
The Woodlands (1828)
The English Gardener (1829)
The Emigrant's Guide (1829)
History of the Regency and Reign of George IV (1830–4)

In even the most banal-sounding of these – Cobbett's *English Grammar*, to name one – will be found examples of surprising inventiveness and humour.

This brief summary of Cobbett's life and works suggests a further, and nearly overlooked, reason for reading *Advice to Young Men* or almost anything else that Cobbett wrote: one meets an extraordinary eccentric whose boastful and often hyperbolic accounts of his own exploits never fail to amuse, who courageously fought for justice and freedom and who, on nearing the end of a long, hard life, was able to say with conviction:

Happiness, or misery, is in the mind. It is the mind that lives; and the length of life ought to be measured by the number and importance of our ideas, and not by the number of our days. Never, therefore, esteem men merely on account of their riches, or their station. Respect goodness, find it where you may. Honour talent wherever you behold it unassociated with vice; but, honour it most when accompanied with exertion, and especially when exerted in the cause of truth and justice; and, above all things, hold it in honour, when it steps forward to protect defenceless innocence against the attacks of powerful guilt. (p. 334)

GEORGE SPATER

COBBETT'S ADVICE
TO YOUNG MEN AND WOMEN

INTRODUCTION

1. IT is the duty, and ought to be the pleasure of age and experience to warn and instruct youth, and to come to the aid of inexperience. When sailors have discovered rocks or breakers, and have had the good luck to escape with life from amidst them, they, unless they be pirates or barbarians as well as sailors, point out the spots for the placing of buoys and of lights, in order that others may not be exposed to the danger which they have so narrowly escaped. What man of common humanity, having, by good luck, missed being engulfed in a quagmire or quicksand, will withhold from his neighbours a knowledge of the peril without which the dangerous spots are not to be approached?

2. The great effect which correct opinions and sound principles, imbibed in early life, together with the good conduct, at that age, which must naturally result from such opinions and principles; the great effect which these have on the whole course of our lives is, and must be, well known to every man of common observation. How many of us, arrived at only forty years, have to repent; nay, which of us has not to repent, or has not had to repent, that he did not, at an earlier age, possess a great stock of knowledge of that kind which has an immediate effect on our personal ease and happiness; that kind

of knowledge upon which the cheerfulness and the harmony of our homes depend!

3. It is to communicate a stock of this sort of knowledge, in particular, that this work is intended; knowledge, indeed, relative to education, to many sciences, to trade, agriculture, horticulture, law, government, and religion; knowledge relating, incidentally, to all these; but, the main object is to furnish that sort of knowledge to the young which but few men acquire until they be old, when it comes too late to be useful.

4. To communicate to others the knowledge that I possess has always been my taste and my delight; and few, who know anything of my progress through life, will be disposed to question my fitness for the task. Talk of rocks and breakers and quagmires and quicksands, who has ever escaped from amidst so many as I have! Thrown (by my own will, indeed) on the wide world at a very early age, not more than eleven or twelve years, without money to support, without friends to advise, and without book-learning to assist me; passing a few years dependent solely on my own labour for my subsistence; then becoming a common soldier, and leading a military life, chiefly in foreign parts, for eight years; quitting that life after really, for me, high promotion, and with, for me, a large sum of money; marrying at an early age, going at once to France to acquire the French language, thence to America; passing eight years there, becoming bookseller and author, and taking a prominent part in all the important discussions of the interesting period from 1793 to 1799, during which

there was, in that country, a continued struggle carried on between the English and the French parties; conducting myself, in the ever-active part which I took in that struggle, in such a way as to call forth marks of unequivocal approbation from the Government at home; returning to England in 1800, resuming my labours here, suffering, during these twenty-nine years, two years of imprisonment, heavy fines, three years' self-banishment to the other side of the Atlantic, and a total breaking of fortune, so as to be left without a bed to lie on, and, during these twenty-nine years of troubles and punishments, writing and publishing, every week of my life, whether in exile or not, eleven weeks only excepted, a periodical paper, containing more or less of matter worthy of public attention; writing and publishing, during the same twenty-nine years, a " Grammar " of the French and another of the English language, a work on the " Economy of the Cottage," a work on " Forest Trees and Woodlands," a work on " Gardening," " An Account of America," a book of " Sermons," a work on the " Corn-plant," a " History of the Protestant Reformation; " all books of great and continued sale, and the last unquestionably the book of greatest circulation in the whole world, the Bible only excepted; having, during these same twenty-nine years of troubles and embarrassments without number, introduced into England the manufacture of straw-plat; also several valuable trees; having introduced, during the same twenty-nine years, the cultivation of the corn-plant, so manifestly valuable as a source of food; having, during the same period, always (whether in exile or not) sustained a shop of some size in London; having, during the whole of the same period, never employed less, on an average, than ten persons, in some capacity or other, exclusive of printers, bookbinders, and others, connected with papers and books; and having, during these twenty-nine years of troubles embarrassments, prisons, fines, and banishments, bred up a family of seven children to man's and woman's state.

5. If such a man be not, after he has survived and accomplished all this, qualified to give advice to young men, no man is qualified for that task. There may have been natural genius: but genius alone, not all the genius in the world, could, without something more, have conducted me through these perils. During these twenty-nine years, I have had for deadly and ever-watchful foes, a Government that has the collecting and distributing of sixty millions of pounds in a year, and also every soul who shares in that distribution. Until very lately, I have had for the far greater part of the time, the whole of the press as my deadly enemy. Yet, at this moment, it will not be pretended that there is another man in the kingdom who has so many cordial friends. For as to the friends of ministers and the great, the friendship is towards the power, the influence; it is, in fact, towards those taxes, of which so many thousands are gaping to get at a share. And, if we could, through so thick a veil, come at the naked fact, we should find the subscription now going on in Dublin for the purpose of erecting a monument in that city, to

commemorate the good recently done, or alleged to be done, to Ireland, by the Duke of Wellington; we should find that the subscribers have the taxes in view; and that, if the monument shall actually be raised, it ought to have selfishness, and not gratitude, engraven on its base. Nearly the same may be said with regard to all the praises that we hear bestowed on men in power. The friendship which is felt towards me is pure and disinterested; it is not founded in any hope that the parties can have, that they can ever profit from professing it; it is founded on the gratitude which they entertain for the good that I have done them; and, of this sort of friendship, and friendship so cordial, no man ever possessed a larger portion.

6. Now, mere genius will not acquire this for a man. There must be something more than genius: there must be industry: there must be perseverance: there must be, before the eyes of the nation, proofs of extraordinary exertion: people must say to themselves, " What wise conduct must there have been in the employing of the time of this man! How sober, how sparing in diet, how early a riser, how little expensive he must have been! " These are the things, and not genius, which have caused my labours to be so incessant and so successful: and, though I do not affect to believe, that every young man, who shall read this work, will become able to perform labours of equal magnitude and importance, I do pretend, that every young man, who will attend to my advice, will become able to perform a great deal more than men generally do perform, whatever may be his

situation in life; and that he will, too, perform it with greater ease and satisfaction than he would, without the advice, be able to perform the smaller portion.

7. I have had from thousands of young men, and men advanced in years also, letters of thanks for the great benefit which they have derived from my labours. Some have thanked me for my " Grammars," some for my " Cottage Economy," others for the " Woodlands " and the " Gardener; " and, in short, for every one of my works have I received letters of thanks from numerous persons, of whom I had never heard before. In many cases I have been told, that, if the parties had had my books to read some years before, the gain to them, whether in time or in other things, would have been very great. Many, and a great many, have told me that, though long at school, and though their parents had paid for their being taught English Grammar, or French, they had, in a short time, learned more from my books, on those subjects, than they had learned, in years. from their teachers. How many gentlemen have thanked me in the strongest terms, for my " Woodlands " and " Gardener," observing (just as Lord Bacon had observed in his time) that they had before seen no books, on these subjects, that they could understand! But, I know not of anything that ever gave me more satisfaction than I derived from the visit of a gentleman of fortune, whom I had never heard of before, and who, about four years ago, came to thank me in person for a complete reformation which had been worked in his son, by the reading of my two sermons on drinking and on gaming.

INTRODUCTION 7

8. I have therefore done, already, a great deal in this way: but, there is still wanting, in a compact form, a body of advice such as that which I now propose to give: and in the giving of which I shall divide my matter as follows: 1. Advice addressed to a Youth; 2. Advice addressed to a Bachelor; 3. Advice addressed to a Lover; 4. To a Husband; 5. To a Father; 6. To a Citizen or Subject.

9. Some persons will smile, and others laugh outright, at the idea of " Cobbett's giving advice for conducting the affairs of love." Yes, but I was once young, and surely I may say with the poet, I forget which of them,

" Though old I am, for ladies' love unfit,
The power of beauty I remember yet."

I forget, indeed, the names of the ladies as completely, pretty nigh, as I do that of the poet; but I remember their influence, and of this influence on the conduct and in the affairs and on the condition of men, I have, and must have, been a witness all my life long. And, when we consider in how great a degree the happiness of all the remainder of a man's life depends, and always must depend, on his taste and judgment in the character of a lover, this may well be considered as the most important period of the whole term of his existence.

10. In my address to the Husband, I shall, of course, introduce advice relative to the important duties of masters and servants; duties of great importance, whether considered as affecting families or as affecting the community. In my address to the

Citizen or Subject, I shall consider all the reciprocal duties of the governors and the governed, and also the duties which man owes to his neighbour. It would be tedious to attempt to lay down rules for conduct exclusively applicable to every distinct calling, profession, and condition of life; but, under the above-described heads, will be conveyed every species of advice of which I deem the utility to be unquestionable.

11. I have thus fully described the nature of my little work, and, before I enter on the first letter, I venture to express a hope, that its good effects will be felt long after its author shall have ceased to exist.

LETTER I

ADVICE TO A YOUTH

12. You are now arrived at that age which the law thinks sufficient to make an oath, taken by you, valid in a court of law. Let us suppose from fourteen to nearly twenty; and reserving, for a future occasion, my remarks on your duty towards parents, let me here offer you my advice as to the means likely to contribute largely towards making you a happy man, useful to all about you, and an honour to those from whom you sprang.

13. Start, I beseech you, with a conviction firmly fixed on your mind, that you have no right to live in this world; that, being of hale body and sound mind, you have no right to any earthly existence, without doing work of some sort or other, unless you have ample fortune whereon to live clear of debt; and, that even in that case, you have no right to breed children to be kept by others, or to be exposed to the chance of being so kept. Start with this conviction thoroughly implanted on your mind. To wish to live on the labour of others is, besides the folly of it, to contemplate a fraud at the least, and, under certain circumstances, to meditate oppression and robbery.

14. I suppose you in the middle rank of life. Happiness ought to be your great object, and it is to

be found only in independence. Turn your back on Whitehall and on Somerset House; leave the Customs and Excise to the feeble and low-minded; look not for success to favour, to partiality, to friendship, or to what is called interest: write it on your heart, that you will depend solely on your own merit and your own exertions. Think not, neither, of any of those situations where gaudy habiliments and sounding titles poorly disguise from the eyes of good sense the mortifications and the heartache of slaves. Answer me not by saying, that these situations "must be filled by somebody;" for, if I were to admit the truth of the proposition, which I do not, it would remain for you to show that they are conducive to happiness, the contrary of which has been proved to me by the observation of a now pretty long life.

15. Indeed, reason tells us that it must be thus: for that which a man owes to favour or to partiality, that same favour or partiality is constantly liable to take from him. He who lives upon anything except his own labour, is incessantly surrounded by rivals: his grand resource is that servility in which he is always liable to be surpassed. He is in daily danger of being out-bidden; his very bread depends upon caprice; and he lives in a state of uncertainty and never-ceasing fear. His is not, indeed, the dog's life, "hunger and idleness;" but it is worse; for it is "idleness with slavery," the latter being the just price of the former. Slaves frequently are well fed and well clad; but slaves dare not speak; they dare not be suspected to think differently from their

masters: hate his acts as much as they may; be he tyrant, be he drunkard, be he fool, or be he all three at once, they must be silent, or, nine times out of ten, affect approbation: though possessing a thousand times his knowledge, they must feign a conviction of his superior understanding; though knowing that it is they who, in fact, do all that he is paid for doing, it is destruction to them to seem as if they thought any portion of the service belonged to them! Far from me be the thought, that any youth who shall read this page would not rather perish than submit to live in a state like this! Such a state is fit only for the refuse of nature; the halt, the half-blind, the un-happy creatures whom nature has marked out for degradation.

16. And how comes it, then, that we see hale and even clever youths voluntarily bending their necks to this slavery; nay, pressing forward in eager rival-ship to assume the yoke that ought to be insupport-able? The cause, and the only cause, is, that the deleterious fashion of the day has created so many artificial wants, and has raised the minds of young men so much above their real rank and state of life, that they look scornfully on the employment, the fare, and the dress, that would become them; and, in order to avoid that state in which they might live free and happy, they become showy slaves.

17. The great source of independence, the French express in a precept of three words, " Vivre de peu," which I have always very much admired. " To live upon little " is the great security against slavery; and this precept extends to dress and other things

besides food and drink. When Doctor Johnson wrote
his Dictionary, he put in the word pensioner thus:—
" Pensioner, a slave of state." After this he himself
became a pensioner! And thus, agreeably to his own
definition, he lived and died "a slave of state!"
What must this man of great genius, and of great
industry, too, have felt at receiving this pension!
Could he be so callous as not to feel a pang upon
seeing his own name placed before his own degrading
definition? And what could induce him to submit to
this? His wants, his artificial wants, his habit of
indulging in the pleasures of the table; his disregard
of the precept " Vivre de peu." This was the cause;
and, be it observed, that indulgences of this sort,
while they tend to make men poor, and expose them
to commit mean acts, tend also to enfeeble the body,
and more especially to cloud and to weaken the mind.

18. When this celebrated author wrote his Dictionary, he had not been debased by luxurious enjoyments: the rich and powerful had not caressed him
into a slave; his writings then bore the stamp of
truth and independence: but, having been debased
by luxury, he who had, while content with plain fare,
been the strenuous advocate of the rights of the
people, became a strenuous advocate for taxation
without representation; and, in a work under the
title of " Taxation no Tyranny," defended, and
greatly assisted to produce, that unjust and bloody
war which finally severed from England that great
country the United States of America, now the most
powerful and dangerous rival that this kingdom ever
had. The statue of Dr. Johnson was the first that

was put into St. Paul's Church! A signal warning to us not to look upon monuments in honour of the dead as a proof of their virtues; for here we see St. Paul's Church holding up to the veneration of posterity a man whose own writings, together with the records of the pension-list, prove him to have been " a slave of state."

19. Endless are the instances of men of bright parts and high spirit having been, by degrees, rendered powerless and despicable, by their imaginary wants. Seldom has there been a man with a fairer prospect of accomplishing great things, and of acquiring lasting renown, than Charles Fox: he had great talents of the most popular sort; the times were singularly favourable to an exertion of them with success; a large part of the nation admired him and were his partisans; he had, as to the great question between him and his rival (Pitt), reason and justice clearly on his side: but he had against him his squandering and luxurious habits: these made him dependent on the rich part of his partisans; made his wisdom subservient to opulent folly or selfishness; deprived his country of all the benefit that it might have derived from his talents; and, finally, sent him to the grave without a single sigh from a people, a great part of whom would, in his earlier years, have wept at his death as at a national calamity.

20. Extravagance in dress, in the haunting of play-houses, in horses, in everything else, is to be avoided, and, in youths and young men, extravagance in dress particularly. This sort of extravagance, this waste of money on the decoration of the body, arises solely

from vanity, and from vanity of the most contemptible sort. It arises from the notion, that all the people
in the street, for instance, will be looking at you as
soon as you walk out; and that they will, in a greater
or less degree, think the better of you on account
of your fine dress. Never was notion more false. All
the sensible people that happen to see you will think
nothing at all about you: those who are filled with
the same vain notion as you are will perceive your
attempt to impose on them, and will despise you
accordingly: rich people will wholly disregard you,
and you will be envied and hated by those who have
the same vanity that you have without the means of
gratifying it. Dress should be suited to your rank
and station: a surgeon or physician should not dress
like a carpenter; but there is no reason why a
tradesman, a merchant's clerk, or clerk of any kind,
or why a shopkeeper, or manufacturer, or even a
merchant; no reason at all why any of these should
dress in an expensive manner. It is a great mistake
to suppose that they derive any advantage from ex-
terior decoration. Men are estimated by other men
according to their capacity and willingness to be in
some way or other useful; and though, with the
foolish and vain part of women, fine clothes frequently do something, yet the greater part of the sex
are much too penetrating to draw their conclusions
solely from the outside show of a man: they look
deeper, and find other criterions whereby to judge.
And, after all, if the fine clothes obtain you a wife,
will they bring you, in that wife, frugality, good
sense, and that sort of attachment that is likely to be

lasting? Natural beauty of person is quite another thing: this always has, it always will and must have, some weight even with men, and great weight with women. But this does not want to be set off by expensive clothes. Female eyes are, in such cases, very sharp; they can discover beauty though half hidden by beard, and even by dirt, and surrounded by rags: and, take this as a secret worth half a fortune to you, that women, however personally vain they may be themselves, despise personal vanity in men.

21. Let your dress be as cheap as may be without shabbiness; think more about the colour of your shirt than about the gloss or texture of your coat; be always as clean as your occupation will, without inconvenience, permit; but never, no, not for one moment, believe, that any human being, with sense in his skull, will love or respect you on account of your fine or costly clothes. A great misfortune of the present day is, that every one is, in his own estimate, raised above his real state of life; every one seems to think himself entitled, if not to title and great estate, at least to live without work. This mischievous, this most destructive, way of thinking has, indeed, been produced, like almost all other evils, by the Acts of our Septennial and Unreformed Parliament. That body, by its Acts, has caused an enormous debt to be created, and, in consequence, a prodigious sum to be raised annually in taxes. It has caused, by these means, a race of loan-mongers and stock-jobbers to arise. These carry on a species of gaming, by which some make fortunes in a day, and others, in a day, become beggars. The unfortunate gamesters, like the

purchasers of blanks in a lottery, are never heard of;
but the fortunate ones become the companions for
lords, and some of them lords themselves. We have,
within these few years, seen many of these gamesters
get fortunes of a quarter of a million in a few days,
and then we have heard them, though notoriously
amongst the lowest and basest of human creatures,
called " honourable gentlemen! " In such a state of
things who is to expect patient industry, laborious
study, frugality and care; who, in such a state of
things, is to expect these to be employed in pursuit
of that competence which it is the laudable wish of
all men to secure? Not long ago a man, who had
served his time to a tradesman in London, became,
instead of pursuing his trade, a stock-jobber, or
gambler; and, in about two years, drove his coach-
and-four, had his town house and country house, and
visited, and was visited by, peers of the highest rank!
A fellow-apprentice of this lucky gambler, though a
tradesman in excellent business, seeing no earthly
reason why he should not have his coach-and-four
also, turned his stock in trade into a stake for the
'Change; but, alas! at the end of a few months,
instead of being in a coach-and-four, he was in the
Gazette.

22. This is one instance out of hundreds of
thousands; not, indeed, exactly of the same description, but all arising from the same copious source.
The words speculate and speculation have been
substituted for gamble and gambling. The hateful-
ness of the pursuit is thus taken away; and, while
taxes to the amount of more than double the whole

of the rental of the kingdom; while these cause such crowds of idlers, every one of whom calls himself a gentleman, and avoids the appearance of working for his bread; while this is the case, who is to wonder, that a great part of the youth of this country, knowing themselves to be as good, as learned, and as well-bred as these gentlemen; who is to wonder that they think that they also ought to be considered as gentlemen? Then, the late war (also the work of the Septennial Parliament) has left us, amongst its many legacies, such swarms of titled men and women; such swarms of " Sirs " and their " Ladies; " men and women who, only the other day, were the fellow-apprentices, fellow-tradesmen's or farmer's sons and daughters, or, indeed, the fellow-servants of those who are now in these several states of life; the late Septennial Parliament has left us such swarms of these, that it is no wonder that the heads of young people are turned, and that they are ashamed of that state of life to act their part well in which ought to be their delight.

23. But, though the cause of the evil is in Acts of the Septennial Parliament; though this universal desire in people to be thought to be above their station; though this arises from such Acts; and, though it is no wonder that young men are thus turned away from patient study and labour; though these things be undoubted, they form no reason why I should not warn you against becoming a victim to this national scourge. For, in spite of every art made use of to avoid labour, the taxes will, after all, maintain only so many idlers. We cannot all be " knights "

and " gentlemen: " there must be a large part of us, after all, to make and mend clothes and houses, and carry on trade and commerce, and in spite of all that we can do, the far greater part of us must actually work at something; for, unless we can get at some of the taxes, we fall under the sentence of Holy Writ, " He who will not work shall not eat." Yet, so strong is the propensity to be thought " gentlemen; " so general is the desire amongst the youth of this formerly laborious and unassuming nation; a nation famed for its pursuit of wealth through the channels of patience, punctuality, and integrity; a nation famed for its love of solid acquisitions and qualities, and its hatred of everything showy and false; so general is this really fraudulent desire amongst the youth of this now " speculating " nation, that thousands upon thousands of them are, at this moment, in a state of half-starvation, not so much because they are too lazy to earn their bread, as because they are too proud! And what are the consequences? Such a youth remains or becomes a burden to his parents, of whom he ought to be the comfort, if not the support. Always aspiring to something higher than he can reach, his life is a life of disappointment and of shame. If marriage befall him, it is a real affliction, involving others as well as himself. His lot is a thousand times worse than that of the common labouring pauper. Nineteen times out of twenty a premature death awaits him: and, alas! how numerous are the cases in which that death is most miserable, not to say ignominious! Stupid pride is one of the symptoms of madness. Of the two madmen mentioned in " Don Quixote," one thought himself Neptune, and the other Jupiter. Shakespeare agrees with Cervantes; for Mad Tom, in " King Lear," being asked who he is, answers, " I am a tailor run mad with pride." How many have we heard of, who claimed relationship with noblemen and kings; while of not a few each has thought himself the Son of God! To the public journals, and to the observations of every one, nay, to the " county lunatic asylums " (things never heard of in England till now), I appeal for the fact of the vast and hideous increase of madness in this country; and, within these very few years, how many scores of young men, who, if their minds had been unperverted by the gambling principles of the day, had a probably long and happy life before them; who had talent, personal endowments, love of parents, love of friends, admiration of large circles; who had, in short, everything to make life desirable, and who, from mortified pride, founded on false pretensions, have put an end to their own existence!

24. As to drunkenness and gluttony, generally so called, these are vices so nasty and beastly, that I deem any one capable of indulging in them to be wholly unworthy of my advice; and, if any youth unhappily initiated in these odious and debasing vices should happen to read what I am now writing, I refer him to the command of God, conveyed to the Israelites by Moses, in Deuteronomy, chap. xxi. The father and mother are to take the bad son " and bring him to the elders of the city; and they shall say to the elders, This our son will not obey our

voice: he is a glutton and a drunkard. And all the men of the city shall stone him with stones, that he die." I refer downright beastly gluttons and drunkards to this; but indulgence short, far short, of this gross and really nasty drunkenness and gluttony is to be deprecated, and that, too, with the more earnestness, because it is too often looked upon as being no crime at all, and as having nothing blamable in it: nay, there are many persons who pride themselves on their refined taste in matters connected with eating and drinking: so far from being ashamed of employing their thoughts on the subject, it is their boast that they do it. St. Gregory, one of the Christian fathers, says: " It is not the quantity or the quality of the meat or drink, but the love of it, that is condemned; " that is to say, the indulgence beyond the absolute demands of nature; the hankering after it; the neglect of some duty or other for the sake of the enjoyments of the table.

25. This love of what are called " good eating and drinking," if very unamiable in grown-up persons, is perfectly hateful in a youth; and, if he indulge in the propensity, he is already half ruined. To warn you against acts of fraud, robbery, and violence, is not my province; that is the business of those who make and administer the law. I am not talking to you against acts which the jailer and the hangman punish; nor against those moral offences which all men condemn; but against indulgences, which, by men in general, are deemed not only harmless, but meritorious; but which the observation of my whole life has taught me to regard as destructive to human happiness, and

against which all ought to be cautioned, even in their boyish days. I have been a great observer, and I can truly say, that I have never known a man " fond of good eating and drinking," as it is called; that I have never known such a man (and hundreds I have known) who was worthy of respect.

26. Such indulgences are, in the first place, very expensive. The materials are costly, and the preparations still more so. What a monstrous thing, that in order to satisfy the appetite of a man, there must be a person or two at work every day! More fuel, culinary implements, kitchen-room; what! all these merely to tickle the palate of four or five people, and especially people who can hardly pay their way! And, then, the loss of time: the time spent in pleasing the palate: it is truly horrible to behold the people who ought to be at work, sitting at the three meals, not less than three of the about fourteen hours that they are out of their beds! A youth, habituated to this sort of indulgence, cannot be valuable to any employer. Such a youth cannot be deprived of his table-enjoyments on any account; his eating and drinking form the momentous concern of his life; if business interfere with that, the business must give way. A young man, some years ago, offered himself to me, on a particular occasion, as an amanuensis, for which he appeared to be perfectly qualified. The terms were settled, and I, who wanted the job despatched, requested him to sit down, and begin; but he, looking out of the window, whence he could see the church clock, said, somewhat hastily, " I cannot stop now, sir; I must go to dinner." " Oh! " said I, " you must

go to dinner, must you! Let the dinner, which you must wait upon to-day have your constant services, then, for you and I shall never agree." He had told me that he was in great distress for want of employment; and yet, when relief was there before his eyes, he could forego it for the sake of getting at his eating and drinking three or four hours, perhaps, sooner than I should have thought it right for him to leave off work. Such a person cannot be sent from home, except at certain times; he must be near the kitchen at three fixed hours of the day; if he be absent more than four or five hours, he is ill-treated. In short, a youth thus pampered is worth nothing as a person to be employed in business.

27. And, as to friends and acquaintances; they will say nothing to you; they will offer you indulgences under their roofs; but the more ready you are to accept of their offers, and, in fact, the better taste you discover, the less they will like you, and the sooner they will find means of shaking you off; for, besides the cost which you occasion them, people do not like to have critics sitting in judgment on their bottles and dishes. Water-drinkers are universally laughed at; but, it has always seemed to me that they are amongst the most welcome of guests, and that, too, though the host be by no means of a niggardly turn. The truth is, they give no trouble; they occasion no anxiety to please them; they are sure not to make their sittings inconveniently long; and, which is the great thing of all, their example teaches moderation to the rest of the company. Your notorious " lovers of good cheer " are, on the contrary, not to be invited

without due reflection—to entertain one of them is a serious business; and as people are not apt voluntarily to undertake such pieces of business, the well-known " lovers of good eating and drinking " are left, very generally, to enjoy it by themselves, and at their own expense.

28. But, all other considerations aside, health, the most valuable of all earthly possessions, and without which all the rest are worth nothing, bids us, not only to refrain from excess in eating and drinking, but bids us to stop short of what might be indulged in without any apparent impropriety. The words of Ecclesiasticus ought to be read once a-week by every young person in the world, and particularly by the young people of this country at this time. " Eat modestly that which is set before thee, and devour not, lest thou be hated. When thou sittest amongst many, reach not thine hand out first of all. How little is sufficient for man well taught! A wholesome sleep cometh of a temperate belly. Such a man riseth up in the morning, and is well at ease with himself. Be not too hasty of meats; for excess of meats bringeth sickness, and choleric disease cometh of gluttony. By surfeit have many perished, and he that dieteth himself prolongeth his life. Show not thy valiantness in wine; for wine hath destroyed many. Wine measurably taken, and in season, bringeth gladness and cheerfulness of mind; but drinking with excess maketh bitterness of mind, brawlings and scoldings." How true are these words! How well worthy of a constant place in our memories! Yet what pains have been taken to apologize for a life contrary to these

precepts! And, good God! what punishment can be too great, what mark of infamy sufficiently signal, for those pernicious villains of talent who have employed that talent in the composition of Bacchanalian songs; that is to say, pieces of fine captivating writing in praise of one of the most odious and destructive vices in the black catalogue of human depravity.

29. In the passage which I have just quoted from chap. xxxi. of Ecclesiasticus, it is said that " wine measurably taken, and in season," is a proper thing. This, and other such passages in the Old Testament, have given a handle to drunkards, and to extravagant people, to insist, that God intended that wine should be commonly drunk. No doubt of that. But, then, He could intend this only in countries in which He had given wine, and to which He had given no cheaper drink except water. If it be said, as it truly may, that, by the means of the sea and the winds, He has given wine to all countries, I answer that this gift is of no use to us now, because our Government steps in between the sea and the winds and us. Formerly, indeed, the case was different: and, here I am about to give you, incidentally, a piece of historical knowledge, which you will not have acquired from Hume, Goldsmith, or any other of the romancers called historians. Before that unfortunate event, the Protestant Reformation, as it is called, took place, the price of red wine, in England, was fourpence a gallon, Winchester measure; and of white wine, sixpence a gallon. At the same time the pay of a labouring man per day, as fixed by law, was fourpence. Now, when a labouring man could

earn four quarts of good wine in a day, it was doubtless allowable, even in England, for people in the
middle rank of life to drink wine rather commonly;
and, therefore, in those happy days of England, these
passages of Scripture were applicable enough. But,
now, when we have got a Protestant Government,
which, by the taxes which it makes people pay to it,
causes the eighth part of a gallon of wine to cost
more than the pay of a labouring man for a day; now,
this passage of Scripture is not applicable to us.
There is no " season " in which we can take wine
without ruining ourselves, however " measurably "
we may take it; and I beg you to regard as perverters
of Scripture and as seducers of youth, all those who
cite passages like that above cited, in justification of,
or as an apology for, the practice of wine-drinking in
England.

30. I beseech you to look again and again at, and
to remember every word of, the passage which I have
just quoted from the book of Ecclesiasticus. How
completely have been, and are, its words verified by
my experience and in my person! How little of eating
and drinking is sufficient for me! How wholesome is
my sleep! How early do I rise; and how " well at
ease " am I " with myself! " I should not have
deserved such blessings, if I had withheld from my
neighbours a knowledge of the means by which they
were obtained; and, therefore, this knowledge I have
been in the constant habit of communicating. When
one gives a dinner to a company, it is an extraordinary
affair, and is intended, by sensible men, for purposes
other than those of eating and drinking. But in

general, in the everyday life, despicable are those who suffer any part of their happiness to depend upon what they have to eat or to drink, provided they have a sufficiency of wholesome food; despicable is the man, and worse than despicable is the youth, that would make any sacrifice, however small, whether of money or of time, or of anything else, in order to secure a dinner different from that which he would have had without such sacrifice. Who, what man, ever performed a greater quantity of labour than I have performed? What man ever did so much? Now, in a great measure, I owe my capability to perform this labour to my disregard of dainties. Being shut up two years in Newgate, with a fine on my head of a thousand pounds to the King, for having expressed my indignation at the flogging of Englishmen under a guard of German bayonets, I ate, during the one whole year, one mutton-chop every day. Being once in town, with one son (then a little boy) and a clerk, while my family was in the country, I had during some weeks nothing but legs of mutton; first day, leg of mutton boiled or roasted; second, cold; third, hashed; then, leg of mutton boiled; and so on. When I have been by myself, or nearly so, I have always proceeded thus: given directions for having every day the same thing, or alternately as above, and every day, exactly at the same hour, so as to prevent the necessity of any talk about the matter. I am certain that, upon an average, I have not, during my life, spent more than thirty-five minutes a-day at table, including all the meals of the day. I like, and I take care to have, good and clean victuals: but, if wholesome and clean, that is enough. If I find it, by chance, too coarse for my appetite, I put the food aside, or let somebody do it, and leave the appetite to gather keenness. But the great security of all is, to eat little, and to drink nothing that intoxicates. He that eats till he is full is little better than a beast; and he that drinks till he is drunk is quite a beast.

31. Before I dismiss this affair of eating and drinking, let me beseech you to resolve to free yourselves from the slavery of the tea and coffee and other slop-kettle, if, unhappily, you have been bred up in such slavery. Experience has taught me that those slops are injurious to health: until I left them off (having taken to them at the age of 26), even my habits of sobriety, moderate eating, early rising; even these were not, until I left off the slops, sufficient to give me that complete health which I have since had. I pretend not to be a " doctor; " but, I assert, that to pour regularly, every day, a pint or two of warm liquid matter down the throat, whether under the name of tea, coffee, soup, grog, or whatever else, is greatly injurious to health. However, at present, what I have to represent to you is the great deduction which the use of these slops makes from your power of being useful, and also from your power to husband your income, whatever it may be, and from whatever source arising. I am to suppose you to be desirous to become a clever and a useful man; a man to be, if not admired and revered, at least to be respected. In order to merit respect beyond that which is due to very common men, you must do something more than very common men; and I am now going to show

you how your course must be impeded by the use of the slops.

32. If the women exclaim, " Nonsense! come and take a cup," take it for that once; but hear what I have to say. In answer to my representation regarding the waste of time which is occasioned by the slops, it has been said, that let what may be the nature of the food, there must be time for taking it. Not so much time, however, to eat a bit of meat or cheese or butter with a bit of bread. But, these may be eaten in a shop, a warehouse, a factory, far from any fire, and even in a carriage on the road. The slops absolutely demand fire and a congregation; so that, be your business what it may; be you shopkeeper, farmer, drover, sportsman, traveller; to the slop-board you must come; you must wait for its assembling, or start from home without your breakfast; and, being used to the warm liquid, you feel out of order for the want of it. If the slops were in fashion amongst ploughmen and carters, we must all be starved, for the food could never be raised. The mechanics are half-ruined by them. Many of them are become poor, enervated creatures; and chiefly from this cause. But is the positive cost nothing? At boarding-schools an additional price is given on account of the tea-slops. Suppose you to be a clerk, in hired lodgings, and going to your counting-house at nine o'clock. You get your dinner, perhaps, near to the scene of your work; but how are you to have the breakfast slops without a servant? Perhaps you find a lodging just to suit you, but the house is occupied by people who keep no servants, and you want a servant

to light a fire, and get the slop ready. You could get
this lodging for several shillings a-week less than
another at the next door; but there they keep a
servant, who will " get you your breakfast," and
preserve you, benevolent creature as she is, from the
cruel necessity of going to the cupboard and cutting
off a slice of meat or cheese and a bit of bread. She
will, most likely, toast your bread for you too, and
melt your butter; and then muffle you up, in winter,
and send you out almost swaddled. Really such a
thing can hardly be expected ever to become a man.
You are weak; you have delicate health; you are
" bilious! " Why, my good fellow, it is these very
slops that make you weak and bilious! And, indeed,
the poverty, the real poverty, that they and their
concomitants bring on you, greatly assists, in more
ways than one, in producing your " delicate health."

33. So much for indulgences in eating, drinking,
and dress. Next, as to amusements. It is recorded of
the famous Alfred, that he devoted eight hours of the
twenty-four to labour, eight to rest, and eight to
recreation. He was, however, a king, and could be
thinking during the eight hours of recreation. It is
certain, that there ought to be hours of recreation,
and I do not know that eight are too many; but then
observe, those hours ought to be well chosen, and
the sort of recreation ought to be attended to. It
ought to be such as is at once innocent in itself and
in its tendency, and not injurious to health. The
sports of the field are the best of all, because they are
conducive to health, because they are enjoyed by
daylight, and because they demand early rising. The

nearer that other amusements approach to these, the
better they are. A town life, which many persons are
compelled, by the nature of their calling, to lead,
precludes the possibility of pursuing amusements of
this description to any very considerable extent; and
young men in towns are, generally speaking, compelled to choose between books on the one hand, or
gaming and the playhouse on the other. Dancing is at
once rational and healthful: it gives animal spirits:
it is the natural amusement of young people, and
such it has been from the days of Moses: it is enjoyed in numerous companies: it makes the parties
to be pleased with themselves and with all about
them; it has no tendency to excite base and malignant
feelings; and none but the most grovelling and hateful
tyranny, or the most stupid and despicable fanaticism,
ever raised its voice against it. The bad modern
habits of England have created one inconvenience
attending the enjoyment of this healthy and innocent
pastime; namely, late hours, which are at once injurious to the health, and destructive of order and of
industry. In other countries people dance by daylight. Here they do not; and, therefore, you must, in
this respect, submit to the custom, though not without robbing the dancing night of as many hours as
you can.

34. As to gaming, it is always criminal either in
itself or in its tendency. The basis of it is covetous-
ness; a desire to take from others something, for
which you have given, and intend to give, no equiva-
lent. No gambler was ever yet a happy man, and very
few gamblers have escaped being miserable; and,

observe, to game for nothing is still gaming, and naturally leads to gaming for something. It is sacrificing time, and that, too, for the worst of purposes. I have kept house for nearly forty years; I have reared a family; I have entertained as many friends as most people; and I have never had cards, dice, a chess-board, nor any implement of gaming, under my roof. The hours that young men spend in this way are hours murdered; precious hours that ought to be spent either in reading, or in writing, or in rest, preparatory to the duties of the dawn. Though I do not agree with the base and nauseous flatterers, who now declare the army to be the best school for statesmen, it is certainly a school in which to learn experimentally many useful lessons; and, in this school I learned, that men, fond of gaming, are very rarely, if ever, trustworthy. I have known many a clever man rejected in the way of promotion only because he was addicted to gaming. Men, in that state of life, cannot ruin themselves by gaming, for they possess no fortune, nor money; but the taste for gaming is always regarded as an indication of a radically bad disposition; and I can truly say, that I never in my whole life knew a man, fond of gaming, who was not, in some way or other, a person unworthy of confidence. This vice creeps on by very slow degrees, till, at last, it becomes an ungovernable passion, swallowing up every good and kind feeling of the heart. The gambler, as portrayed by Regnard, in a comedy, the translation of which into English resembles the original much about as nearly as Sir J. Graham's plagiarisms resembled the Registers on which they had been committed, is a fine instance of the contempt and scorn to which gaming, at last, reduces its votaries; but, if any young man be engaged in this fatal career, and be not yet wholly lost, let him behold Hogarth's gambler just when he has made his last throw, and when disappointment has bereft him of his senses. If, after this sight, he remain obdurate, he is doomed to be a disgrace to his name.

35. The theatre may be a source not only of amusement, but also of instruction; but, as things now are in this country, what, that is not bad, is to be learned in this school? In the first place, not a word is allowed to be uttered on the stage which has not been previously approved of by the Lord Chamberlain; that is to say, by a person appointed by the Ministry, who, at his pleasure, allows, or disallows, of any piece, or any words in a piece, submitted to his inspection. In short, those who go to playhouses pay their money to hear uttered such words as the Government approve of, and no others. It is now just twenty-six years since I first well understood how this matter was managed; and, from that moment to this, I have never been in an English playhouse. Besides this, the meanness, the abject servility of the players, and the slavish conduct of the audience, are sufficient to corrupt and debase the heart of any young man who is a frequent beholder of them. Homage is here paid to every one clothed with power, be he who or what he may; real virtue and public spirit are subjects of ridicule; and mock sentiment and mock liberality and mock loyalty are applauded to the skies.

36. " Show me a man's companions," says the proverb, " and I will tell you what the man is; " and this is, and must be, true; because all men seek the society of those who think and act somewhat like themselves; sober men will not associate with drunkards, frugal men will not like spendthrifts, and the orderly and decent shun the noisy, the disorderly, and the debauched. It is for the very vulgar to herd together as singers, ringers, and smokers; but there is a class rather higher still more blamable; I mean the tavern-hunters, the gay companions who herd together to do little but talk, and who are so fond of talk that they go from home to get at it. The conversation amongst such persons has nothing of instruction in it, and is generally of a vicious tendency. Young people naturally and commendably seek the society of those of their own age; but, be careful in choosing your companions; and lay this down as a rule never to be departed from, that no youth, nor man, ought to be called your friend who is addicted to indecent talk, or who is fond of the society of prostitutes. Either of these argues a depraved taste, and even a depraved heart; an absence of all principle and of all trustworthiness; and I have remarked it all my life long, that young men addicted to these vices never succeed in the end, whatever advantages they may have, whether in fortune or in talent. Fond mothers and fathers are but too apt to be over-lenient to such offenders; and as long as youth lasts and fortune smiles, the punishment is deferred; but it comes at last; it is sure to come; and the gay and dissolute youth is a dejected and miserable man.

After the early part of a life spent in illicit indulgences, a man is unworthy of being the husband of a virtuous woman; and, if he have anything like justice in him, how is he to reprove, in his children, vices in which he himself so long indulged? These vices of youth are varnished over by the saying, that there must be time for " sowing the wild oats," and that " wildest colts make the best horses." These figurative oats are, however, generally like the literal ones; they are never to be eradicated from the soil; and as to the colts, wildness in them is an indication of high animal spirit, having nothing at all to do with the mind, which is invariably debilitated and debased by profligate indulgences. Yet this miserable piece of sophistry, the offspring of parental weakness, is in constant use, to the incalculable injury of the rising generation. What so amiable as a steady, trustworthy boy? He is of real use at an early age: he can be trusted far out of the sight of parent or employer, while the " pickle," as the poor fond parents call the profligate, is a great deal worse than useless, because there must be some one to see that he does no harm. If you have to choose, choose companions of your own rank in life as nearly as may be; but, at any rate, none to whom you acknowledge inferiority; for, slavery is too soon learned; and, if the mind be bowed down in the youth, it will seldom rise up in the man. In the schools of those best of teachers, the Jesuits, there is a perfect equality as to rank in life; the boy, who enters there, leaves all family pride behind him: intrinsic merit alone is the standard of preference; and the masters are so scrupulous upon this head, that they do not suffer one scholar, of whatever rank, to have more money to spend than the poorest. These wise men know well the mischiefs that must arise from inequality of pecuniary means amongst their scholars: they know how injurious it would be to learning, if deference were, by the learned, paid to the dunce; and they, therefore, take the most effectual means to prevent it. Hence, amongst other causes, it is, that the scholars have, ever since the existence of their Order, been the most celebrated for learning of any men in the world.

37. In your manners be neither boorish nor blunt, but even these are preferable to simpering and crawling. I wish every English youth could see those of the United States of America; always civil, never servile. Be obedient, where obedience is due; for it is no act of meanness, and no indication of want of spirit, to yield implicit and ready obedience to those who have a right to demand it at your hands. In this respect England has been, and I hope always will be, an example to the whole world. To this habit of willing and prompt obedience in apprentices, in servants, in all inferiors in station, she owes, in a great measure, her multitudes of matchless merchants, tradesmen, and workmen of every description, and also the achievements of her armies and navies. It is no disgrace, but the contrary, to obey, cheerfully, lawful and just commands. None are so saucy and disobedient as slaves; and, when you come to read history, you will find that in proportion as nations have been free has been their reverence for the laws. But, there is a wide difference between lawful and

cheerful obedience, and that servility which repre-
sents people as laying petitions " at the king's feet,"
which makes us imagine that we behold the suppli-
cants actually crawling upon their bellies. There is
something so abject in this expression; there is such
horrible self-abasement in it, that I hope that every
youth, who shall read this, will hold in detestation
the reptiles who make use of it. In all other countries,
the lowest individual can put a petition into the
hands of the chief magistrate, be he king or emperor:
let us hope, that the time will yet come when
Englishmen will be able to do the same. In the
meanwhile I beg you to despise these worse than
pagan parasites.

38. Hitherto I have addressed you chiefly relative
to things to be avoided; let me now turn to the things
which you ought to do. And, first of all, the husbanding of your time. The respect that you will receive, the
real and sincere respect, will depend entirely on what
you are able to do. If you be rich, you may purchase
what is called respect; but it is not worth having.
To obtain respect worth possessing you must, as I
observed before, do more than the common run of
men in your state of life; and, to be enabled to do
this, you must manage well your time; and, to
manage it well, you must have as much of the daylight and as little of the candle-light as is consistent
with the due discharge of your duties. When people
get into the habit of sitting up merely for the purpose
of talking, it is no easy matter to break themselves off
it; and if they do not go to bed early, they cannot rise
early. Young people require more sleep than those

that are grown up: there must be the number of hours, and that number cannot well be, on an average, less than eight; and if it be more in winter time it is all the better; for an hour in bed is better than an hour spent over fire and candle in an idle gossip. People never should sit talking till they do not know what to talk about. It is said by the country-people that one hour's sleep before midnight is worth more than two are worth after midnight; and this I believe to be a fact; but it is useless to go to bed early, and even to rise early, if the time be not well employed after rising. In general half the morning is loitered away, the party being in a sort of half-dressed half-naked state; out of bed, indeed, but still in a sort of bedding. Those who first invented morning-gowns and slippers could have very little else to do. These things are very suitable to those who have had fortunes gained for them by others; very suitable to those who have nothing to do, and who merely live for the purpose of assisting to consume the produce of the earth; but he who has his bread to earn, or who means to be worthy of respect on account of his labours, has no business with morning-gown and slippers. In short, be your business or calling what it may, dress at once for the day; and learn to do it as quickly as possible. A looking-glass is a piece of furniture a great deal worse than useless. Looking at the face will not alter its shape or its colour; and, perhaps, of all wasted time, none is so foolishly wasted, as that which is employed in surveying one's own face. Nothing can be of little importance if one be compelled to attend to it every day of our lives;

if we shaved but once a year, or once a month, the execution of the thing would be hardly worth naming; but this is a piece of work that must be done once every day; and as it may cost only about five minutes of time, and may be, and frequently is, made to cost thirty, or even fifty minutes; and as only fifteen minutes make about a fifty-eighth part of the hours of our average daylight, this being the case, this is a matter or real importance. I once heard Sir John Sinclair ask Mr. Cochrane Johnstone whether he meaned to have a son of his (then a little boy) taught Latin. " No," said Mr. Johnstone, " but I mean to do something a great deal better for him." " What is that? " said Sir John. " Why," said the other, " teach him to shave with cold water and without a glass." Which, I dare say, he did; and for which benefit I am sure that son has good reason to be grateful. Only think of the inconvenience attending the common practice! There must be hot water; to have this there must be a fire, and, in some cases, a fire for that purpose alone; to have these there must be a servant, or you must light a fire yourself. For the want of these the job is put off until a later hour; this causes a stripping and another dressing bout; or you go in a slovenly state all that day, and the next day the thing must be done, or cleanliness must be abandoned altogether. If you be on a journey, you must wait the pleasure of the servants at the inn, before you can dress and set out in the morning; the pleasant time for travelling is gone before you can move from the spot; instead of being at the end of your day's journey in good time, you are benighted, and have to endure all the great inconveniences attendant on tardy movements. And all this from the apparently insignificant affair of shaving! How many a piece of important business has failed from a short delay! And how many thousand of such delays daily proceed from this unworthy cause! " Toujours prêt! " was the motto of a famous French general; and, pray, let it be yours: be " always ready; " and never, during your whole life, have to say, " I cannot go till I be shaved and dressed." Do the whole at once for the day, whatever may be your state of life; and then you have a day unbroken by those indispensable performances. Begin thus, in the days of your youth, and, having felt the superiority which this practice will give you over those in all other respects your equals, the practice will stick by you to the end of your life. Till you be shaved and dressed for the day, you cannot set steadily about any business; you know that you must presently quit your labour to return to the dressing affair; you therefore put it off until that be over; the interval, the precious interval, is spent in lounging about; and, by the time that you are ready for business, the best part of the day is gone.

39. Trifling as this matter appears upon naming it, it is, in fact, one of the great concerns of life; and, for my part, I can truly say, that I owe more of my great labours to my strict adherence to the precepts that I have here given you, than to all the natural abilities with which I have been endowed; for these, whatever may have been their amount, would have been of comparatively little use, even aided by great

sobriety and abstinence, if I had not, in early life, contracted the blessed habit of husbanding well my time. To this, more than to any other thing, I owed my very extraordinary promotion in the army. I was always ready: if I had to mount guard at ten, I was ready at nine: never did any man, or anything, wait one moment for me. Being, at an age under twenty years, raised from corporal to sergeant-major at once, over the heads of thirty sergeants, I naturally should have been an object of envy and hatred; but this habit of early rising and of rigid adherence to the precepts which I had given you, really subdued these passions; because every one felt that what I did he had never done, and never could do. Before my promotion, a clerk was wanted to make out the morning report of the regiment. I rendered the clerk unnecessary; and long before any other man was dressed for parade, my work for the morning was well done, and I myself was on the parade, walking, in fine weather, for an hour perhaps. My custom was this: to get up, in summer, at daylight, and in winter at four o'clock; shave, dress, even to the putting of my sword-belt over my shoulder, and having my sword lying on the table before me, ready to hang by my side. Then I ate a bit of cheese, or pork, and bread. Then I prepared my report, which was filled up as fast as the companies brought me in the materials. After this I had an hour or two to read, before the time came for any duty out of doors, unless when the regiment or part of it went out to exercise in the morning. When this was the case, and the matter was left to me, I always had it on the ground in such time as that the bayonets glistened in the rising sun, a sight which gave me delight, of which I often think, but which I should in vain endeavour to describe. If the officers were to go out, eight or ten o'clock was the hour, sweating the men in the heat of the day, breaking in upon the time for cooking their dinner, putting all things out of order and all men out of humour. When I was commander, the men had a long day of leisure before them: they could ramble into the town or into the woods; go to get raspberries, to catch birds, to catch fish, or to pursue any other recreation, and such of them as chose, and were qualified, to work at their trades. So that here, arising solely from the early habits of one very young man, were pleasant and happy days given to hundreds.

40. Money is said to be power, which is, in some cases, true; and the same may be said of knowledge: but superior sobriety, industry, and activity, are a still more certain source of power; for, without these, knowledge is of little use; and as to the power which money gives, it is that of brute force, it is the power of the bludgeon and the bayonet, and of the bribed press, tongue, and pen. Superior sobriety, industry, activity, though accompanied with but a moderate portion of knowledge, command respect, because they have great and visible influence. The drunken, the lazy, and the inert, stand abashed before the sober and the active. Besides, all those whose interests are at stake prefer, of necessity, those whose exertions produce the greatest and most immediate and visible effect. Self-interest is no respecter of persons: it

asks, not who knows best what ought to be done, but who is most likely to do it; we may, and often do, admire the talents of lazy and even dissipated men, but we do not trust them with the care of our interests. If, therefore, you would have respect and influence in the circle in which you move, be more sober, more industrious, more active than the general run of those amongst whom you live.

41. As to education, this word is now applied exclusively to things which are taught in schools; but education means rearing up, and the French speak of the education of pigs and sheep. In a very famous French book on rural affairs, there is a chapter entitled " Education du Cochon," that is, education of the hog. The word has the same meaning in both languages, for both take it from the Latin. Neither is the word learning properly confined to things taught in schools, or by books, for learning means knowledge; and but a comparatively small part of useful knowledge comes from books. Men are not to be called ignorant merely because they cannot make upon paper certain marks with a pen, or because they do not know the meaning of such marks when made by others. A ploughman may be very learned in his line, though he does not know what the letters p-l-o-u-g-h mean when he sees them combined upon paper. The first thing to be required of a man is, that he understand well his own calling or profession; and, be you in what state of life you may, to acquire this knowledge ought to be your first and greatest care. A man who has had a new-built house tumble down will derive little more

consolation from being told that the architect is a great astronomer, than this distressed nation now derives from being assured that its distresses arise from the measures of a long list of the greatest orators and greatest heroes that the world ever beheld.

42. Nevertheless, book-learning is by no means to be despised; and it is a thing which may be laudably sought after by persons in all states of life. In those pursuits which are called professions, it is necessary, and also in certain trades; and, in persons in the middle ranks of life, a total absence of such learning is somewhat disgraceful. There is, however, one danger to be carefully guarded against; namely, the opinion that your genius, or your literary acquirements are such as to warrant you in disregarding the calling in which you are, and by which you gain your bread. Parents have an uncommon portion of solid sense to counterbalance their natural affection, sufficient to make them competent judges in such a case. Friends are partial; and those who are not, you deem enemies. Stick, therefore, to the shop; rely upon your mercantile or mechanical or professional calling; try your strength in literature, if you like, but rely on the shop. If Bloomfield, who wrote a poem, called the " Farmer's Boy," had placed no reliance on the faithless Muses, his unfortunate and much to be pitied family would, in all probability, have not been in a state to solicit relief from charity. I remember that this loyal shoemaker was flattered to the skies, and (ominous sign, if he had understood it) feasted at the tables of some of the great. Have, I

beseech you, no hope of this sort; and, if you find
it creeping towards your heart, drive it instantly
away as the mortal foe of your independence and
your peace.

43. With this precaution, however, book-learning
is not only proper, but highly commendable; and
portions of it are absolutely necessary in every case
of trade or profession. One of these portions is
distinct reading, plain and neat writing, and arithmetic. The two former are mere child's work; the
latter not quite so easily acquired, but equally
indispensable; and of it you ought to have a thorough
knowledge before you attempt to study even the
grammar of your own language. Arithmetic is soon
learned; it is not a thing that requires much natural
talent; it is not a thing that loads the memory or
puzzles the mind; and it is a thing of every-day
utility. Therefore, this is, to a certain extent, an
absolute necessary; an indispensable acquisition.
Every man is not to be a surveyor or an actuary; and,
therefore, you may stop far short of the knowledge
of this sort which is demanded by these professions;
but, as far as common accounts and calculations go,
you ought to be perfect; and this you may make
yourself, without any assistance from a master, by
bestowing upon this science, during six months, only
one-half of the time that is, by persons of your age,
usually wasted over the tea-slops, or other kettle-
slops alone! If you become fond of this science, there
may be a little danger of your wasting your time on
it. When, therefore, you have got as much of it as
your business or profession can possibly render

necessary, turn the time to some other purpose. As to books, on this subject, they are in everybody's hand; but there is one book, on the subject of calculations, which I must point out to you, " The Cambist," by Dr. Kelly. This is a bad title, because, to men in general, it gives no idea of what the book treats of. It is a book which shows the value of the several pieces of money of one country when stated in the money of another country. For instance, it tells us what a Spanish dollar, a Dutch dollar, a French franc, and so on, is worth in English money. It does the same with regard to weights and measures; and it extends its information to all the countries in the world. It is a work of rare merit; and every youth, be his state of life what it may, if it permit him to pursue book-learning of any sort, and particularly, if he be destined, or at all likely to meddle with commercial matters, ought, as soon as convenient, to possess this valuable and instructive book.

44. The next thing is the grammar of your own language. Without understanding this, you can never hope to become fit for anything beyond mere trade or agriculture. It is true, that we do (God knows!) but too often see men have great wealth, high titles, and boundless power heaped upon them, who can hardly write ten lines together correctly; but, remember, it is not merit that has been the cause of their advancement; the cause has been, in almost every such case, the subserviency of the party to the will of some government, and the baseness of some nation who have quietly submitted to be governed by brazen fools. Do not you imagine that

you will have luck of this sort: do not you hope to be
rewarded and honoured for that ignorance which
shall prove a scourge to your country, and which
will earn you the curses of the children yet unborn.
Rely you upon your merit, and upon nothing else.
Without a knowledge of grammar, it is impossible
for you to write correctly; and, it is by mere accident
if you speak correctly; and, pray, bear in mind, that
all well-informed persons judge of a man's mind
(until they have other means of judging) by his
writing or speaking. The labour necessary to acquire
this knowledge is, indeed, not trifling; grammar is
not like arithmetic, a science consisting of several
distinct departments, some of which may be dis-
pensed with: it is a whole, and the whole must be
learned, or no part is learned. The subject is abstruse:
it demands much reflection and much patience; but,
when once the task is performed, it is performed for
life, and in every day of that life it will be found to
be, in a greater or less degree, a source of pleasure
or of profit, or both together. And, what is the
labour? It consists of no bodily exertion; it exposes
the student to no cold, no hunger, no suffering of
any sort. The study need subtract from the hours of
no business, nor, indeed, from the hours of necessary
exercise: the hours usually spent on the tea and coffee
slops, and in the mere gossip which accompany them;
those wasted hours, of only one year, employed in
the study of English grammar, would make you a
correct speaker and writer for the rest of your life.
You want no school, no room to study in, no expenses, and no troublesome circumstances of any

sort. I learned grammar when I was a private soldier on the pay of sixpence a day. The edge of my berth, or that of the guard-bed, was my seat to study in; my knapsack was my bookcase; a bit of board lying on my lap was my writing-table; and the task did not demand anything like a year of my life. I had no money to purchase candle or oil; in winter time it was rarely that I could get any evening light but that of the fire, and only my turn even of that. And if I, under such circumstances, and without parent or friend to advise or encourage me, accomplished this undertaking, what excuse can there be for any youth, however poor, however pressed with business, or however circumstanced as to room or other conveniences? To buy a pen or a sheet of paper I was compelled to forego some portion of food, though in a state of half-starvation: I had no moment of time that I could call my own; and I had to read and to write amidst the talking, laughing, singing, whistling, and brawling of at least half a score of the most thoughtless of men, and that, too, in the hours of their freedom from all control. Think not lightly of the farthing that I had to give, now and then, for ink, pen, or paper. That farthing was, alas! a great sum to me! I was as tall as I am now; I had great health and great exercise. The whole of the money, not expended for us at market, was twopence a week for each man. I remember, and well I may! that, upon one occasion, I, after all absolutely necessary expenses, had, on a Friday, made shift to have a halfpenny in reserve, which I had destined for the purchase of a red-herring in the morning; but, when

I pulled off my clothes at night, so hungry then as to be hardly able to endure life, I found that I had lost my halfpenny! I buried my head under the miserable sheet and rag, and cried like a child! And, again I say, if I, under circumstances like these, could encounter and overcome this task, is there, can there be, in the whole world, a youth to find an excuse for the non-performance? What youth, who shall read this, will not be ashamed to say, that he is not able to find time and opportunity for this most essential of all the branches of book-learning.

45. I press this matter with such earnestness, because a knowledge of grammar is the foundation of all literature; and because without this knowledge opportunities for writing and speaking are only occasions for men to display their unfitness to write and speak. How many false pretenders to erudition have I exposed to shame merely by my knowledge of grammar! How many of the insolent and ignorant great and powerful have I pulled down and made little and despicable! And, with what ease have I conveyed, upon numerous important subjects, information and instruction to millions now alive, and provided a store of both for millions yet unborn! As to the course to be pursued in this great undertaking, it is, first, to read the grammar from the first word to the last very attentively, several times over; then, to copy the whole of it very correctly and neatly; and then to study the chapters one by one. And what does this reading and writing require as to time? Both together not more than the tea-slops and their gossips for three months! There are about three

hundred pages in my English Grammar. Four of those little pages in a day, which is a mere trifle of work, do the thing in three months. Two hours a day are quite sufficient for the purpose; and these may, in any town that I have ever known, or in any village, be taken from that part of the morning during which the main part of the people are in bed. I do not like the evening candle-light work: it wears the eyes much more than the same sort of light in the morning, because then the faculties are in vigour and wholly unexhausted. But for this purpose there is sufficient of that daylight which is usually wasted, usually gossipped or lounged away, or spent in some other manner productive of no pleasure, and generally producing pain in the end. It is very becoming in all persons, and particularly in the young, to be civil and even polite; but it becomes neither young nor old to have an everlasting simper on their faces, and their bodies sawing in an everlasting bow; and how many youths have I seen who, if they had spent, in the learning of grammar, a tenth part of the time that they had consumed in earning merited contempt for their affected gentility, would have laid the foundation of sincere respect towards them for the whole of their lives!

46. Perseverance is a prime quality in every pursuit, and particularly in this. Yours, is, too, the time of life to acquire this inestimable habit. Men fail much oftener from want of perseverance than from want of talent and of good disposition: as the race was not to the hare but to the tortoise; so the meed of success in study is to him who is not in haste, but

to him who proceeds with a steady and even step. It is not to a want of taste or of desire or of disposition to learn that we have to ascribe the rareness of good scholars, so much as to the want of patient perseverance. Grammar is a branch of knowledge, like all other things of high value, which is of difficult acquirement: the study is dry; the subject is intricate; it engages not the passions; and, if the great end be not kept constantly in view; if you lose, for a moment, sight of the ample reward, indifference begins, that is followed by weariness, and disgust and despair close the book. To guard against this result be not in haste; keep steadily on; and, when you find weariness approaching, rouse yourself, and remember that, if you give up, all that you have done has been done in vain. This is a matter of great moment; for out of every ten, who undertake this task, there are, perhaps, nine who abandon it in despair; and this, too, merely for the want of resolution to overcome the first approaches of weariness. The most effectual means of security against this mortifying result is to lay down a rule to write or to read a certain fixed quantity every day, Sunday excepted. Our minds are not always in the same state; they have not, at all times, the same elasticity; to-day we are full of hope on the very grounds which, to-morrow, afford us no hope at all; every human being is liable to those flows and ebbs of the mind; but, if reason interfere and bid you overcome the fits of lassitude, and almost mechanically to go on without the stimulus of hope, the buoyant fit speedily returns; you congratulate yourself that you did not yield to the temptation to abandon your pursuit, and you proceed with more vigour than ever. Five or six triumphs over temptation to indolence or despair lay the foundation of certain success; and what is of still more importance, fix in you the habit of perseverance.

47. If I have bestowed a large portion of my space on this topic, it has been because I know from experience, as well as from observation, that it is of more importance than all the other branches of book-learning put together. It gives you, when you possess it thoroughly, a real and practical superiority over the far greater part of men. How often did I experience this even long before I became what is called an author! The adjutant, under whom it was my duty to act when I was a sergeant-major, was, as almost all military officers are, or at least were, a very illiterate man, perceiving that every sentence of mine was in the same form and manner as sentences in print, became shy of letting me see pieces of his writing. The writing of orders, and other things, therefore, fell to me; and thus, though no nominal addition was made to my pay, and no nominal addition to my authority, I acquired the latter as effectually as if a law had been passed to confer it upon me. In short, I owe to the possession of this branch of knowledge everything that has enabled me to do so many things that very few other men have done, and that now gives me a degree of influence, such as is possessed by few others, in the most weighty concerns of the country. The possession of this branch of knowledge raises you in your own esteem, gives

just confidence in yourself, and prevents you from being the willing slave of the rich and the titled part of the community. It enables you to discover that riches and titles do not confer merit; you think comparatively little of them; and, as far as relates to you, at any rate, their insolence is innoxious.

48. Hoping that I have said enough to induce you to set resolutely about the study of grammar, I might here leave the subject of learning, arithmetic and grammar, both well learned, being as much as I would wish in a mere youth. But these need not occupy the whole of your spare time; and there are other branches of learning which ought immediately to follow. If your own calling or profession require book-study, books treating of that are to be preferred to all others; for, the first thing, the first object in life, is to secure the honest means of obtaining sustenance, raiment, and a state of being suitable to your rank, be that rank what it may: excellence in your own calling is, therefore, the first thing to be aimed at. After this may come general knowledge, and of this, the first is a thorough knowledge of your own country; for how ridiculous it is to see an English youth engaged in reading about the customs of the Chinese, or of the Hindoos, while he is content to be totally ignorant of those of Kent or of Cornwall. Well employed he must be in ascertaining how Greece was divided, and how the Romans parcelled out their territory, while he knows not, and, apparently, does not want to know, how England came to be divided into counties, hundreds, parishes, and tithings!

49. Geography naturally follows grammar; and

you should begin with that of this kingdom, which you ought to understand well, perfectly well, before you venture to look abroad. A rather slight knowledge of the divisions and customs of other countries is, generally speaking, sufficient; but, not to know these full well, as far as relates to our own country, is, in one who pretends to be a gentleman or a scholar, somewhat disgraceful. Yet, how many men are there, and those called gentlemen too, who seem to think that counties and parishes, and churches and parsons, and tithes and glebes, and manors and courtsleet, and paupers and poor-houses, all grew up in England, or dropped down upon it, immediately after Noah's flood! Surely, it is necessary for every man, having any pretensions to scholarship, to know how these things came; and, the sooner this knowledge is acquired, the better; for, until it be acquired, you read the history of your country in vain. Indeed, to communicate this knowledge is one main part of the business of history; but it is a part which no historian, commonly so called, has, that I know of, ever yet performed, except, in part, myself in the " History of the Protestant Reformation." I had read Hume's " History of England," and the continuation by Smollett; but, in 1802, when I wanted to write on the subject of the non-residence of the clergy, I found, to my great mortification, that I knew not the foundation of the office and the claims of the parsons, and that I could not even guess at the origin of parishes. This gave a new turn to my inquiries; and I soon found the romancers, called historians, had given me no information that I could rely on, and besides had done, apparently, all they could to keep me in the dark.

50. When you come to history, begin also with that of your own country; and here it is my bounden duty to put you well on your guard; for, in this respect, we are peculiarly unfortunate, and for the following reasons, to which I beg you to attend. Three hundred years ago, the religion of England had been, during nine hundred years, the Catholic religion; the Catholic clergy possessed about a third part of all the lands and houses, which they held in trust for their own support, for the building and repairing of churches, and for the relief of the poor, the widow, the orphan, and the stranger; but, at the time just mentioned, the king and the aristocracy changed the religion to Protestant, took the estates of the Church and the poor to themselves as their own property, and taxed the people at large for the building and repairing of churches, and for the relief of the poor. This great and terrible change, effected partly by force against the people, and partly by the most artful means of deception, gave rise to a series of efforts, which has been continued from that day to this, to cause us all to believe that that change was for the better; that it was for our good; and that, before that time, our forefathers were a set of the most miserable slaves that the sun ever warmed with his beams. It happened, too, that the art of printing was not discovered, or, at least, it was very little understood, until about the time when this change took place; so that the books relating to former times were confined to manuscript; and, besides, even these

manuscript libraries were destroyed with great care by those who had made the change and had grasped the property of the poor and the Church. Our " historians," as they are called, have written under the fear of the powerful, or have been bribed by them; and, generally speaking, both at the same time: and, accordingly, their works are, as far as they relate to former times, masses of lies, unmatched by any others that the world has ever seen.

51. The great object of these lies always has been to make the main body of the people believe that the nation is now more happy, more populous, more powerful, than it was before it was Protestant, and thereby to induce us to conclude that it was a good thing for us that the aristocracy should take to themselves the property of the poor and the Church, and make the people at large pay taxes for the support of both. This has been, and still is, the great object of all those heaps of lies; and those lies are continually spread about amongst us in all forms of publication, from heavy folios down to halfpenny tracts. In refutation of those lies we have only very few and rare ancient books to refer to, and their information is incidental, seeing that their authors never dreamed of the possibility of the lying generations which were to come. We have the ancient Acts of Parliament, the common law, the customs, the canons of the Church, and the churches themselves; but these demand analyses and argument, and they demand also a really free press and unprejudiced and patient readers. Never in this world before had truth to struggle with so many and such great disadvantages!

52. To refute lies is not, at present, my business; but it is my business to give you, in as small a compass as possible, one striking proof that they are lies; and thereby to put you well upon your guard for the whole of the rest of your life. The opinion sedulously inculcated by these " historians " is this: that, before the Protestant times came, England was, comparatively, an insignificant country, having few people in it, and those few wretchedly poor and miserable. Now, take the following undeniable facts. All the parishes in England are now (except where they have been united, and two, three, or four have been made into one), in point of size, what they were a thousand years ago. The county of Norfolk is the best cultivated of any one in England. This county has now 731 parishes, and the number was formerly greater. Of these parishes 22 have now no churches at all; 74 contain less than 100 souls each; and 268 have no parsonage-houses. Now, observe, every parish had, in old times, a church and a parsonage-house. The county contains 2,092 square miles; that is to say, something less than three square miles to each parish, and that is 1,920 statute acres of land; and the size of each parish is, on an average, that of a piece of ground about one mile and a half each way; so that the churches are, even now, on an average, only about a mile and a half from each other. Now, the questions for you to put to yourself are these: Were churches formerly built and kept up without being wanted, and especially by a poor and miserable people? Did these miserable people build 74 churches out of 731, each of which 74 had

not a hundred souls belonging to it? Is it a sign of an augmented population, that 22 churches out of 731 have tumbled down and been effaced? Was it a country thinly inhabited by miserable people that could build and keep a church in every piece of ground a mile and a half each way, besides having, in this same county, 77 monastic establishments and 142 free chapels? Is it a sign of augmented population, ease, and plenty, that out of 731 parishes, 268 have suffered the parsonage-houses to fall into ruins, and their sites to become patches of nettles and of brambles? Put these questions calmly to yourself; common sense will dictate the answers; and truth will call for an expression of your indignation against the lying historians and the still more lying population-mongers.

LETTER II

TO A YOUNG MAN

53. IN the foregoing Letter, I have given my advice to a Youth. In addressing myself to you, I am to presume that you have entered upon your present stage of life, having acted upon the precepts contained in that letter; and that, of course, you are a sober, abstinent, industrious, and well-informed young man. In the succeeding letters, which will be addressed to the Lover, the Husband, the Father, and the Citizen, I shall, of course, have to include my notion of your duties as a master, and as a person employed by another. In the present letter, therefore, I shall confine myself principally to the conduct of a young man with regard to the management of his means, or money.

54. Be you in what line of life you may, it will be amongst your misfortunes if you have not time properly to attend to this matter; for, it very frequently happens, it has happened to thousands upon thousands, not only to be ruined, according to the common acceptation of the word; not only to be made poor, and to suffer from poverty, in consequence of want of attention to pecuniary matters; but it has frequently, and even generally, happened, that a want of attention to these matters has impeded the

progress of science, and of genius itself. A man, oppressed with pecuniary cares and dangers, must be next to a miracle, if he have his mind in a state fit for intellectual labours; to say nothing of the temptations arising from such distress, to abandon good principles, to suppress useful opinions and useful facts; and, in short, to become a disgrace to his kindred, and an evil to his country, instead of being an honour to the former and a blessing to the latter. To be poor and independent is very nearly an impossibility.

55. But then, poverty is not a positive, but a relative term. Burke observed, and very truly, that a labourer who earned a sufficiency to maintain him as a labourer, and to maintain him in a suitable manner; to give him a sufficiency of good food, of clothing, of lodging, and of fuel, ought not to be called a poor man; for that, though he has little riches, though his, compared with that of a lord, was a state of poverty, it was not a state of poverty in itself. When, therefore, I say that poverty is the cause of a depression of spirit, of inactivity and of servility in men of literary talent, I must say, at the same time, that the evil arises from their own fault; from them having created for themselves imaginary wants; from their having indulged in unnecessary enjoyments, and from their having caused that to be poverty, which would not have been poverty, if they had been moderate in their enjoyments.

56. As it may be your lot (such has been mine) to live by your literary talent, I will here, before I proceed to matter more applicable to persons in other

states of life, observe, that I cannot form an idea of a mortal more wretched than a man of real talent, compelled to curb his genius, and to submit himself, in the exercise of that genius, to those whom he knows to be far inferior to himself, and whom he must despise from the bottom of his soul. The late Mr. William Gifford, who was the son of a shoemaker at Ashburton in Devonshire; who was put to school and sent to the University at the expense of a generous and good clergyman of the name of Cookson, and who died, the other day, a sort of whipper-in of Murray's *Quarterly Review:* this was a man of real genius; and, to my certain personal knowledge, he detested, from the bottom of his soul, the whole of the paper-money and borough-mongering system, and despised those by whom the system was carried on. But he had imaginary wants; he had been bred up in company with the rich and the extravagant; expensive indulgences had been made necessary to him by habit; and when, in the year 1798, or thereabouts, he had to choose between a bit of bacon, a scrag of mutton, and a lodging at ten shillings a week, on the one side, and made-dishes, wine, a fine house and a footman, on the other side, he chose the latter. He became the servile editor of Canning's anti-Jacobin newspaper; and he who had more wit and learning than all the rest of the writers put together, became the miserable tool in circulating their attacks upon everything that was hostile to a system which he deplored and detested. But, he secured the made-dishes, the wine, the footman and the coachman. A sinecure as Clerk of the Foreign

Estreats, gave him £329 a year, a double commis-
sionership of the lottery gave him £600 or £700
more; and, at a later period, his editorship of the
Quarterly Review gave him perhaps as much more.
He rolled in his carriage for several years; he fared
sumptuously; he was buried at Westminster Abbey,
of which his friend, and formerly his brother pamphleteer in defence of Pitt, was the Dean; and never
is he to be heard of more! Mr. Gifford would have
been fully as happy; his health would have been better,
his life longer, and his name would have lived for
ages, if he could have turned to the bit of bacon and
scrag of mutton in 1798; for his learning and talents
were such, his reasonings so clear and conclusive,
and his wit so pointed and keen, that his writings
must have been generally read, must have been of
long duration; and, indeed, must have enabled him
(he being always a single man) to live in his latter
days in as good style as that which he procured by
becoming a sinecurist, a pensioner, and a hack—all
which he was from the moment he lent himself to
the *Quarterly Review*. Think of the mortification of
such a man, when he was called upon to justify the
Power-of-imprisonment Bill in 1817! But to go into
particulars would be tedious: his life was a life of
luxurious misery, than which a worse is not to be
imagined.

57. So that poverty is, except where there is an
actual want of food and raiment, a thing much more
imaginary than real. The shame of poverty, the shame
of being thought poor, is a great and fatal weakness,
though arising, in this country, from the fashion of

the times themselves. When a good man, as in the phraseology of the city, means a rich man, we are not to wonder that every one wishes to be thought richer than he is. When adulation is sure to follow wealth, and when contempt would be awarded to many, if they were not wealthy, who are spoken of with deference, and even lauded to the skies, because their riches are great and notorious; when this is the case, we are not to be surprised that men are ashamed to be thought to be poor. This is one of the greatest of all the dangers at the outset of life: it has brought thousands and hundreds of thousands to ruin, even to pecuniary ruin. One of the most amiable features in the character of American society is this: that men never boast of their riches, and never disguise their poverty; but they talk of both as of any other matter fit for public conversation. No man shuns another because he is poor: no man is preferred to another because he is rich. In hundreds and hundreds of instances, men not worth a shilling have been chosen by the people and entrusted with their rights and interests in preference to men who ride in their carriages.

58. This shame of being thought poor is not only dishonourable in itself, and fatally injurious to men of talent, but it is ruinous even in a pecuniary point of view, and equally destructive to farmers, traders, and even gentlemen of landed estate. It leads to everlasting efforts to disguise one's poverty; the carriage, the servants, the wine, (oh, that fatal wine!) the spirits, the decanters, the glasses, all the table apparatus, the dress, the horses, the dinners, the

parties, all must be kept up; not so much because he or she who keeps or gives them has any pleasure arising therefrom, as because not to keep and give them would give rise to a suspicion of the want of means so to give and keep; and thus thousands upon thousands are yearly brought into a state of real poverty by their great anxiety not to be thought poor. Look round you, mark well what you behold, and say if this be not the case. In how many instances have you seen most amiable and even most industrious families brought to ruin by nothing but this? Mark it well; resolve to set this false shame at defiance; and when you have done that, you have laid the first stone of the surest foundation of your future tranquillity of mind. There are thousands of families, at this very moment, who are thus struggling to keep up appearances. The farmers accommodate themselves to circumstances more easily than tradesmen and professional men. They live at a greater distance from their neighbours; they can change their style of living unperceived; they can banish the decanter, change the dishes for a bit of bacon, make a treat out of a rasher and eggs, and the world is none the wiser all the while. But the tradesman, the doctor, the attorney, and the trader, cannot make the change so quietly and unseen. The accursed wine, which is a sort of criterion of the style of living, a sort of scale to the plan, a sort of key to the tune; this is the thing to banish first of all; because all the rest follow, and come down to their proper level in a short time. The accursed decanter cries footman or waiting-maid, puts bells

to the side of the wall, screams aloud for carpets;
and when I am asked, " Lord, what is a glass of
wine? " my answer is, that, in this country, it is
everything; it is the pitcher of the key; it demands
all the other unnecessary expenses; it is injurious to
health, and must be injurious, every bottle of wine
that is drunk containing a certain portion of ardent
spirits, besides other drugs deleterious in their
nature; and, of all the friends to the doctor, this
fashionable beverage is the greatest. And, which
adds greatly to the folly, or, I should say, the real
vice of using it, is, that the parties themselves, nine
times out of ten, do not drink it by choice; do not
like it: do not relish it; but use it from mere ostenta-
tion, being ashamed to be seen, even by their own
servants, not to drink wine. At the very moment I
am writing this, there are thousands of families in
and near London, who daily have wine upon their
tables, and who drink it too, merely because their
own servants should not suspect them to be poor,
and not deem them to be genteel: and thus families
by thousands are ruined, only because they are
ashamed to be thought poor.

59. There is no shame belonging to poverty,
which frequently arises from the virtues of the im-
poverished parties. Not so frequently, indeed, as
from vice, folly, and indiscretion; but still very
frequently. And as the Scripture tells us, that we are
not to " despise the poor because he is poor," so
ought we not to honour the rich because he is rich.
The true way is, to take a fair survey of the character
of a man as depicted in his conduct, and to respect

him, or despise him, according to a due estimate of that character. No country upon earth exhibits so many, as this, of those fatal terminations of life, called suicides. These arise, in nine instances out of ten, from this very source. The victims are, in general, what may be fairly called insane; but their insanity always arises from the dread of poverty; not from the dread of a want of the means of sustaining life, or even decent living, but from the dread of being thought or known to be poor; from the dread of what is called falling in the scale of society; a dread which is prevalent hardly in any country but this. Looked at in its true light, what is there in poverty to make a man take away his own life? He is the same man that he was before: he has the same body and the same mind: if he even foresee a great alteration in his dress or his diet, why should he kill himself on that account? Are these all the things that a man wishes to live for? But such is the fact; so great is the disgrace upon this country, and so numerous and terrible are the evils arising from this dread of being thought to be poor.

60. Nevertheless, men ought to take care of their means, ought to use them prudently and sparingly, and to keep their expenses always within the bounds of their income, be it what it may. One of the effectual means of doing this is to purchase with ready money. St. Paul says, " Owe no man anything," and, of his numerous precepts, this is by no means the least worthy of our attention. Credit has been boasted of as a very fine thing; to decry credit seems to be setting oneself up against the opinions of the whole

world; and I remember a paper in the *Freeholder* or the *Spectator*, published just after the funding system had begun, representing " Public Credit " as a goddess, enthroned in a temple dedicated to her by her votaries, amongst whom she is dispensing blessings of every description. It must be more than forty years since I read this paper, which I read soon after the time when the late Mr. Pitt uttered in Parliament an expression of his anxious hope, that his " name would be inscribed on the monument which he should raise to public credit." Time has taught me that public credit means the contracting of debts which a nation never can pay; and I have lived to see this goddess produce effects, in my country, which Satan himself never could have produced. It is a very bewitching goddess; and not less fatal in her influence in private than in public affairs. It has been carried in this latter respect to such a pitch, that scarcely any transaction, however low and inconsiderable in amount, takes place in any other way. There is a trade in London, called the " tally trade," by which household goods, coals, clothing, all sorts of things, are sold upon credit, the seller keeping a tally, and receiving payment for the goods little by little; so that the income and the earnings of the buyers are always anticipated; are always gone, in fact, before they come in or are earned; the sellers receiving, of course, a great deal more than the proper profit.

61. Without supposing you to descend to so low a grade as this, and even supposing you to be lawyer, doctor, parson, or merchant; it is still the same

thing, if you purchase on credit, and not, perhaps, in a much less degree of disadvantage. Besides the higher price that you pay, there is the temptation to have what you really do not want. The cost seems a trifle, when you have not to pay the money until a future time. It has been observed, and very truly observed, that men used to lay out a one-pound note when they would not lay out a sovereign; a consciousness of the intrinsic value of the things produces a retentiveness in the latter case more than in the former: the sight and the touch assist the mind in forming its conclusions, and the one-pound note was parted with, when the sovereign would have been kept. Far greater is the difference between credit and ready money. Innumerable things are not bought at all with ready money, which would be bought in case of trust; it is so much easier to order a thing than to pay for it. A future day; a day of payment must come, to be sure, but that is little thought of at the time; but if the money were to be drawn out the moment the thing was received or offered, this question would arise, " Can I do without it? " Is this thing indispensable; am I compelled to have it, or, suffer a loss or injury greater in amount than the cost of the thing? If this question were put every time we make a purchase, seldom should we hear of those suicides which are such a disgrace to this country.

62. I am aware that it will be said, and very truly said, that the concerns of merchants; that the purchasing of great estates, and various other great transactions cannot be carried on in this manner;

but these are rare exceptions to the rule; even in these cases there might be much less of bills and bonds, and all the sources of litigation; but in the everyday business of life; in transactions with the butcher, the baker, the tailor, the shoemaker, what excuse can there be for pleading the example of the merchant, who carries on his work by ships and exchanges? I was delighted, some time ago, by being told of a young man, who, upon being advised to keep a little account of all he received and expended, answered, " that his business was not to keep account-books; that he was sure not to make a mistake as to his income; and that, as to his expenditure, the little bag that held his sovereigns would be an infallible guide, as he never bought anything that he did not immediately pay for."

63. I believe that nobody will deny, that, generally speaking, you pay for the same article a fourth part more in the case of trust than you do in the case of ready money. Suppose, then, the baker, butcher, tailor, and shoemaker, receive from you only one hundred pounds a year. Put that together; that is to say, multiply twenty-five by twenty, and you will find, that at the end of twenty years, you have £500 besides the accumulating and growing interest. The Fathers of the Church (I mean the ancient ones), and also the canons of the Church, forbade selling on trust at a higher price than for ready money, which was, in effect, to forbid trust; and this, doubtless, was one of the great objects which those wise and pious men had in view; for they were fathers in legislation and morals as well as in religion.

But the doctrine of these Fathers and canons no longer prevails; they are set at naught by the present age, even in the countries that adhere to their religion. Addison's goddess has prevailed over the Fathers and the canons; and men not only make a difference in the price, regulated by the difference in the mode of payment, but it would be absurd to expect them to do otherwise. They must not only charge something for the want of the use of the money; but they must charge something additional for the risk of its loss, which may frequently arise, and most frequently does arise, from the misfortunes of those to whom they have assigned their goods on trust. The man, therefore, who purchases on trust, not only pays for the trust, but he also pays his due share of what the tradesman loses by trust; and, after all, he is not so good a customer as the man who purchases cheaply with ready money; for there is his name indeed in the tradesman's book, but with that name the tradesman cannot go to the market to get a fresh supply.

64. Infinite are the ways in which gentlemen lose by this sort of dealing. Servants go and order, sometimes, things not wanted at all; at other times, more than is wanted; at others, things of a higher quality; and all this would be obviated by purchasing with ready money; for, whether through the hands of the party himself, or through those of an inferior, there would always be an actual counting out of the money; somebody would see the thing bought and see the money paid; and as the master would give the house-keeper or steward a bag of money, at the time, he

would see the money too, would set a proper value upon it, and would just desire to know upon what it had been expended.

65. How is it that farmers are so exact, and show such a disposition to retrench in the article of labour, when they seem to think little or nothing about the sums which they pay in tax upon malt, wine, sugar, tea, soap, candles, tobacco, and various other things? You find the utmost difficulty in making them understand that they are affected by these. The reason is that they see the money which they give to the labourer on each succeeding Saturday night; but they do not see that which they give in taxes on the articles before mentioned. Why is it that they make such an outcry about the six or seven millions a year which are paid in poor-rates, and say not a word about the sixty millions a year raised in other taxes? The consumer pays all; and therefore they are as much interested in the one as in the other; and yet the farmers think of no tax but the poor-tax. The reason is, that the latter is collected from them in money; they see it go out of their hands into the hands of another; and therefore they are everlastingly anxious to reduce the poor-rates, and they take care to keep them within the smallest possible bounds.

66. Just thus would it be with every man that never purchased but with ready money: he would make the amount as low as possible in proportion to his means. This care and frugality would make an addition to his means, and therefore, in the end, at the end of his life, he would have had a great deal more to spend, and still be as rich, as if he had gone

in trust; while he would have lived in tranquillity all the while; and would have avoided all the endless papers and writings and receipts and bills and disputes and lawsuits inseparable from a system of credit. This is by no means a lesson of stinginess; by no means tends to inculcate heaping up of money; for, the purchasing with ready money really gives you more money to purchase with; you can afford to have a greater quantity and variety of things; and I will engage that, if horses or servants be your taste, the saving in this way gives you an additional horse or an additional servant, if you be in any profession or engaged in any considerable trade. In towns it tends to accelerate your pace along the streets; for the temptation of the windows is answered in a moment by clapping your hand upon your thigh; and the question, " Do I really want that? " is sure to occur to you immediately; because the touch of the money is sure to put that thought in your mind.

67. Now, supposing you to have a plenty; to have a fortune beyond your wants; would not the money which you would save in this way, be very well applied in acts of real benevolence? Can you walk many yards in the streets; can you ride a mile in the country; can you go to half a dozen cottages; can you, in short, open your eyes, without seeing some human being; some one born in the same country with yourself, and who, on that account alone, has some claim upon your good wishes and your charity; can you open your eyes without seeing some person to whom even a small portion of your annual savings would convey gladness of heart? Your own heart

will suggest the answer; and if there were no motive
but this, what need I say more in the advice which
I have here tendered to you?

68. Another great evil arising from this desire to
be thought rich, or rather, from the desire not to be
thought poor, is the destructive thing which has
been honoured by the name of " speculation," but
which ought to be called gambling. It is a purchasing
of something which you do not want either in your
family or in the way of ordinary trade: a something
to be sold again with a great profit; and on the sale
of which there is a considerable hazard. When purchases of this sort are made with ready money, they
are not so offensive to reason, and not attended with
such risk; but when they are made with money
borrowed for the purpose, they are neither more nor
less than gambling transactions; and they have been,
in this country, a source of ruin, misery, and suicide,
admitting of no adequate description. I grant that
this gambling has arisen from the influence of the
" goddess " before mentioned; I grant that it has
arisen from the facility of obtaining the fictitious
means of making the purchases; and I grant that
that facility has been created by the system under
the baneful influence of which we live. But it is not
the less necessary that I beseech you not to practise
such gambling; that I beseech you, if you be engaged
in it, to disentangle yourself from it as soon as you
can. Your life, while you are thus engaged, is the life
of a gamester; a life of constant anxiety; constant
desire to overreach; constant apprehension: general
gloom; enlivened, now and then, by a gleam of hope

or of success. Even that success is sure to lead to further adventures; and, at last, a thousand to one, that your fate is that of the pitcher to the well.

69. The great temptation to this gambling is, as is the case in other gambling, the success of the few. As young men who crowd to the army, in search of rank and renown, never look into the ditch that holds their slaughtered companions, but have their eye constantly fixed on the general-in-chief; and as each of them belongs to the same profession, and is sure to be conscious that he has equal merit, every one deems himself the suitable successor of him who is surrounded with aides-de-camp, and who moves battalions and columns by his nod: so with the rising generation of " speculators; " they see the great estates that have succeeded the pencil-box and the orange-basket; they see those whom nature and good laws made to black shoes, sweep chimneys or the streets, rolling in carriages, or sitting in saloons surrounded by gaudy footmen with napkins twisted round their thumbs; and they can see no earthly reason why they should not all do the same; forgetting the thousands and thousands who, in making the attempt, have reduced themselves to that beggary which, before the attempt, they would have regarded as a thing wholly impossible.

70. In all situations of life avoid the trammels of the law. Man's nature must be changed before law-suits will cease; and perhaps it would be next to impossible to make them less frequent than they are in the present state of this country; but though no man, who has any property at all, can say that he

will have nothing to do with lawsuits, it is in the power of most men to avoid them in a considerable degree. One good rule is to have as little as possible to do with any man who is fond of lawsuits; and who, upon every slight occasion, talks of an appeal to the law. Such persons, from their frequent litigations, contract a habit of using the technical terms of the courts, in which they take a pride, and are, therefore, companions peculiarly disgusting to men of sense. To such men a lawsuit is a luxury, instead of being, as it is to men or ordinary minds, a source of anxiety and a real and substantial scourge. Such men are always of a quarrelsome disposition, and avail themselves of every opportunity to indulge in that which is mischievous to their neighbours. In thousands of instances men go to law for the indulgence of mere anger. The Germans are said to bring spite-actions against one another, and to harass their poorer neighbours from motives of pure revenge. They have carried this their disposition with them to America; for which reason no one likes to live in a German neighbourhood.

71. Before you go to law consider well the cost; for if you win your suit, and are poorer than you were before, what do you accomplish? You only imbibe a little additional anger against your opponent; you injure him, but do harm to yourself. Better to put up with the loss of one pound than two, to which latter is to be added all the loss of time, all the trouble, and all the mortification and anxiety attending a lawsuit. To set an attorney to work to worry and torment another man is a very base act;

to alarm his family as well as himself, while you are sitting quietly at home. If a man owe you money which he cannot pay, why add to his distress, without the chance of benefit to yourself? Thousands of men have injured themselves by resorting to the law; while very few ever bettered themselves by it, except such resort were unavoidable.

72. Nothing is much more discreditable than what is called hard dealing. They say of the Turks, that they know nothing of two prices for the same article, and that to ask an abatement of the lowest shop-keeper is to insult him. It would be well if Christians imitated Mohammedans in this respect. To ask one price and take another, or to offer one price and give another, besides the loss of time that it occasions, is highly dishonourable to the parties, and especially when pushed to the extent of solemn protestations. It is, in fact, a species of lying, and it answers no one advantageous purpose to either buyer or seller. I hope that every young man who reads this will start in life with a resolution never to higgle and lie in dealings. There is this circumstance in favour of the bookseller's business; every book has its fixed price, and no one ever asks an abatement. If it were thus in all other trades, how much time would be saved, and how much immorality prevented!

73. As to the spending of your time, your business or your profession is to claim the priority of every-thing else. Unless that be duly attended to, there can be no real pleasure in any other employment of a portion of your time. Men, however, must have some leisure, some relaxation from business; and in

the choice of this relaxation much of your happiness will depend. Where fields and gardens are at hand, they present the most rational scenes for leisure. As to company, I have said enough in the former letter to deter any young man from that of drunkards and rioting companions; but there is such a thing as your quiet " pipe and pot companions," which are, perhaps, the most fatal of all. Nothing can be conceived more dull, more stupid, more the contrary of edification and rational amusement, than sitting, sotting, over a pot and a glass, sending out smoke from the head, and articulating, at intervals, nonsense about all sorts of things. Seven years' service as a galley-slave would be more bearable to a man of sense than seven months' confinement to society like this. Yet, such is the effect of habit, that if a young man become a frequenter of such scenes, the idle propensity sticks to him for life. Some companions, however, every man must have; but these every well-behaved man will find in private houses, where families are found residing, and where the suitable intercourse takes place between women and men. A man that cannot pass an evening without drink, merits the name of a sot. Why should there be drink for the purpose of carrying on conversation? Women stand in need of no drink to stimulate them to converse; and I have a thousand times admired their patience in sitting quietly at their work, while their husbands are engaged, in the same room, with bottles and glasses before them, thinking nothing of the expense, and still less of the shame which the distinction reflects upon them. We have to thank the women for many things, and particularly for their sobriety, for fear of following their example in which men drive them from the table, as if they said to them, " You have had enough; food is sufficient for you; but we must remain to fill ourselves with drink, and to talk in language which your ears ought not to endure." When women are getting up to retire from the table, men rise in honour of them; but they take special care not to follow their excellent example. That which is not fit to be uttered before women is not fit to be uttered at all; and it is next to a pro- clamation, tolerating drunkenness and indecency, to send women from the table the moment they have swallowed their food. The practice has been ascribed to a desire to leave them to themselves; but why should they be left to themselves? Their conversation is always the most lively, while their persons are generally the most agreeable objects. No: the plain truth is, that it is the love of the drink and of the indecent talk that send women from the table; and it is a practice which I have always abhorred. I like to see young men especially follow them out of the room, and prefer their company to that of the sots who are left behind.

74. Another mode of spending the leisure time is that of books. Rational and well-informed com- panions may be still more instructive; but books never annoy; they cost little, and they are always at hand, and ready at your call. The sort of books must, in some degree, depend upon your pursuit in life; but there are some books necessary to every one who aims at the character of a well-informed man.

I have slightly mentioned history and geography in the preceding letter; but I must here observe, that as to both these, you should begin with your own country, and make yourself well acquainted, not only with its ancient state, but with the origin of all its principal institutions. To read of the battles which it has fought, and of the intrigues by which one king or one minister has succeeded another, is very little more profitable than the reading of a romance. To understand well the history of the country, you should first understand how it came to be divided into counties, hundreds, and into parishes; how judges, sheriffs, and juries first arose; to what end they were all invented, and how the changes with respect to any of them have been produced. But it is of particular consequence that you ascertain the state of the people in former times, which is to be ascertained by comparing the then price of labour with the then price of food. You hear enough, and you read enough, about the glorious wars in the reign of King Edward the Third; and it is very proper that those glories should be recorded and remembered; but you never read, in the works of the historians, that, in that reign, a common labourer earned threepence-halfpenny a day; and that a fat sheep was sold, at the same time, for one shilling and twopence, and a fat hog, two years old, for three shillings and fourpence, and a fat goose for twopence-halfpenny. You never read that women received a penny a day for hay-making or weeding in the corn, and that a gallon of red wine was sold for fourpence. These are matters which historians have deemed to be beneath their notice; but they are matters of real importance; they are matters which ought to have practical effect at this time: for these furnish the criterion whereby we are to judge of our condition compared with that of our forefathers. The poor-rates form a great feature in the laws and customs of this country. Put to a thousand persons who have read what is called the History of England; put to them the question, how the poor-rates came; and nine hundred and ninety-nine of the thousand will tell you that they know nothing at all of the matter. This is not history; a list of battles and a string of intrigues are not history; they communicate no knowledge applicable to our present state; and it really is better to amuse oneself with an avowed romance, which latter is a great deal worse than passing one's time in counting the trees.

75. History has been described as affording arguments of experience; as a record of what has been, in order to guide us as to what is likely to be, or what ought to be; but from this romancing history no such experience is to be derived: for it furnishes no facts on which to found arguments relative to the existing or future state of things. To come at the true history of a country, you must read its laws: you must read books treating of its usages and customs in former times; and you must particularly inform yourself as to prices of labour and of food. By reading the single Act of the 23rd year of Edward the Third, specifying the price of labour at that time; by reading an Act of Parliament passed in the 24th year of Henry the Eighth; by reading these two Acts, and then reading

the Preciosum of Bishop Fleetwood, which shows the price of food in the former reign, you come into full possession of the knowledge of what England was in former times. Divers books teach how the divisions of the country arose, and how its great institutions were established; and the result of this reading is a store of knowledge which will afford you pleasure for the whole of your life.

76. History, however, is by no means the only thing about which every man's leisure furnishes him with the means of reading; besides which, every man has not the same taste. Poetry, Geography, Moral Essays, the divers subjects of Philosophy, Travels, Natural History, books on Sciences, and, in short, the whole range of book-knowledge is before you; but there is one thing always to be guarded against, and that is, not to admire and applaud anything you read, merely because it is the fashion to admire and applaud it. Read, consider well what you read, form your own judgment, and stand by that judgment in despite of the sayings of what are called learned men, until fact or argument be offered to convince you of your error. One writer praises another; and it is very possible for writers so to combine as to cry down and, in some sort, to destroy the reputation of any one who meddles with the combination, unless the person thus assailed be blessed with uncommon talent and uncommon perseverance. When I read the works of Pope and of Swift, I was greatly delighted with their lashing of Dennis; but wondered at the same time, why they should have taken so much pains in running down such a fool. By the

merest accident in the world, being at a tavern in the woods of America, I took up an old book, in order to pass away the time while my travelling companions were drinking in the next room; but, seeing the book contained the criticisms of Dennis, I was about to lay it down, when the play of " Cato " caught my eye; and, having been accustomed to read books in which this play was lauded to the skies, and knowing it to have been written by Addison, every line of whose works I had been taught to believe teemed with wisdom and genius, I condescended to begin to read, though the work was from the pen of that fool Dennis. I read on, and soon began to laugh, not at Dennis, but at Addison. I laughed so much and so loud that the landlord, who was in the passage, came in to see what I was laughing at. In short, I found it a most masterly production, one of the most witty things that I had ever read in my life. I was delighted with Dennis, and was heartily ashamed of my former admiration of " Cato," and felt no little resentment against Pope and Swift for their endless reviling of this most able and witty critic. This, as far as I recollect, was the first emancipation that had assisted me in my reading. I have, since that time, never taken anything upon trust; I have judged for myself, trusting neither to the opinions of writers nor in the fashions of the day. Having been told by Dr. Blair, in his " Lectures of Rhetoric," that if I meant to write correctly, I must " give my days and nights to Addison," I read a few numbers of the *Spectator* at the time I was writing my " English Grammar; " I gave neither my nights nor my days to him; but I found an abundance of matter to afford examples of false grammar; and, upon a re-perusal, I found that the criticisms of Dennis might have been extended to this book too.

77. But that which never ought to have been forgotten by those who were men at the time, and that which ought to be made known to every young man of the present day, in order that he may be induced to exercise his own judgment with regard to books, is, the transactions relative to the writings of Shakspeare, which transactions took place about thirty years ago. It is still, and it was then much more, the practice to extol every line of Shakspeare to the skies: not to admire Shakspeare has been deemed to be a proof of want of understanding and taste. Mr. Garrick, and some others after him, had their own good and profitable reasons for crying up the works of this poet. When I was a very little boy there was a jubilee in honour of Shakspeare; and as he was said to have planted a mulberry-tree, boxes, and other little ornamental things in wood, were sold all over the country, as having been made out of the trunk or limbs of this ancient and sacred tree. We Protestants laugh at the relics so highly prized by Catholics; but never was a Catholic people half so much duped by the relics of saints, as this nation was by the mulberry-tree, of which, probably, more wood was sold than would have been sufficient in quantity to build a ship of war, or a large house. This madness abated for some years; but, towards the end of the last century, it broke out again with more fury than ever. Shakspeare's works were published by Boy-

dell, an Alderman of London, at a subscription of five hundred pounds for each copy, accompanied by plates, each forming a large picture. Amongst the madmen of the day was a Mr. Ireland, who seemed to be more mad than any of the rest. His adoration of the poet led him to perform a pilgrimage to an old farmhouse, near Stratford-upon-Avon, said to have been the birthplace of the poet. Arrived at the spot, he requested the farmer and his wife to let him search the house for papers, first going upon his knees, and praying, in the poetic style, the gods to aid him in his quest. He found no papers; but he found that the farmer's wife, in clearing out a garret some years before, had found some rubbishy old papers which she had burnt, and which had probably been papers used in the wrapping up of pigs' cheeks, to keep them from the bats. " Oh, wretched woman! " exclaimed he; " do you know what you have done? " " Oh dear no! " said the woman, half frightened out of her wits: " no harm, I hope, for the papers were very old; I dare say as old as the house itself." This threw him into an additional degree of excitement, as it is now fashionably called; he raved, he stamped, he foamed, and at last quitted the house, covering the poor woman with every term of reproach; and hastening back to Stratford, took post-chaise for London, to relate to his brother madmen the horrible sacrilege of this heathenish woman. Unfortunately for Mr. Ireland, unfortunately for his learned brothers in the metropolis, and unfortunately for the reputation of Shakspeare, Mr. Ireland took with him to the scene of his adoration, a son, about sixteen years of age, who was articled to an attorney in London. The son was by no means so sharply bitten as the father; and, upon returning to town, he conceived the idea of supplying the place of the invaluable papers which the farmhouse heathen had destroyed. He thought, and he thought rightly, that he should have little difficulty in writing plays just like those of Shakspeare! To get paper that should seem to have been made in the reign of Queen Elizabeth, and ink that should give to writing the appearance of having the same age, was somewhat difficult; but both were overcome. Young Ireland was acquainted with a son of a bookseller, who dealt in old books; the blank leaves of these books supplied the young author with paper: and he found out the way of making proper ink for his purpose. To work he went, wrote several plays, some love-letters, and other things; and, having got a Bible, extant in the time of Shakspeare, he wrote notes in the margin. All these, together with sonnets in abundance, and other little detached pieces, he produced to his father, telling him he got them from a gentleman, who had made him swear that he would not divulge his name. The father announced the invaluable discovery to the literary world; the literary world rushed to him; the manuscripts were regarded as genuine by the most grave and learned doctors, some of whom (and amongst these were Doctors Parr and Warton) gave, under their hands, an opinion that the manuscripts must have been written by Shakspeare; for that no other man in the world could have been capable of writing them!

78. Mr. Ireland opened a subscription, published these new and invaluable manuscripts at an enormous price; and preparations were instantly made for performing one of the plays, called " Vortigern." Soon after the acting of the play, the indiscretion of the lad caused the secret to explode; and, instantly, those who had declared that he had written as well as Shakspeare, did everything in their power to destroy him! The attorney drove him from his office; the father drove him from his house; and, in short, he was hunted down as if he had been a malefactor of the worst description. The truth of this relation is undeniable; it is recorded in numberless books. The young man is, I believe, yet alive; and, in short, no man will question any one of the facts.

79. After this, where is the person of sense who will be guided in these matters by fashion; where is the man, who wishes not to be deluded, who will not, when he has read a book, judge for himself? After all these jubilees and pilgrimages; after Boydell's subscription of £500 for one single copy; after it had been deemed almost impiety to doubt of the genius of Shakspeare surpassing that of all the rest of mankind; after he had been called the " immortal bard," as a matter of course, as we speak of Moses and Aaron, there having been but one of each in the world; after all this, comes a lad of sixteen years of age, writes that which learned doctors declare could have been written by no man but Shakspeare, and when it is discovered that this laughing boy is the real author, the doctors turn round upon him, with all the newspapers, magazines, and reviews, and, of

course, the public at their back, revile him as an
impostor; and, under that odious name, hunt him
out of society, and doom him to starve! This lesson,
at any rate, he has given us, not to rely on the judgment of doctors and other pretenders to literary
superiority. Every young man, when he takes up a
book for the first time, ought to remember this
story; and if he do remember it, he will disregard
fashion with regard to the book, and will pay little
attention to the decision of those who call themselves
critics.

80. I hope that your taste will keep you aloof from
the writings of those detestable villains, who employ
the powers of their mind in debauching the minds of
others, or in endeavours to do it. They present their
poison in such captivating forms, that it requires
great virtue and resolution to withstand their
temptations; and they have, perhaps, done a thousand times as much mischief in the world as all the
infidels and atheists put together. These men ought
to be called literary pimps; they ought to be held in
universal abhorrence, and never spoken of but with
execration. Any appeal to bad passions is to be
despised; any appeal to ignorance and prejudice;
but here is an appeal to the frailties of human nature,
and an endeavour to make the mind corrupt, just as
it is beginning to possess its powers. I never have
known any but bad men, worthless men, men unworthy of any portion of respect, who took delight
in, or even kept in their possession, writings of the
description to which I here allude. The writings of
Swift have this blemish; and, though he is not a

teacher of lewdness, but rather the contrary, there are certain parts of his poems which are much too filthy for any decent person to read. It was beneath him to stoop to such means of setting forth that wit which would have been far more brilliant without them. I have heard that in the library of what is called an " illustrious person," sold some time ago, there was an immense collection of books of this infamous description; and from this circumstance, if from no other, I should have formed my judgment of the character of that person.

81. Besides reading, a young man ought to write, if he have the capacity and the leisure. If you wish to remember a thing well, put it into writing, even if you burn the paper immediately after you have done; for the eye greatly assists the mind. Memory consists of a concatenation of ideas, the place, the time, and other circumstances, lead to the recollection of facts; and no circumstance more effectually than stating the facts upon paper. A journal should be kept by every young man. Put down something against every day in the year, if it be merely a description of the weather. You will not have done this for one year without finding the benefit of it. It disburdens the mind of many things to be recollected; it is amusing and useful, and ought by no means to be neglected. How often does it happen that we cannot make a statement of facts, sometimes very interesting to ourselves and our friends, for the want of a record of the places where we were, and of things that occurred on such and such a day! How often does it happen that we get into disagree-

able disputes about things that have passed, and about the time and other circumstances attending them! As a thing of mere curiosity it is of some value, and may frequently prove of very great utility. It demands not more than a minute in the twenty-four hours; and that minute is most agreeably and advantageously employed. It tends greatly to produce regularity in the conducting of affairs; it is a thing demanding a small portion of attention once in every day; I myself have found it to be attended with great and numerous benefits, and I therefore strongly recommend it to the practice of every reader.

LETTER III

ADVICE TO A LOVER

82. THERE are two descriptions of lovers on whom all advice would be wasted; namely, those in whose minds passion so wholly overpowers reason as to deprive the party of his sober senses. Few people are entitled to more compassion than young men thus affected: it is a species of insanity that assails them; and when it produces self-destruction, which it does in England more frequently than in all the other countries in the world put together, the mortal remains of the sufferer ought to be dealt with in as tender a manner as that of which the most merciful construction of the law will allow. If Sir Samuel Romilly's remains were, as they were, in fact, treated as those of a person labouring under " temporary mental derangement," surely the youth who destroys his life on account of unrequited love, ought to be considered in as mild a light! Sir Samuel was represented, in the evidence taken before the coroner's jury, to have been inconsolable for the loss of his wife; that his loss had so dreadful an effect upon his mind that it bereft him of his reason, made life insupportable, and led him to commit the act of suicide; and, on this ground alone, his remains and his estate were rescued from the awful, though just and

wise, sentence of the law. But, unfortunately for the reputation of the administration of that just and wise law, there had been, only about two years before, a poor man, at Manchester, buried in cross roads, and under circumstances which entitled his remains to mercy much more clearly than in the case of Sir Samuel Romilly.

83. This unfortunate youth, whose name was Smith, and who was a shoemaker, was in love with a young woman, who, in spite of all his importunities and his proofs of ardent passion, refused to marry him, and even discovered her liking for another; and he, unable to support life, accompanied by the thought of her being in possession of anybody but himself, put an end to his life by the means of a rope. If, in any case, we are to presume the existence of insanity; if, in any case, we are led to believe the thing without positive proof; if, in any case, there can be an apology in human nature itself, for such an act, this was that case. We all know (as I observed at the time), that is to say, all of us who cannot wait to calculate upon the gains and losses of the affair; all of us, except those who are endowed with this provident frigidity, know well what youthful love is, and what its torments are, when accompanied by even the smallest portion of jealousy. Every man, and especially every Englishman (for here we seldom love or hate by halves), will recollect how many mad pranks he has played; how many wild and ridiculous things he has said and done between the age of sixteen and that of twenty-two; how many times a kind glance has scattered all his reasoning and reso-

lutions to the winds; how many times a cool look
has plunged him into the deepest misery! Poor
Smith, who was at this age of love and madness,
might surely be presumed to have done the deed in
a moment of " temporary mental derangement."
He was an object of compassion in every humane
breast: he had parents and brethren and kindred and
friends to lament his death, and to feel shame at the
disgrace inflicted on his lifeless body: yet *he* was
pronounced to be a *felo de se*, or self-murderer, and
his body was put into a hole by the wayside, with a
stake driven down through it; while that of Romilly
had mercy extended to it, on the ground that the
act had been occasioned by " temporary mental
derangement," caused by his grief for the death of
his wife!

84. To reason with passion like that of the unfortunate Smith, is perfectly useless; you may, with
as much chance of success, reason and remonstrate
with the winds or the waves: if you make impression,
it lasts but for a moment: your effort, like an in-
adequate stoppage of waters, only adds, in the end,
to the violence of the torrent: the current must have
and will have its course, be the consequences what
they may. In cases not quite so decided, absence, the
sight of new faces, the sound of new voices, generally
serve, if not as a radical cure, as a mitigation, at least,
of the disease. But the worst of it is, that, on this
point, we have the girls (and women too) against us!
For they look upon it as right that every lover should
be a little maddish; and every attempt to rescue him
from the thraldom imposed by their charms, they

look upon as an overt act of treason against their
natural sovereignty. No girl ever liked a young man
less for his having done things foolish and wild and
ridiculous, provided she was sure that love of her
had been the cause: let her but be satisfied upon this
score, and there are very few things which she will
not forgive. And, though wholly unconscious of the
fact, she is a great and sound philosopher after all;
for, from the nature of things, the rearing of a family
always has been, is, and must ever be, attended with
cares and troubles, which must infallibly produce, at
times, feelings to be combated and overcome by
nothing short of that ardent affection which first
brought the parties together. So that, talk as long as
Parson Malthus likes about " moral restraint," and
report as long as the Committees of Parliament please
about preventing " premature and improvident marriages " amongst the labouring classes, the passion
that they would restrain, while it is necessary to the
existence of mankind, is the greatest of all the com-
pensations for the inevitable cares, troubles, hardships, and sorrows of life; and as to the marriages, if
they could once be rendered universally provident,
every generous sentiment would quickly be banished
from the world.

85. The other description of lovers, with whom it
is useless to reason, are those who love according to
the rules of arithemtic, or who measure their matrimonial expectations by the chain of the land surveyor. These are not love and marriage; they are
bargain and sale. Young men will naturally, and
almost necessarily, fix their choice on young women

in their own rank in life, because from habit and intercourse they will know them best. But if the length of the girl's purse, present or contingent, be a consideration with the man, or the length of his purse, present or contingent, be a consideration with her, it is an affair of bargain and sale. I know that kings, princes, and princesses, are, in respect of marriage, restrained by the law: I know that nobles, if not thus restrained by positive law, are restrained, in fact, by the very nature of their order. And here is a disadvantage which, as far as real enjoyment of life is concerned, more than counterbalances all the advantages that they possess over the rest of the community. This disadvantage, generally speaking, pursues rank and riches downwards, till you approach very nearly to that numerous class who live by manual labour, becoming, however, less and less as you descend. You generally find even very vulgar rich men making a sacrifice of their natural and rational taste to their mean and ridiculous pride, and thereby providing for themselves an ample supply of misery for life. By preferring " provident marriages " to marriages of love, they think to secure themselves against all the evils of poverty; but if poverty come, and come it may, and frequently does, in spite of the best-laid plans, and best modes of conduct; if poverty come, then where is the counterbalance for that ardent mutual affection which troubles, and losses, and crosses, always increase rather than diminish, and which, amidst all the calamities that can befall a man, whispers to his heart, that his best possession is still left him unimpaired? The Worcestershire

Baronet, who has had to endure the sneers of fools on account of his marriage with a beautiful and virtuous barmaid, would, were the present ruinous measures of the Government to drive him from his mansion to a cottage, still have a source of happiness; while many of those who might fall in company with him, would, in addition to all their other troubles, have, perhaps, to endure the reproaches of wives to whom poverty, or even humble life, would be insupportable.

86. If marrying for the sake of money be, under any circumstances, despicable, if not disgraceful: if it be, generally speaking, a species of legal prostitution, only a little less shameful than that which, under some governments, is openly licensed for the sake of a tax, if this be the case generally, what ought to be said of a young man, who, in the hey-dey of youth, should couple himself on to a libidinous woman, old enough, perhaps, to be his grandmother, ugly as the nightmare, offensive alike to the sight and the smell, and who should pretend to love her too; and all this merely for the sake of her money? Why, it ought, and it doubtless would be said of him, that his conduct was a libel on both man and woman-kind; that his name ought, for ever, to be synonymous with baseness and nastiness, and that in no age and in no nation, not marked by a general depravity of manners, and total absence of all sense of shame, every associate, male or female, of such a man, or of his filthy mate, would be held in abhorrence. Public morality would drive such a hateful pair from society, and strict justice would hunt them from the face of the earth.

87. Buonaparte could not be said to marry for money, but his motive was little better. It was for dominion, for power, for ambition, and that, too, of the most contemptible kind. I knew an American gentleman, with whom Buonaparte had always been a great favourite; but the moment the news arrived of his divorce and second marriage, he gave him up. This piece of grand prostitution was too much to be defended. And the truth is, that Buonaparte might have dated his decline from the day of that marriage. My American friend said, " If I had been he, I would, in the first place, have married the poorest and prettiest girl in all France." If he had done this, he would, in all probability, have now been on an imperial throne, instead of being eaten by worms at the bottom of a very deep hole in St. Helena; whence, however, his bones convey to the world the moral, that to marry for money, for ambition, or from any motive other than the one pointed out by affection, is not the road to glory, to happiness, or to peace.

88. Let me now turn from these two descriptions of lovers, with whom it is useless to reason, and address myself to you, my reader, whom I suppose to be a real lover, but not so smitten as to be bereft of your reason. You should never forget that marriage, which is a state that every young person ought to have in view, is a thing to last for life; and that, generally speaking, it is to make life happy or miserable; for, though a man may bring his mind to something nearly a state of indifference, even that is misery, except with those who can hardly be reckoned among sensitive beings. Marriage brings

numerous cares, which are amply compensated by the more numerous delights which are their companions. But to have the delights, as well as the cares, the choice of the partner must be fortunate. Say fortunate; for, after all, love, real love, impassioned affection, is an ingredient so absolutely necessary, that no perfect reliance can be placed on the judgment. Yet the judgment may do something; reason may have some influence; and, therefore, I here offer you my advice with regard to the exercise of that reason.

89. The things which you ought to desire in a wife are, 1. Chastity; 2. Sobriety; 3. Industry; 4. Frugality; 5. Cleanliness; 6. Knowledge of domestic affairs; 7. Good temper; 8. Beauty.

90. Chastity, perfect modesty, in word, deed, and even thought, is so essential, that, without it, no female is fit to be a wife. It is not enough that a young woman abstain from everything approaching towards indecorum in her behaviour towards men; it is, with me, not enough that she cast down her eyes, or turn aside her head with a smile when she hears an indelicate allusion: she ought to appear not to understand it, and to receive from it no more impression than if she were a post. A loose woman is a disagreeable acquaintance: what must she be, then, as a wife? Love is so blind, and vanity is so busy in persuading us that our own qualities will be sufficient to ensure fidelity, that we are very apt to think nothing or, at any rate, very little of trifling symptoms of levity; but if such symptoms show themselves now, we may be well assured that we shall never possess

the power of effecting a cure. If prudery mean false modesty, it is to be despised; but if it mean modesty pushed to the utmost extent, I confess that I like it. Your " free and hearty " girls I have liked very well to talk and laugh with; but never, for one moment, did it enter into my mind that I could have endured a " free and hearty " girl for a wife. The thing is, I repeat, to last for life; it is to be a counterbalance for troubles and misfortunes; and it must, therefore, be perfect, or it had been better not be at all. To say that one despises jealousy is foolish: it is a thing to be lamented; but the very elements of it ought to be avoided. Gross indeed is the beast, for he is unworthy the name of man; nasty indeed is the wretch, who can even entertain a thought of putting himself between a pair of sheets with a wife of whose in-fidelity he possesses the proof; but, in such cases, a man ought to be very slow to believe appearances: and he ought not to decide against his wife but upon the clearest proof. The last, and, indeed, the only effectual safeguard, is to begin well; to make a good choice; to let the beginning be such as to render infidelity and jealousy next to impossible. If you begin in grossness; if you couple yourself on to one with whom you have taken liberties, infidelity is the natural and just consequence. When a peer of the realm, who had not been over-fortunate in his matrimonial affairs, was urging Major Cartwright to seek for nothing more than " moderate reform," the Major (forgetting the domestic circumstances of his Lordship), asked him how he should relish " mode-rate chastity " in a wife! The bare use of the two words, thus coupled together, is sufficient to excite disgust. Yet with this "moderate chastity" you must be, and ought to be, content, if you have entered into marriage with one, in whom you have ever discovered the slightest approach towards lewdness, either in deeds, words, or looks. To marry has been your own act; you have made the contract for your own gratification; you knew the character of the other party; and the children, if any, or the community, are not to be the sufferers for your gross and corrupt passion. "Moderate chastity" is all that you have, in fact, contracted for: you have it, and you have no reason to complain. When I come to address myself to the husband, I shall have to say more upon this subject, which I dismiss for the present with observing, that my observation has convinced me that, when families are rendered unhappy from the existence of "moderate chastity," the fault, first or last, has been in the man, ninety-nine times out of every hundred.

91. Sobriety. By Sobriety I do not mean merely an absence of drinking to a state of intoxication; for, if that be hateful in a man, what must it be in a woman! There is a Latin proverb which says, that wine, that is to say, intoxication, brings forth truth. Whatever it may do in this way in men, in women it is sure, unless prevented by age or by salutary ugliness, to produce a moderate, and a very moderate portion of chastity. There never was a drunken woman, a woman who loved strong drink, who was chaste, if the opportunity of being the contrary presented itself to her. There are cases where health requires wine, and even small portions of more

ardent liquor; but (reserving what I have further to say on this point till I come to the conduct of the husband) young unmarried women can seldom stand in need of these stimulants; and, at any rate, only in cases of well-known definite ailments. Wine! " only a glass or two of wine at dinner, or so! " As soon as have married a girl whom I had thought liable to be persuaded to drink, habitually, " only a glass or two of wine at dinner, or so; " as soon as have married such a girl, I would have taken a strumpet from the streets. And it has not required age to give me this way of thinking: it has always been rooted in my mind from the moment that I began to think the girls prettier than posts. There are few things so disgusting as a guzzling woman. A gormandizing one is bad enough; but one who tips off the liquor with an appetite, and exclaims, " Good, good! " by a smack of her lips, is fit for nothing but a brothel. There may be cases, amongst the hard-labouring women, such as reapers, for instance, especially when they have children at the breast: there may be cases, where very hard-working women may stand in need of a little good beer, beer which, if taken in immoderate quantities, would produce intoxication. But while I only allow the possibility of the existence of such cases, I deny the necessity of any strong drink at all in every other case. Yet, in this metropolis, it is the general custom for tradesmen, journeymen, and even labourers, to have regularly on their tables the big brewers' poison twice in every day, and at the rate of not less than a pot to a person, women as well as men, as the allowance for the day. A pot of

poison a day, at five-pence the pot, amounts to seven
pounds and two shillings in the year! Man and wife
suck down, in this way, fourteen pounds four shillings a year! Is it any wonder that they are clad in
rags, that they are skin and bone, and that their
children are covered with filth?

92. But by the word sobriety, in a young woman,
I mean a great deal more than even a rigid abstinence
from that love of drink which I am not to suppose,
and which I do not believe, to exist anything like
generally amongst the young women of this country.
I mean a great deal more than this; I mean sobriety
of conduct. The word sober, and its derivatives, do
not confine themselves to matters of drink; they
express steadiness, seriousness, carefulness, scrupulous propriety of conduct; and they are thus used
amongst country people in many parts of England.
When a Somersetshire fellow makes too free with a
girl, she reproves him with, " Come! be sober!"
And when we wish a team, or anything to be moved
on steadily and with great care, we cry out to the
carter or other operator, " Soberly, soberly." Now,
this species of sobriety is a great qualification in the
person you mean to make your wife. Skipping,
capering, romping, rattling girls are very amusing,
where all costs and other consequences are out of the
question; and they may become sober in the Somersetshire sense of the word. But while you have no
certainty of this, you have a presumptive argument
on the other side. To be sure, when girls are mere
children, they are to play and romp like children.
But when they arrive at that age which turns their

thoughts towards that sort of connection which is to be theirs for life; when they begin to think of having the command of a house, however small or poor, it is time for them to cast away the levity of the child. It is natural, nor is it very wrong, that I know of, for children to like to gad about and to see all sorts of strange sights, though I do not approve of this even in children; but if I could not have found a young woman (and I am sure I never should have married an old one) who I was not sure possessed all the qualities expressed by the word sobriety, I should have remained a bachelor to the end of that life, which, in that case, would, I am satisfied, have terminated without my having performed a thousandth part of those labours which have been, and are, in spite of all political prejudice, the wonder of all who have seen or heard of them. Scores of gentlemen have, at different times, expressed to me their surprise, that I was " always in spirits; " that nothing pulled me down; and the truth is, that, throughout nearly forty years of troubles, losses, and crosses, assailed all the while by more numerous and powerful enemies than ever man had before to contend with, and performing, at the same time, labours greater than man ever before performed, all those labours requiring mental exertion, and some of them mental exertion of the highest order,—the truth is, that, throughout the whole of this long time of troubles and of labours, I have never known a single hour of real anxiety; the troubles have been no troubles to me; I have not known what lowness of spirits meaned; have been more gay, and felt less

care, than any bachelor that ever lived. " You are
always in spirits, Cobbett! " To be sure; for why
should I not? Poverty I have always set at defiance,
and I could, therefore, defy the temptations of riches;
and, as to home and children, I had taken care to
provide myself with an inexhaustible store of that
" sobriety " which I am so strongly recommending
my reader to provide himself with; or, if he cannot
do that, to deliberate long before he ventures on the
life-enduring matrimonial voyage. This sobriety is a
title to trustworthiness; and this, young man, is the
treasure that you ought to prize far above all others.
Miserable is the husband, who, when he crosses the
threshold of his house, carries with him doubts and
fears and suspicions. I do not mean suspicions of the
fidelity of his wife, but of her care, frugality, attention
to his interests, and to the health and morals of his
children. Miserable is the man who cannot leave all
unlocked, and who is not sure, quite certain, that all
is safe as if grasped in his own hand. He is the happy
husband, who can go away at a moment's warning,
leaving his house and his family with as little anxiety
as he quits an inn, not more fearing to find, on his
return, anything wrong than he would fear a dis-
continuance of the rising and setting of the sun;
and if, as in my case, leaving books and papers all
lying about at sixes and sevens, finding them arranged
in proper order, and the room, during the lucky
interval, freed from the effects of his and his ploughman's or gardener's dirty shoes. Such a man has no
real cares; such a man has no troubles; and this is
the sort of life that I have led. I have had all the

numerous and indescribable delights of home and children, and, at the same time, all the bachelor's freedom from domestic cares: and to this cause, far more than to any other, my readers owe those labours, which I never could have performed, if even the slightest degree of want of confidence at home had ever once entered into my mind.

93. But, in order to possess this precious trustworthiness, you must, if you can, exercise your reason in the choice of your partner. If she be vain of her person, very fond of her dress, fond of flattery, at all given to gadding about, fond of what are called parties of pleasure, or coquettish, though in the least degree; if either of these, she never will be trustworthy; she cannot change her nature; and if you marry her, you will be unjust if you expect trustworthiness at her hands. But, besides this, even if you find in her that innate " sobriety," of which I have been speaking, there requires on your part, and that at once, too, confidence and trust without any limit. Confidence is, in this case, nothing unless it be reciprocal. To have a trustworthy wife, you must begin by showing her, even before you are married, that you have no suspicions, no fears, no doubts, with regard to her. Many a man has been discarded by a virtuous girl, merely on account of his querulous conduct. All women despise jealous men; and, if they marry such, their motive is other than that of affection. Therefore, begin by proofs of unlimited confidence; and, as example may serve to assist precept, and as I never have preached that which I have not practised, I will

give you the history of my own conduct in this respect.

94. When I first saw my wife, she was thirteen years old, and I was within about a month of twenty-one. She was the daughter of a sergeant of artillery, and I was the sergeant-major of a regiment of foot, both stationed in forts near the city of St. John, in the province of New Brunswick. I sat in the same room with her for about an hour, in company with others, and I made up my mind that she was the very girl for me. That I thought her beautiful is certain, for that I had always said should be an indispensable qualification; but I saw in her what I deemed marks of that sobriety of conduct of which I have said so much, which has been by far the greatest blessing of my life. It was now dead of winter, and, of course, the snow several feet deep on the ground, and the weather piercing cold. It was my habit, when I had done my morning's writing, to go out at break of day to take a walk on a hill at the foot of which our barracks lay. In about three mornings after I had first seen her, I had, by an invitation to breakfast with me, got up two young men to join me in my walk; and our road lay by the house of her father and mother. It was hardly light, but she was out on the snow, scrubbing out a washing-tub. " That's the girl for me," said I, when we had got out of her hearing. One of these young men came to England soon afterwards; and he, who keeps an inn in Yorkshire, came over to Preston, at the time of the election, to verify whether I were the same man. When he found that I was, he appeared

surprised; but what was his surprise when I told him that those tall young men whom he saw around me were the sons of that pretty little girl that he and I saw scrubbing out the washing-tub on the snow in New Brunswick at daybreak in the morning!

95. From the day that I first spoke to her, I never had a thought of her ever being the wife of any other man, more than I had a thought of her being transformed into a chest of drawers; and I formed my resolution at once, to marry her as soon as we could get permission, and to get out of the army as soon as I could. So that this matter was at once settled as firmly as if written in the book of fate. At the end of about six months, my regiment, and I along with it, were removed to Frederickton, a distance of a hundred miles up the river of St. John; and, which was worse, the artillery was expected to go off to England a year or two before our regiment! The artillery went, and she along with them; and now it was that I acted a part becoming a real and sensible lover. I was aware that, when she got to that gay place Woolwich, the house of her father and mother, necessarily visited by numerous persons not the most select, might become unpleasant to her, and I did not like, besides, that she should continue to work hard. I had saved a hundred and fifty guineas, the earnings of my early hours, in writing for the paymaster, the quartermaster, and others, in addition to the savings of my own pay. I sent her all my money before she sailed; and wrote to her, to beg of her, if she found her home uncomfortable, to hire a lodging with respectable people: and, at any rate,

not to spare the money, by any means, but to buy herself good clothes, and to live without hard work, until I arrived in England; and I, in order to induce her to lay out the money, told her that I should get plenty more before I came home.

96. As the malignity of the devil would have it, we were kept abroad two years longer than our time, Mr. Pitt (England not being so tame then as she is now) having knocked up a dust with Spain about Nootka Sound. Oh how I cursed Nootka Sound, and poor brawling Pitt too, I am afraid! At the end of four years, however, home I came, landed at Portsmouth, and got my discharge from the army by the great kindness of poor Lord Edward Fitzgerald, who was then the major of my regiment. I found my little girl a servant of all work (and hard work it was), at five pounds a year, in the house of a Captain Brisac; and, without hardly saying a word about the matter, she put into my hands the whole of my hundred and fifty guineas unbroken!

97. Need I tell the reader what my feelings were? Need I tell kind-hearted English parents what effect this anecdote must have produced on the minds of our children? Need I attempt to describe what effect this example ought to have on every young woman who shall do me the honour to read this book? Admiration of her conduct, and self-gratulation on this indubitable proof of the soundness of my own judgment, were now added to my love of her beautiful person.

98. Now, I do not say that there are not many young women of this country who would, under

similar circumstances, have acted as my wife did in this case; on the contrary, I hope, and do sincerely believe, that there are. But when her age is considered; when we reflect that she was living in a place crowded, literally crowded, with gaily-dressed and handsome young men, many of whom really far richer and in higher rank than I was, and scores of them ready to offer her their hand; when we reflect that she was living amongst young women who put upon their backs every shilling that they could come at; when we see her keeping the bag of gold untouched, and working hard to provide herself with but mere necessary apparel, and doing this while she was passing from fourteen to eighteen years of age; when we view the whole of the circumstances, we must say that here is an example which, while it reflects honour on her sex, ought to have weight with every young woman whose eyes or ears this relation shall reach.

99. If any young man imagine that this great sobriety of conduct in young women must be accompanied with seriousness approaching to gloom, he is, according to my experience and observation, very much deceived. The contrary is the fact; for I have found that as, amongst men, your jovial companions are, except over the bottle, the dullest and most insipid of souls; so amongst women, the gay, the rattling, and laughing, are, unless some party of pleasure, or something out of domestic life, is going on, generally in the dumps and blue-devils. Some stimulus is always craved after by this description of women; some sight to be seen, something to see or

hear other than what is to be found at home, which, as it affords no incitement, nothing " to raise and keep up the spirits," is looked upon merely as a place to be at for want of a better; merely a place for eating and drinking, and the like; merely a biding-place, whence to sally in search of enjoyments. A greater curse than a wife of this description it would be somewhat difficult to find; and, in your character of lover, you are to provide against it. I hate a dull, melancholy, moping thing; I could not have existed in the same house with such a thing for a single month. The mopers are, too, all giggle at other times; the gaiety is for others, and the moping for the husband, to comfort him, happy man, when he is alone: plenty of smiles and of badinage for others, and for him to participate with others; but the moping is reserved exclusively for him. One hour she is capering about, as if rehearsing a jig; and the next, sighing to the motion of a lazy needle, or weeping over a novel: and this is called sentiment! Music, indeed! Give me a mother singing to her clean and fat and rosy baby, and making the house ring with her extravagant and hyperbolical encomiums on it. That is the music which is " the food of love," and not the formal, pedantic noises, an affectation of skill in which is now-a-days the ruin of half the young couples in the middle rank of life. Let any man observe, as I so frequently have with delight, the excessive fondness of the labouring people for their children. Let him observe with what pride they dress them out on a Sunday, with means deducted from their own scanty meals. Let him observe the husband, who has toiled all the week like a horse, nursing the baby, while the wife is preparing the bit of dinner. Let him observe them both abstaining from a sufficiency, lest the children should feel the pinchings of hunger. Let him observe, in short, the whole of their demeanour, the real mutual affection, evinced, not in words, but in unequivocal deeds. Let him observe these things, and, having then cast a look at the lives of the great and wealthy, he will say, with me, that when a man is choosing his partner for life, the dread of poverty ought to be cast to the winds. A labourer's cottage, on a Sunday; the husband or wife having a baby in arms, looking at two or three older ones playing between the flower-borders going from the wicket to the door, is, according to my taste, the most interesting object that eyes ever beheld; and it is an object to be beheld in no country upon earth but in England. In France, a labourer's cottage means a shed with a dung-heap before the door; and it means much about the same in America, where it is wholly inexcusable. In riding once, about five years ago, from Petworth to Horsham, on a Sunday in the afternoon, I came to a solitary cottage, which stood at about twenty yards distance from the road. There was the wife with the baby in her arms, the husband teaching another child to walk, while four more were at play before them. I stopped and looked at them for some time, and then, turning my horse, rode up to the wicket, getting into talk by asking the distance to Horsham. I found that the man worked chiefly in the woods, and that he was doing pretty well. The wife was then only twenty-two, and the man only twenty-five. She was a pretty woman, even for Sussex, which, not excepting Lancashire, contains the prettiest women in England. He was a very fine and stout young man. " Why," said I, " how many children do you reckon to have at last? " " I do not care how many," said the man: " God never sends mouths without sending meat." " Did you ever hear," said I, " of one Parson Malthus? " " No, sir." " Why, if he were to hear of your works, he would be outrageous; for he wants an Act of Parliament to prevent poor people from marrying young, and from having such lots of children." " Oh! the brute! " exclaimed the wife; while the husband laughed, thinking that I was joking. I asked the man whether he had ever had relief from the parish; and upon his answering in the negative, I took out my purse, took from it enough to bait my horse at Horsham, and to clear my turnpikes to Worth, whither I was going to stay awhile, and gave him all the rest. Now, is it not a shame, is it not a sin of all sins, that people like these should, by acts of the Government, be reduced to such misery as to be induced to abandon their homes and their country, to seek, in a foreign land, the means of preventing themselves and their children from starving? And this has been, and now is, actually the case with many such families in this same county of Sussex!

100. An ardent-minded young man (who, by-the-by, will, as I am afraid, have been wearied by this rambling digression) may fear that this great sobriety of conduct in a young woman, for which I have been

so strenuously contending, argues a want of that warmth which he naturally so much desires; and if my observation and experience warranted the entertaining of this fear, I should say, had I to live my life over again, give me the warmth, and I will stand my chance as to the rest. But this observation and this experience tell me the contrary; they tell me that levity is, ninety-nine times out of a hundred, the companion of a want of ardent feeling. Prostitutes never love, and, for the far greater part, never did. Their passion, which is more mere animal than anything else, is easily gratified; they, like rakes, change, not only without pain, but with pleasure; that is to say, pleasure as great as they can enjoy. Women of light minds have seldom any ardent passion; love is a mere name, unless confined to one object; and young women, in whom levity of conduct is observable, will not be thus restricted. I do not, however, recommend a young man to be too severe in judging, where the conduct does not go beyond mere levity, and is not bordering on loose conduct; for something here depends upon constitution and animal spirits, and something also upon the manners of the country. That levity, which in a French girl I should not have thought a great deal of, would have frightened me away from an English or an American girl. When I was in France, just after I was married, there happened to be amongst our acquaintance a gay, sprightly girl, of about seventeen. I was remonstrating with her, one day, on the facility with which she seemed to shift her smiles from object to object; and she, stretching one arm out in an upward

direction, the other in a downward direction, raising
herself upon one foot, leaning her body on one side,
and thus throwing herself into a flying attitude,
answered my grave lecture by singing, in a very
sweet voice (significantly bowing her head, and
smiling at the same time), the following lines from
the vaudeville, in the play of Figaro:

> " Si l'amour a des ailles,
>   N'est-ce pas pour voltiger? "

that is, if love has wings, is it not to flutter about
with? The wit, argument, and manner, all together,
silenced me. She, after I left France, married a very
worthy man, has had a large family, and has been,
and is, a most excellent wife and mother. But that
which does sometimes well in France does not do
here at all. Our manners are more grave: steadiness
is the rule, and levity the exception. Love may voltige
in France; but in England it cannot, with safety to
the lover: and it is a truth which, I believe, no man
of attentive observation will deny, that, as, in
general, English wives are more warm in their conjugal attachments than those of France, so, with
regard to individuals, that those English women
who are the most light in their manners, and who
are the least constant in their attachments, have the
smallest portion of that warmth, that indescribable
passion which God has given to human beings as the
great counterbalance to all the sorrows and sufferings
of life.

101. Industry. By industry, I do not mean merely
laboriousness, merely labour or activity of body, for

purposes of gain or of saving; for there may be industry amongst those who have more money than they know well what to do with, and there may be lazy ladies, as well as lazy farmers' and tradesmen's wives. There is no state of life in which industry in a wife is not necessary to the happiness and prosperity of the family, at the head of the household affairs of which she is placed. If she be lazy there will be lazy servants, and which is a great deal worse, children habitually lazy: everything, however necessary to be done, will be put off to the last moment: then it will be done badly, and in many cases not at all; the dinner will be too late; the journey or the visit will be tardy; inconveniences of all sorts will be continually arising: there will always be a heavy arrear of things unperformed; and this, even amongst the most wealthy of all, is a great curse; for if they have no business imposed upon them by necessity, they make business for themselves; life would be unbearable without it: and therefore a lazy woman must always be a curse, be her rank or station what it may.

102. But who is to tell whether a girl will make an industrious woman? How is the purblind lover especially, to be able to ascertain whether she, whose smiles and dimples, and bewitching lips have half bereft him of his senses; how is he to be able to judge, from anything that he can see, whether the beloved object will be industrious or lazy? Why, it is very difficult: it is a matter that reason has very little to do with; but there are, nevertheless, certain outward and visible signs, from which a man, not wholly deprived of the use of his reason, may form a pretty

accurate judgment as to this matter. It was a story in
Philadelphia, some years ago, that a young man, who
was courting one of three sisters, happened to be on
a visit to her, when all the three were present, and
when one said to the others, " I wonder where our
needle is." Upon which he withdrew, as soon as was
consistent with the rules of politeness, resolved never
to think more of a girl who possessed a needle only
in partnership, and who, it appeared, was not too
well informed as to the place where even that share
was deposited.

103. This was, to be sure, a very flagrant instance
of a want of industry; for if the third part of the use
of a needle satisfied her when single, it was reasonable
to anticipate that marriage would banish that useful
implement altogether. But such instances are seldom
suffered to come in contact with the eyes and ears
of the lover, to disguise all defects from whom is the
great business, not only of the girl herself, but of her
whole family. There are, however, certain outward
signs, which, if attended to with care, will serve as
pretty sure guides. And, first, if you find the tongue
lazy, you may be nearly certain that the hands and
feet are the same. By laziness of the tongue I do not
mean silence; I do not mean an absence of talk, for
that is, in most cases, very good; but I mean a slow
and soft utterance; a sort of sighing out of the words
instead of speaking them; a sort of letting the sounds
fall out, as if the party were sick at stomach. The
pronunciation of an industrious person is generally
quick, distinct, and the voice, if not strong, firm at
the least. Not masculine; as feminine as possible; not

a croak nor a bawl, but a quick, distinct, and sound voice. Nothing is much more disgusting than what the sensible country people call a maw-mouthed woman. A maw-mouthed man is bad enough: he is sure to be a lazy fellow; but a woman of this description, in addition to her laziness, soon becomes the most disgusting of mates. In this whole world nothing is much more hateful than a female's underjaw lazily moving up and down, and letting out a long string of half-articulate sounds. It is impossible for any man, who has any spirit in him, to love such a woman for any length of time.

104. Look a little, also, at the labours of the teeth, for these correspond with those of the other members of the body, and with the operations of the mind. " Quick at meals, quick at work," is a saying as old as the hills, in this, the most industrious nation upon earth; and never was there a truer saying. But fashion comes in here, and decides that you shall not be quick at meals; that you shall sit and be carrying on the affair of eating for an hour or more. Good God! what have I not suffered on this account! However, though she must sit as long as the rest, and though she join in the performance (for it is a real performance) unto the end of the last scene, she cannot make her teeth abandon their character. She may, and must suffer the slice to linger on the plate, and must make the supply slow, in order to fill up the time; but when she does bite, she cannot well disguise what nature has taught her to do; and you may be assured, that if her jaws move in slow time, and if she rather squeeze than bite the food; if she

so deal with it as to leave you in doubt as to whether she mean finally to admit or reject it; if she deal with it thus, set her down as being, in her very nature, incorrigibly lazy. Never mind the pieces of needle-work, the tambouring, the maps of the world made by her needle. Get to see her at work upon a mutton-chop, or a bit of bread and cheese; and if she deal quickly with these, you have a pretty good security for that activity, that stirring industry, without which a wife is a burden instead of being a help. And, as to love, it cannot live for more than a month or two (in the breast of a man of spirit) towards a lazy woman.

105. Another mark of industry is, a quick step, and a somewhat heavy tread, showing that the foot comes down with a hearty good will; and if the body lean a little forward, and the eyes keep steadily in the same direction, while the feet are going, so much the better, for these discover earnestness to arrive at the intended point. I do not like, and I never liked, your sauntering, soft-stepping girls, who move as if they were perfectly indifferent as to the result; and, as to the love part of the story, whoever expects ardent and lasting affection from one of these sauntering girls, will, when too late, find his mistake: the character runs the same all the way through; and no man ever yet saw a sauntering girl, who did not, when married, make a mawkish wife, and a cold-hearted mother; cared very little for either by husband or children; and, of course, having no store of those blessings which are the natural resources to apply to in sickness and in old age.

106. Early rising is another mark of industry; and though, in the higher situations of life, it may be of no importance in a mere pecuniary point of view, it is, even there, of importance in other respects; for it is, I should imagine, pretty difficult to keep love alive towards a woman who never sees the dew, never beholds the rising sun, and who constantly comes directly from a reeking bed to the breakfast table, and there chews about without appetite the choicest morsels of human food. A man might, perhaps, endure this for a month or two, without being disgusted; but that is ample allowance of time. And as to people in the middle rank of life, where a living and a provision for children is to be sought by labour of some sort or other, late rising in the wife is certain ruin; and never was there yet an early rising wife who had been a late rising girl. If brought up to late rising, she will like it; it will be her habit; she will, when married, never want excuses for indulging in the habit; at first she will be indulged without bounds; to make a change afterwards will be difficult; it will be deemed a wrong done to her; she will ascribe it to diminished affection; a quarrel must ensue, or the husband must submit to be ruined, or, at the very least, to see half the fruit of his labour snored and lounged away. And is this being rigid? is it being harsh? is it being hard upon women? Is it the offspring of the frigid severity of age? It is none of these: it arises from an ardent desire to promote the happiness, and to add to the natural, legitimate, and salutary influence of the female sex. The tendency of this advice is to promote

the preservation of their health; to prolong the duration of their beauty; to cause them to be beloved to the last day of their lives; and to give them during the whole of those lives, weight and consequence, of which laziness would render them wholly unworthy.

107. Frugality. This means the contrary of extravagance. It does not mean stinginess; it does not mean a pinching of the belly, nor a stripping of the back; but it means an abstaining from all unnecessary expenditure, and all unnecessary use of goods of any and of every sort; and a quality of great importance it is, whether the rank in life be high or low. Some people are, indeed, so rich, they have such an over-abundance of money and goods, that how to get rid of them would, to a looker-on, seem to be their only difficulty. But while the inconvenience of even these immense masses is not too great to be overcome by a really extravagant woman, who jumps with joy at a basket of strawberries at a guinea an ounce, and who would not give a straw for green peas later in the year than January; while such a dame would lighten the bags of a loan-monger, or shorten the rent-roll of half a dozen peerages amalgamated into one possession, she would, with very little study and application of her talent, send a nobleman of ordinary estate to the poor-house or the pension-list, which last may be justly regarded as the poor-book of the aristocracy. How many noblemen and gentlemen of fine estates have been ruined and degraded by the extravagance of their wives! More frequently by their own extravagance, perhaps; but, in numerous instances, by that of those whose duty

it is to assist in upholding their stations by husbanding their fortunes.

108. If this be the case amongst the opulent, who
have estates to draw upon, what must be the consequences of a want of frugality in the middle and
lower ranks of life? Here it must be fatal, and
especially amongst that description of persons whose
wives have, in many cases, the receiving as well as
the expending of money. In such a case, there wants
nothing but extravagance in the wife to make ruin
as sure as the arrival of old age. To obtain security
against this is very difficult; yet, if the lover be not
quite blind, he may easily discover a propensity
towards extravagance. The object of his addresses
will, nine times out of ten, not be the manager of a
house; but she must have her dress, and other little
matters under her control. If she be costly in these;
if, in these, she step above her rank, or even to the
top of it; if she purchase all she is able to purchase,
and prefer the showy to the useful, the gay and the
fragile to the less sightly and more durable, he may
be sure that the disposition will cling to her through
life. If he perceive in her a taste for costly food,
costly furniture, costly amusements; if he find her
love of gratification to be bounded only by her want
of means: if he find her full of admiration of the
trappings of the rich, and of desire to be able to
imitate them, he may be pretty sure that she will
not spare his purse when once she gets her hand
into it; and, therefore, if he can bid adieu to her
charms, the sooner he does it the better.

109. The outward and visible and vulgar signs of

extravagance are rings, brooches, bracelets, buckles, necklaces, diamonds (real or mock), and, in short, all the hardware which women put upon their persons. These things may be proper enough in palaces, or in scenes resembling palaces; but when they make their appearance amongst people in the middle rank of life, where, after all, they only serve to show that poverty in the parties which they wish to disguise: when the nasty, mean, tawdry things make their appearance in this rank of life, they are the sure indications of a disposition that will always be straining at what it can never attain. To marry a girl of this disposition is really self-destruction. You never can have either property or peace. Earn her a horse to ride, she will want a gig; earn the gig, she will want a chariot; get her that, she will long for a coach-and-four; and, from stage to stage, she will torment you to the end of her or your days; for still there will be somebody with a finer equipage than you can give her; and as long as this is the case, you will never have rest. Reason would tell her that she could never be at the top; that she must stop at some point short of that; and that, therefore, all expenses in the rivalship are so much thrown away. But reason and brooches and bracelets do not go in company: the girl who has not the sense to perceive that her person is disfigured, and not beautified, by parcels of brass and tin (for they are generally little better) and other hardware, stuck about her body; the girl that is so foolish as not to perceive, that when silks and cottons and cambrics, in their neatest form, have done their best, nothing more is to be done;—the girl that cannot perceive this, is too great a fool to be trusted with the purse of any man.

110. Cleanliness. This is a capital ingredient; for there never yet was, and there never will be, love of long duration, sincere and ardent love, in any man towards a " filthy mate." I mean any man in England, or in those parts of America where the people have descended from the English. I do not say that there are not men enough, even in England, to live peaceably and even contentedly, with dirty, sluttish women; for there are some who seem to like the filth well enough. But what I contend for is this, that there never can exist, for any length of time, ardent affection in any man towards a woman who is filthy either in her person or in her house affairs. Men may be careless as to their own persons; they may, from the nature of their business, or from their want of time to adhere to neatness in dress, be slovenly in their own dress and habits; but they do not relish this in their wives, who must still have charms; and charms and filth do not go together.

111. It is not dress that the husband wants to be perpetual: it is not finery; but cleanliness is everything. The French women dress enough, especially when they sally forth. My excellent neighbour, Mr. John Tredwell, of Long Island, used to say that the French were " pigs in the parlour and peacocks on the promenade; " an alliteration which " Canning's self " might have envied! This occasional cleanliness is not the thing that an English or an American husband wants: he wants it always: indoors as well as out; by night as well as by day; on the floor as well

as on the table; and, however he may grumble about the " fuss " and the " expense " of it, he would grumble more if he had it not. I once saw a picture representing the amusements of Portuguese lovers; that is to say, three or four young men, dressed in gold or silver laced clothes, each having a young girl, dressed like a princess, and affectionately engaged in hunting down and killing the vermin in his head! This was, perhaps, an exaggeration; but that it should have had the shadow of foundation, was enough to fill me with contempt for the whole nation.

112. The signs of cleanliness are, in the first place, a clean skin. An English girl will hardly let her lover see the stale dirt between her fingers, as I have many times seen it between those of French women, and even ladies, of all ages. An English girl will have her face clean, to be sure, if there be soap and water within her reach; but get a glance, just a glance, at her poll, if you have any doubt upon the subject; and if you find there, or behind the ears, what the York-shire people call grime, the sooner you cease your visits the better. I hope now, that no young woman will be offended at this, and think me too severe on her sex. I am only saying, I am only telling the women, that which all men think; and it is a decided advantage to them to be fully informed of our thoughts on the subject. If any one who shall read this, find, upon self-examination, that she is defective in this respect, there is plenty of time for correcting the defect.

113. In the dress you can, amongst rich people,

find little whereon to form a judgment as to cleanliness, because they have not only the dress prepared for them, but put upon them into the bargain. But in the middle rank of life, the dress is a good criterion in two respects; first, as to its colour; for if the white be a sort of yellow, cleanly hands would have been at work to prevent that. A white-yellow cravat, or shirt, on a man, speaks at once the character of his wife; and, be you assured, that she will not take with your dress pains which she has never taken with her own. Then the manner of putting on the dress is no bad foundation for judging. If it be careless, slovenly, if it do not fit properly, no matter for its mean quality: mean as it may be, it may be neatly and trimly put on; and if it be not, take care of yourself; for as you will soon find to your cost, a sloven in one thing is a sloven in all things. The country people judge greatly from the state of the covering of the ankles, and if that be not clean and tight, they conclude that all out of sight is not what it ought to be. Look at the shoes! If they be trodden on one side, loose on the foot, or run down at the heel, it is a very bad sign; and, as to slip-shod, though at coming down in the morning and even before daylight, make up your mind to a rope, rather than to live with a slip-shod wife.

114. Oh! how much do women lose by inattention to these matters? Men, in general, say nothing about it to their wives; but they think about it; they envy their luckier neighbours; and, in numerous cases, consequences the most serious arise from this apparently trifling cause. Beauty is valuable; it is

one of the ties; and a strong tie too: that, however, cannot last to old age; but the charm of cleanliness never ends but with life itself. I dismiss this part of my subject with a quotation from my " Year's Residence in America," containing words which I venture to recommend to every young woman to engrave on her heart: " The sweetest flowers, when they become putrid, stink the most; and a nasty woman is the nastiest thing in nature."

115. Knowledge of Domestic Affairs. Without more or less of this knowledge, a lady, even the wife of a peer, is but a poorish thing. It was the fashion, in former times, for ladies to understand a great deal about these affairs, and it would be very hard to make me believe that this did not tend to promote the interests and honour of their husbands. The affairs of a great family never can be well managed if left wholly to hirelings; and there are many parts of these affairs in which it would be unseemly for the husband to meddle. Surely, no lady can be too high in rank to make it proper for her to be well acquainted with the character and general demeanour of all the female servants. To receive and give them characters is too much to be left to a servant, however good, and of service however long. Much of the ease and happiness of the great and rich must depend on the character of those by whom they are served: they live under the same roof with them; they are frequently the children of their tenants, or poorer neighbours; the conduct of their whole lives must be influenced by the examples and precepts which they here imbibe; and when ladies consider how much

more weight there must be in one word from them than in ten thousand words from a person who, call her what you like, is still a fellow-servant, it does appear strange that they should forego the performance of this at once important and pleasing part of their duty. It was from the mansions of noblemen and gentlemen, and not from boarding-schools, that farmers and tradesmen formerly took their wives; and though these days are gone, with little chance of returning, there is still something left for ladies to do in checking that torrent of immorality which is now crowding the streets with prostitutes, and cramming the jails with thieves.

116. I am, however, addressing myself, in this work, to persons in the middle rank of life; and here a knowledge of domestic affairs is so necessary in every wife, that the lover ought to have it continually in his eye. Not only a knowledge of these affairs, not only to know how things ought to be done, but how to do them, not only to know what ingredients ought to be put into a pie or a pudding, but to be able to make the pie or the pudding. Young people, when they come together, ought not, unless they have fortunes, or are in a great way of business, to think about servants. Servants for what! To help them to eat and drink and sleep? When children come, there must be some help in a farmer's or tradesman's house; but until then, what call for a servant in a house, the master of which has to earn every mouthful that is consumed?

117. I shall, when I come to address myself to the husband, have much more to say upon this subject

of keeping servants; but what the lover, if he be not quite blind, has to look to, is, that his intended wife know how to do the work of a house, unless he have fortune sufficient to keep her like a lady. " Eating and drinking," as I observe in " Cottage Economy," come three times every day: they must come; and however little we may, in the days of our health and vigour, care about choice food and about cookery, we very soon get tired of heavy or burnt bread, and of spoiled joints of meat: we bear them for a time, or for two, perhaps, but about the third time, we lament inwardly; about the fifth time, it must be an extra-ordinary honeymoon that will keep us from com-plaining: if the like continue for a month or two, we begin to repent; and then adieu to all our anticipated delights. We discover, when it is too late, that we have not got a helpmate, but a burden; and the fire of love being damped, the unfortunately educated creature, whose parents are more to blame than she, is, unless she resolve to learn her duty, doomed to lead a life very nearly approaching to that of misery; for, how-ever considerate the husband, he never can esteem her as he would have done, had she been skilled and able in domestic affairs.

118. The mere manual performance of domestic labours is not, indeed, absolutely necessary in the female head of the family of professional men, such as lawyers, doctors, and parsons; but, even here, and also in the case of great merchants, and of gentlemen living on their fortunes, surely the head of the household ought to be able to give directions as to the purchasing of meat, salting meat, making bread,

making preserves of all sorts, and ought to see the things done, or that they be done. She ought to take care that food be well cooked, drink properly prepared and kept; that there be always a sufficient supply; that there be good living without waste; and that, in her department, nothing shall be seen inconsistent with the rank, station, and character of her husband, who, if he have a skilful and industrious wife, will, unless he be of a singularly foolish turn, gladly leave all these things to her absolute dominion, controlled only by the extent of the whole expenditure, of which he must be the best, and, indeed, the sole judge.

119. But, in a farmer's or a tradesman's family, the manual performance is absolute necessary, whether there be servants or not. No one knows how to teach another so well as one who has done, and can do, the thing himself. It was said of a famous French commander, that, in attacking an enemy, he did not say to his men " Go on," but, " Come on; " and whoever have well observed the movements of servants, must know what a prodigious difference there is in the effect of the words *go* and *come*. A very good rule would be, to have nothing to eat in a farmer's or tradesman's house that the mistress did not know how to prepare and cook; no pudding, tart, pie, or cake, that she did not know how to make. Never fear the toil to her: exercise is good for health; and without health there is no beauty; a sick beauty may excite pity; but pity is a short-lived passion. Besides, what is the labour in such a case? And how many thousands of ladies, who loll away the day,

would give half their fortunes for that sound sleep which the stirring housewife seldom fails to enjoy!

120. Yet, if a young farmer or tradesman marry a girl who has been brought up to play music, to what is called draw, to sing, to waste paper, pen, and ink, in writing long and half-romantic letters, and to see shows, and plays, and read novels; if a young man do marry such an unfortunate young creature, let him bear the consequences with temper; let him be just; and justice will teach him to treat her with great indulgence; to endeavour to cause her to learn her business as a wife; to be patient with her; to reflect that he has taken her, being apprized of her inability; to bear in mind that he was, or seemed to be, pleased with her showy and useless acquire- ments; and that, when the gratification of his passion has been accomplished, he is unjust and cruel and unmanly, if he turn round upon her, and accuse her of a want of that knowledge which he well knew that she did not possess.

121. For my part, I do not know, nor can I form an idea of, a more unfortunate being than a girl with a mere boarding-school education, and without a fortune to enable her to keep a servant when married. Of what use are her accomplishments? Of what use her music, her drawing, and her romantic epistles? If she be good in her nature, the first little faint cry of her first baby drives all the tunes, and all the landscapes, and all the Clarissa Harlowes, out of her head for ever. I once saw a very striking instance of this sort. It was a climb-over-the-wall match, and I gave the bride away, at St. Margaret's Church,

Westminster; the pair being as handsome a pair as
ever I saw in my life. Beauty, however, though in
double quantity, would not pay the baker and
butcher; and, after an absence of little better than a
year, I found the husband in prison for debt; but I
there found also his wife, with her baby, and she,
who had never, before her marriage, known what it
was to get water to wash her own hands, and whose
talk was all about music, and the like, was now the
cheerful sustainer of her husband, and the most
affectionate of mothers. All the music and all the
drawing, and all the plays and romances, were gone
to the winds! The husband and baby had fairly sup-
planted them; and even this prison-scene was a
blessing, as it gave her, at this early stage, an opportunity of proving her devotion to her husband, who,
though I have not seen him for about fifteen years,
he being in a part of America which I could not
reach when last there, has, I am sure, amply repaid
her for that devotion. They have now a numerous
family (not less than twelve children, I believe), and
she is, I am told, a most excellent and able mistress
of a respectable house.

122. But this is a rare instance: the husband, like
his countrymen in general, was at once brave,
humane, gentle, and considerate; and the love was
so sincere and ardent on both sides, that it made
losses and sufferings appear as nothing. When I,
in a sort of half-whisper, asked Mrs. Dickens where
her piano was, she smiled, and turned her face
towards her baby that was sitting on her knee; as
much as to say, " This little fellow has beaten the

piano;" and if what I am now writing should ever have the honour to be read by her, let it be the bearer of a renewed expression of my admiration of her conduct, and of that regard for her kind and sensible husband, which time and distance have not in the least diminished, and which will be an inmate of my heart until it shall cease to beat.

123. The like of this is, however, not to be expected: no man ought to think that he has even a chance of it: besides, the husband was, in this case, a man of learning and of great natural ability: he has not had to get his bread by farming or trade; and, in all probability, his wife has had the leisure to practise those acquirements which she possessed at the time of her marriage. But can this be the case with the farmer or the tradesman's wife? She has to help to earn a provision for her children; or, at the least, to help to earn a store for sickness or old age. She, therefore, ought to be qualified to begin at once to assist her husband in his earnings: the way in which she can most efficiently assist, is by taking care of his property; by expending his money to the greatest advantage; by wasting nothing; by making the table sufficiently abundant with the least expense. And how is she to do these things unless she have been brought up to understand domestic affairs? How is she to do these things if she have been taught to think these matters beneath her study? How is any man to expect her to do these things if she have been so bred up as to make her habitually look upon them as worthy the attention of none but low and ignorant women?

124. Ignorant, indeed! Ignorance consists in a want of knowledge of those things which your calling or state of life naturally supposes you to understand. A ploughman is not an ignorant man because he does not know how to read: if he knows how to plough, he is not to be called an ignorant man; but a wife may be justly called an ignorant woman if she does not know how to provide a dinner for her husband. It is a cold comfort for a hungry man to tell him how delightfully his wife plays and sings: lovers may live on very aerial diet, but husbands stand in need of the solids; and young women may take my word for it, that a constantly clean board, well-cooked victuals, a house in order, and a cheerful fire, will do more in preserving a husband's heart, than all the " accomplishments " taught in all the " establishments " in the world.

125. Good temper. This is a very difficult thing to ascertain beforehand. Smiles are so cheap; they are so easily put on for the occasion; and besides, the frowns are, according to the lover's whim, interpreted into the contrary. By " good temper," I do not mean easy temper, a serenity which nothing disturbs, for that is a mark of laziness. Sulkiness, if you be not too blind to perceive it, is a temper to be avoided by all means. A sulky man is bad enough; what, then, must be a sulky woman, and that woman a wife; a constant inmate, a companion day and night! Only think of the delight of sitting at the same table, and sleeping in the same bed, for a week, and not exchange a word all the while! Very bad to be scolding for such a length of time; but this is far

better than the sulks. If you have your eyes, and look sharp, you will discover symptoms of this, if it unhappily exist. She will, at some time or other, show it towards some one or other of the family; or perhaps towards yourself; and you may be sure that, in this respect, marriage will not mend her. Sulkiness arises from capricious displeasure, displeasure not founded on reason. The party takes offence unjustifiably, is unable to frame a complaint, and therefore expresses displeasure by silence. The remedy for sulkiness is, to suffer it to take its full swing; but it is better not to have the disease in your house; and to be married to it is little short of madness.

126. Querulousness is a great fault. No man, and especially, no woman, likes to hear eternal plaintiveness. That she complain, and roundly complain, of your want of punctuality, of your coolness, of your neglect, of your liking the company of others: these are all very well, more especially as they are frequently but too just. But an everlasting complaining, without rhyme or reason, is a bad sign. It shows want of patience, and, indeed, want of sense. But the contrary of this, a cold indifference, is still worse. "When will you come again? You can never find time to come here. You like any company better than mine." These, when groundless, are very teasing, and demonstrate a disposition too full of anxiousness; but from a girl who always receives you with the same civil smile, lets you, at your own good pleasure, depart with the same; and who, when you take her by the hand, holds her cold fingers as straight as

sticks, I say (or should if I were young), God in his mercy preserve me!

127. Pertinacity is a very bad thing in anybody, and especially in a young woman; and it is sure to increase in force with the age of the party. To have the last word is a poor triumph; but with some people it is a species of disease of the mind. In a wife it must be extremely troublesome; and if you find an ounce of it in the maid, it will become a pound in the wife. An eternal disputer is a most disagreeable companion; and where young women thrust their say into conversations carried on by older persons, fire their opinions in a positive manner, and court a contest of the tongue, those must be very bold men who will encounter them as wives.

128. Still, of all the faults as to temper, your melancholy ladies have the worst, unless you have the same mental disease. Most wives are, at times, misery-makers; but these carry it on as a regular trade. They are always unhappy about something, either past, present, or to come. Both arms full of children is a pretty efficient remedy in most cases; but if the ingredients be wanting, a little want, a little real trouble, a little genuine affliction must, if you would effect a cure, be resorted to. But this is very painful to a man of any feeling; and, therefore, the best way is to avoid a connection which is to give you a life of wailing and sighs.

129. Beauty. Though I have reserved this to the last of the things to be desired in a wife, I by no means think it the last in point of importance. The less favoured part of the sex say, that " beauty is but

skin deep;" and this is very true; but it is very agreeable, though, for all that. Pictures are only paint-deep, or pencil-deep; but we admire them, nevertheless. "Handsome is that handsome does," used to say to me an old man, who had marked me out for his not over-handsome daughter. "Please your eye and plague your heart," is an adage that want of beauty invented, I dare say, more than a thousand years ago. These adages would say, if they had but the courage, that beauty is inconsistent with chastity, with sobriety of conduct, and with all the female virtues. The argument is, that beauty exposes the possessor to greater temptation than women not beautiful are exposed to; and that, therefore, their fall is more probable. Let us see a little how this matter stands.

130. It is certainly true that pretty girls will have more, and more ardent, admirers than ugly ones; but as to the temptation when in their unmarried state, there are few so very ugly as to be exposed to no temptation at all; and which is the most likely to resist; she who has a choice of lovers, or she who, if she let the occasion slip, may never have it again? Which of the two is most likely to set a high value upon her reputation; she whom all beholders admire, or she who is admired, at best, by mere chance? And as to women in the married state, this argument assumes, that when they fall, it is from their own vicious disposition; when the fact is, that, if you search the annals of conjugal infidelity, you will find that, nine cases out of ten, the fault is in the husband. It is his neglect, his flagrant disregard, his

frosty indifference, his foul example; it is to these
that, nine times out of ten, he owes the infidelity of
his wife; and if I were to say ninety-nine times out
of a hundred, the facts, if verified, would, I am
certain, bear me out. And whence this neglect, this
disregard, this frosty indifference; whence this foul
example? Because it is easy, in so many cases, to find
some woman more beautiful than the wife. This is
no justification for the husband to plead; for he has,
with his eyes open, made a solemn contract: if she
have not beauty enough to please him, he should have
sought it in some other woman: if, as is frequently
the case, he have preferred rank or money to beauty,
he is an unprincipled man, if he do anything to make
her unhappy who has brought him the rank or the
money. At any rate, as conjugal infidelity is, in so
many cases; as it is generally caused by the want of
affection and due attention in the husband, it follows,
of course, that it must more frequently happen in the
case of ugly than in that of handsome women.

131. In point of dress, nothing need be said to
convince any reasonable man, that beautiful women
will be less expensive in this respect than women of
a contrary description. Experience teaches us, that
ugly women are always the most studious about their
dress; and if we had never observed upon the subject,
reason would tell us that it must be so. Few women
are handsome without knowing it; and if they know
that their features naturally attract admiration, will
they desire to draw it off, and to fix it on lace, and
silks, and jewels?

132. As to manners and temper, there are certainly

some handsome women who are conceited and arrogant; but as they have all the best reasons in the world for being pleased with themselves, they afford you the best chance of general good-humour; and this good-humour is a very valuable commodity in the married state. Some that are called handsome, and that are such at the first glance, are dull, inanimate things, that might as well have been made of wax, or of wood. But the truth is, that this is not beauty, for this is not to be found only in the form of the features, but in the movements of them also. Besides, here nature is very impartial; for she gives animation promiscuously to the handsome as well as to the ugly; and the want of this in the former is surely as bearable as in the latter.

133. But the great use of female beauty, the great practical advantage of it is, that it naturally and unavoidably tends to keep the husband in good-humour with himself, to make him, to use the dealer's phrase, pleased with his bargain. When old age approaches, and the parties have become endeared to each other by a long series of joint cares and interests, and when children have come and bound them together by the strongest ties that nature has in store, at this age the features and the person are of less consequence; but in the young days of matrimony, when the roving eye of the bachelor is scarcely become steady in the head of the husband, it is dangerous for him to see, every time he stirs out, a face more captivating than that of the person to whom he is bound for life. Beauty is, in some degree, a matter of taste: what one man admires, another does not; and it is fortunate

for us that it is thus. But still there are certain things that all men admire; and a husband is always pleased when he perceives that a portion, at least, of these things are in his own possession: he takes this possession as a compliment to himself: there must, he will think the world will believe, have been some merit in him, some charm, seen or unseen, to have caused him to be blessed with the acquisition.

134. And then there arise so many things, sickness, misfortune in business, losses, many, many things, wholly unexpected; and there are so many circumstances, perfectly nameless, to communicate to the new-married man the fact, that it is not a real angel of whom he has got the possession; there are so many things of this sort, so many and such powerful dampers of the passions, and so many incentives to cool reflection, that it requires something, and a good deal too, to keep the husband in countenance in this his altered and enlightened state. The passion of women does not cool so soon; the lamp of their love burns more steadily, and even brightens as it burns; and there is, the young man may be assured, a vast difference in the effect of the fondness of a pretty woman and that of one of a different description; and let reason and philosophy say what they will, a man will come downstairs of a morning better pleased after seeing the former, than he would after seeing the latter, in her night-cap.

135. To be sure, when a man has, from whatever inducement, once married a woman, he is unjust and cruel if he even slight her on account of her want of beauty, and if he treat her harshly on this account,

he is a brute. But it requires a greater degree of reflection and consideration than falls to the lot of men in general to make them act with justice in such a case; and, therefore, the best way is to guard, if you can, against the temptation to commit such injustice, which is to be done in no other way, than by not marrying any one that you do not think handsome.

136. I must not conclude this address to the Lover without something on the subject of seduction and inconstancy. In, perhaps, nineteen cases out of twenty, there is, in the unfortunate cases of illicit gratification, no seduction at all, the passion, the absence of virtue, and the crime, being all mutual. But there are other cases of a very different description; and where a man goes coolly and deliberately to work, first to gain and rivet the affections of a young girl, then to take advantage of those affections to accomplish that which he knows must be her ruin, and plunge her into misery for life; when a man does this merely for the sake of a momentary gratification, he must be either a selfish and unfeeling brute, unworthy of the name of man, or he must have a heart little inferior, in point of obduracy, to that of the murderer. Let young women, however, be aware; let them be well aware, that few, indeed, are the cases in which this apology can possibly avail them. Their character is not solely theirs, but belongs, in part, to their family and kindred. They may, in the case contemplated, be objects of compassion with the world; but what contrition, what repentance, what remorse, what that even the tenderest

benevolence can suggest, is to heal the wounded hearts of humbled, disgraced, but still affectionate, parents, brethren, and sisters?

137. As to constancy in lovers, though I do not approve of the saying, " At lovers' lies Jove laughs; " yet, when people are young, one object may supplant another in their affections, not only without crimin- ality in the party experiencing the change, but without blame; and it is honest, and even humane, to act upon the change; because it would be both foolish and cruel to marry one girl while you liked another better: and the same holds good with regard to the other sex. Even when marriage has been promised, and that, too, in the most solemn manner, it is better for both parties to break off, than to be coupled together with the reluctant assent of either; and I have always thought, that actions for damages on this score, if brought by the girl, show a want of delicacy as well as of spirit; and if brought by the man, excessive meanness. Some damage may, in- deed, have been done to the complaining party; but no damage equal to what that party would have sus- tained from a marriage, to which the other would have yielded by a sort of compulsion, producing to almost a certainty what Hogarth, in his " Marriage à la Mode," most aptly typifies by two curs, of different sexes, fastened together by what sportsmen call couples, pulling different ways, and snarling and barking and foaming like furies.

138. But when promises have been made to a young woman; when they have been relied on for any considerable time; when it is manifest that her

peace and happiness, and perhaps her life, depend upon their fulfilment; when things have been carried to this length, the change in the lover ought to be announced in the manner most likely to make the disappointment as supportable as the case will admit of; for though it is better to break the promise than to marry one while you like another better; though it is better for both parties, you have no right to break the heart of her who has, and that, too, with your own accordance, and, indeed, at your instigation, or at least by your encouragement, confided it to your fidelity. You cannot help your change of affections; but you can help making the transfer in such a way as to cause the destruction, or even probable destruction, nay, if it were but the deep misery, of her, to gain whose heart you had pledged your own. You ought to proceed by slow degrees; you ought to call time to your aid in executing the painful task; you ought scrupulously to avoid everything calculated to aggravate the sufferings of the disconsolate party.

139. A striking, a monstrous instance of conduct the contrary of this has recently been placed upon the melancholy records of the Coroner of Middlesex, which have informed an indignant public, that a young man, having first secured the affections of a virtuous young woman, next promised her marriage, then caused the banns to be published, and then, on the very day appointed for the performance of the ceremony, married another woman, in the same church; and this, too, without, as he avowed, any provocation, and without the smallest intimation or

hint of his intention to the disappointed party, who, unable to support existence under a blow so cruel, put an end to that existence by the most deadly and the swiftest poison. If anything could wipe from our country the stain of having given birth to a monster so barbarous as this, it would be the abhorrence of him which the jury expressed; and which, from every tongue, he ought to hear to the last moment of his life.

140. Nor has a man any right to sport with the affections of a young woman, though he stop short of positive promises. Vanity is generally the tempter in this case; a desire to be regarded as being admired by the women: a very despicable species of vanity, but frequently greatly mischievous, notwithstanding. You do not, indeed, actually, in so many words, promise to marry; but the general tenor of your language and deportment has that meaning; you know that your meaning is so understood; and if you have not such meaning; if you be fixed by some previous engagement with, or greater liking for, another; if you know you are here sowing the seeds of disappointment; and if you, keeping your previous engagement, or greater liking, a secret, persevere, in spite of the admonitions of conscience, you are guilty of deliberate deception, injustice, and cruelty: you make to God an ungrateful return for those endowments which have enabled you to achieve this inglorious and unmanly triumph; and if, as is frequently the case, you glory in such triumph; you may have person, riches, talents to excite envy; but every just and humane man will abhor your heart.

141. There are, however, certain cases in which you deceive, or nearly deceive, yourself; cases in which you are, by degrees and by circumstances, deluded into something very nearly resembling sincere love for a second object, the first still, however, maintaining her ground in your heart; cases in which you are not actuated by vanity, in which you are not guilty of injustice and cruelty; but cases in which you, nevertheless, do wrong: and as I once did a wrong of this sort myself, I will here give you a history of it, as a warning to every young man who shall read this little book; that being the best and, indeed, the only atonement that I can make, or ever could have made, for this only serious sin that I ever committed against the female sex.

142. The Province of New Brunswick, in North America, in which I passed my years from the age of eighteen to that of twenty-six, consists, in general, of heaps of rocks, in the interstices of which grow the pine, the spruce, and various sorts of fir-trees, or, where the woods have been burned down, the bushes of the raspberry or those of the huckleberry. The province is cut asunder lengthwise by a great river, called the St. John, about two hundred miles in length, and, at half-way from the mouth, full a mile wide. Into this main river run innumerable smaller rivers, there called creeks. On the sides of these creeks the land is, in places, clear of rocks; it is, in these places, generally good and productive; the trees that grow here are the birch, the maple, and others of the deciduous class; natural meadows here and there present themselves; and some of these

spots far surpass in rural beauty any other that my eyes ever beheld; the creeks abounding towards their sources in waterfalls of endless variety, as well in form as in magnitude, and always teeming with fish, while water-fowl enliven their surface, and wild-pigeons, of the gayest plumage, flutter, in thousands upon thousands, amongst the branches of the beautiful trees, which sometimes, for miles together, form an arch over the creeks.

143. I, in one of my rambles in the woods, in which I took great delight, came to a spot at a very short distance from the source of one of these creeks. Here was everything to delight the eye, and especially of one like me, who seem to have been born to love rural life, and trees and plants of all sorts. Here were about two hundred acres of natural meadow, interspersed with patches of maple-trees in various forms and of various extent; the creek (there about thirty miles from its point of joining the St. John) ran down the middle of the spot, which formed a sort of dish, the high and rocky hills rising all round it, except at the outlet of the creek, and these hills crowned with lofty pines: in the hills were the sources of the creek, the waters of which came down in cascades, for any one of which many a nobleman in England would, if he could transfer it, give a good slice of his fertile estate; and in the creek, at the foot of the cascades, there were, in the season, salmon, the finest in the world, and so abundant, and so easily taken, as to be used for manuring the land.

144. If nature, in her very best humour, had made a spot for the express purpose of captivating me, she

could not have exceeded the efforts which she had here made. But I found something here besides these rude works of nature; I found something in the fashioning of which man had had something to do. I found a large and well-built log dwelling-house, standing (in the month of September) on the edge of a very good field of Indian corn, by the side of which there was a piece of buckwheat just then mowed. I found a homestead, and some very pretty cows. I found all the things by which an easy and happy farmer is surrounded; and I found still something besides all these, something that was destined to give me a great deal of pleasure and also a great deal of pain, both in their extreme degree; and both of which, in spite of the lapse of forty years, now make an attempt to rush back into my heart.

145. Partly from misinformation, and partly from miscalculation, I had lost my way; and, quite alone, but armed with my sword and a brace of pistols, to defend myself against the bears, I arrived at the log-house in the middle of a moonlight night, the hoar frost covering the trees and the grass. A stout and clamorous dog, kept off by the gleaming of my sword, waked the master of the house, who got up, received me with great hospitality, got me something to eat, and put me into a feather-bed, a thing that I had been a stranger to for some years. I, being very tired, had tried to pass the night in the woods, between the trunks of two large trees, which had fallen side by side, and within a yard of each other. I had made a nest for myself of dry fern, and had made a covering by laying boughs of spruce across

the trunks of the trees. But unable to sleep on account of the cold; becoming sick from the great quantity of water that I had drunk during the heat of the day, and being, moreover, alarmed at the noise of the bears, and lest one of them should find me in a defenceless state, I had roused myself up, and had crept along as well as I could. So that no hero of Eastern romance ever experienced a more enchanting change.

146. I had got into the house of one of those Yankee Loyalists, who, at the close of the revolutionary war (which, until it had succeeded, was called a rebellion), had accepted of grants of land in the King's Province of New Brunswick; and who, to the great honour of England, had been furnished with all the means of making new and comfortable settlements. I was suffered to sleep till breakfast time, when I found a table, the like of which I have since seen so many in the United States, loaded with good things. The master and mistress of the house, aged about fifty, were like what an English farmer and his wife were half a century ago. There were two sons, tall and stout, who appeared to have come in from work, and the youngest of whom was about my age, then twenty-three. But there was another member of the family, aged nineteen, who (dressed according to the neat and simple fashion of New England, whence she had come with her parents five or six years before) had her long light-brown hair twisted nicely up, and fastened on the top of her head, in which head were a pair of lively blue eyes, associated with features of which that softness and

that sweetness, so characteristic of American girls, were the predominant expressions, the whole being set off by a complexion indicative of glowing health, and forming, figure, movements, and all taken together, an assemblage of beauties, far surpassing any that I had ever seen but once in my life. That once was, too, two years agone; and, in such a case and at such an age, two years, two whole years, is a long, long while! It was a space as long as the eleventh part of my then life. Here was the present against the absent: here was the power of the eyes pitted against that of the memory: here were all the senses up in arms to subdue the influence of the thoughts: here was vanity, here was passion, here was the spot of all spots in the world, and here were also the life, and the manners and the habits and the pursuits that I delighted in: here was everything that imagination can conceive, united in a conspiracy against the poor little brunette in England! What, then, did I fall in love at once with this bouquet of lilies and rose? Oh! by no means. I was, however, so enchanted with the place; I so much enjoyed its tranquillity, the shade of the maple trees, the business of the farm, the sports of the water and of the woods, that I stayed at it to the last possible minute, promising, at my departure, to come again as often as I possibly could; a promise which I most punctually fulfilled.

147. Winter is the great season for jaunting and dancing (called frolicking) in America. In this province the river and the creeks were the only roads from settlement to settlement. In summer we travelled in canoes; in winter in sleighs on the ice or snow.

During more than two years I spent all the time I could with my Yankee friends: they were all fond of me: I talked to them about country affairs, my evident delight in which they took as a compliment to themselves: the father and mother treated me as one of their children; the sons as a brother; and the daughter, who was as modest and as full of sensibility as she was beautiful, in a way to which a chap much less sanguine than I was would have given the tenderest interpretation; which treatment I, especially in the last-mentioned case, most cordially repaid.

148. It is when you meet in company with others of your own age that you are, in love matters, put most frequently to the test, and exposed to detection. The next-door neighbour might, in that country, be ten miles off. We used to have a frolic, sometimes at one house and sometimes at another. Here, where female eyes are very much on the alert, no secret can long be kept; and very soon father, mother, brothers, and the whole neighbourhood looked upon the thing as certain, not excepting herself, to whom I, however, had never once even talked of marriage, and had never even told her that I loved her. But I had a thousand times done these by implication, taking into view the interpretation that she would naturally put upon my looks, appellations, and acts; and it was of this that I had to accuse myself. Yet I was not a deceiver; for my affection for her was very great: I spent no really pleasant hours but with her; I was uneasy if she showed the slightest regard for any other young man; I was unhappy if the smallest matter affected her health or spirits: I quitted her

in dejection, and returned to her with eager delight: many a time when I could get leave but for a day, I paddled in a canoe two whole succeeding nights, in order to pass that day with her. If this was not love, it was first cousin to it; for as to any criminal intention, I no more thought of it, in her case, than if she had been my sister. Many times I put to myself the questions: " What am I at? Is not this wrong? Why do I go? " But still I went.

149. Then, further in my excuse, my prior engagement, though carefully left unalluded to by both parties, was, in that thin population, and owing to the singular circumstances of it, and to the great talk that there always was about me, perfectly well known to her and all her family. It was matter of so much notoriety and conversation in the province, that General Carleton (brother of the late Lord Dorchester) who was the Governor when I was there, when he, about fifteen years afterwards, did me the honour, on his return to England, to come and see me at my house in Duke Street, Westminster, asked, before he went away, to see my wife, of whom he had heard so much before her marriage. So that here was no deception on my part; but still I ought not to have suffered even the most distant hope to be entertained by a person so innocent, so amiable, for whom I had so much affection, and to whose heart I had no right to give a single twinge. I ought, from the very first, to have prevented the possibility of her ever feeling pain on my account. I was young, to be sure; but I was old enough to know what was my duty in this case, and I ought, dismissing

my own feelings, to have had the resolution to perform it.

150. The last parting came; and now came my just punishment! The time was known to everybody, and was irrevocably fixed; for I had to move with a regiment, and the embarkation of a regiment is an epoch in a thinly-settled province. To describe this parting would be too painful even at this distant day, and with this frost of age upon my head. The kind and virtuous father came forty miles to see me, just as I was going on board in the river. His looks and words I have never forgotten. As the vessel descended, she passed the mouth of that creek, which I had so often entered with delight; and though England, and all that England contained, were before me, I lost sight of this creek with an aching heart.

151. On what trifles turn the great events in the life of man! If I had received a cool letter from my intended wife; if I had only heard a rumour of anything from which fickleness in her might have been inferred: if I had but found in her any, even the smallest, abatement of affection: if she had but let go any one of the hundred strings by which she held my heart: if any of these, never would the world have heard of me. Young as I was; able as I was as a soldier; proud as I was of the admiration and commendations of which I was the object; fond as I was, too, of the command, which, at so early an age, my rare conduct and great natural talents had given me; sanguine as was my mind, and brilliant as were my prospects: yet I had seen so much of the meannesses,

the unjust partialities, the insolent pomposity, the disgusting dissipations of that way of life, that I was weary of it: I longed, exchanging my fine laced coat for the Yankee farmer's homespun, to be where I should never behold the supple crouch of servility, and never hear the hectoring voice of authority again; and, on the lonely banks of this branch-covered creek, which contained (she out of the question) everything congenial to my taste and dear to my heart, I, unapplauded, unfeared, unenvied and un-calumniated, should have lived and died.

LETTER IV

ADVICE TO A HUSBAND

152. IT is in this capacity that your conduct will
have the greatest effect on your happiness; and a
great deal will depend on the manner in which you
begin. I am to suppose that you have made a good
choice; but a good young woman may be made, by a
weak, a harsh, a neglectful, an extravagant, or a
profligate husband, a really bad wife and mother.
All in a wife, beyond her own natural disposition and
education is, nine times out of ten, the work of her
husband.

153. The first thing of all, be the rank in life what
it may, is to convince her of the necessity of moderation in expense; and to make her clearly see the
justice of beginning to act upon the presumption,
that there are children coming, that they are to be
provided for, and that she is to assist in the making
of that provision. Legally speaking, we have a right
to do what we please with our own property, which,
however, is not our own unless it exceed our debts.
And, morally speaking, we, at the moment of our
marriage, contract a debt with the naturally to be
expected fruit of it; and, therefore (reserving further
remarks upon this subject till I come to speak of the
education of children), the scale of expense should,

at the beginning, be as low as that of which a due attention to rank in life will admit.

154. The great danger of all is, beginning with servants, or a servant. Where there are riches, or where the business is so great as to demand help in the carrying on of the affairs of a house, one or more female servants must be kept; but where the work of a house can be done by one pair of hands, why should there be two: especially as you cannot have the hands without having the mouth, and, which is frequently not less costly, inconvenient, and injurious, the tongue? When children come, there must, at times, be some foreign aid; but until then, what need can the wife of a young tradesman, or even farmer (unless the family be great), have of a servant? The wife is young, and why is she not to work as well as the husband? What justice is there in wanting you to keep two women instead of one? You have not married them both in form; but if they be inseparable, you have married them in substance; and if you are free from the crime of bigamy, you have the far most burdensome part of its consequences.

155. I am well aware of the unpopularity of this doctrine; well aware of its hostility to prevalent habits; well aware that almost every tradesman and every farmer, though with scarcely a shilling to call his own; and that every clerk, and every such person, begins by keeping a servant, and that the latter is generally provided before the wife be installed: I am well aware of all this; but knowing, from long and attentive observation, that it is the great bane

of the marriage life; the great cause of that penury, and of those numerous and tormenting embarrassments, amidst which conjugal felicity can seldom long be kept alive, I give the advice, and state the reasons on which it was founded.

156. In London, or near it, a maid-servant cannot be kept at an expense so low as that of thirty pounds a year; for, besides her wages, board and lodging, there must be a fire solely for her; or she must sit with the husband and wife, hear every word that passes between them, and between them and their friends, which will, of course, greatly add to the pleasures of their fireside! To keep her tongue still would be impossible, and, indeed, unreasonable; and if, as may frequently happen, she be prettier than the wife, she will know how to give the suitable interpretation to the looks which, next to a certainty, she will occasionally get from him, who, as it were in mockery, she calls by the name of " master." This is almost downright bigamy; but this can never do; and therefore she must have a fire to herself. Besides the blaze of coals, however, there is another sort of flame that she will inevitably covet. She will by no means be sparing of the coals; but, well fed and lodged, as she will be, whatever you may be, she will naturally sigh for the fire of love, for which she carries in her bosom a match always ready prepared. In plain language, you have a man to keep, a part, at least, of every week; and the leg of lamb, which might have lasted you and your wife for three days, will, by this gentleman's sighs, be borne away in one. Shut the door against this intruder; out she goes herself:

and if she go empty-handed, she is no true Christian, or, at least, will not be looked upon as such by the charitable friend at whose house she meets the longing soul, dying partly with love and partly with hunger.

157. The cost, altogether, is nearer fifty pounds a year than thirty. How many thousands of tradesmen and clerks, and the like, who might have passed through life without a single embarrassment, have lived in continual trouble and fear, and found a premature grave, from this very cause, and this cause alone! When I, on my return from America, in 1800, lived a short time in Saint James's Street, following my habit of early rising, I used to see the servant-maids, at almost every house, dispensing charity at the expense of their masters, long before they, good men, opened their eyes; who thus did deeds of benevolence, not only without boasting of them, but without knowing of them. Meat, bread, cheese, butter, coals, candles; all came with equal freedom from these liberal hands. I have observed the same, in my early walks and rides, in every part of this great place and its environs. Where there is one servant it is worse than when there are two or more; for, happily for their employers, they do not always agree: so that the oppression is most heavy on those who are the least able to bear it; and particularly on clerks, and such like people, whose wives seem to think that, because the husband's work is of a genteel description, they ought to live the life of ladies. Poor fellows! their work is not hard and rough to be sure; but it is work, and work for many hours too, and

painful enough; and as to their income, it scarcely exceeds, on an average, the double, at any rate, of that of a journeyman carpenter, bricklayer, or tailor.

158. Besides, the man and wife will live on cheaper diet and drink than a servant will live. Thousands who would never have had beer in their house have it for the servant, who will not live without it. However frugal your wife, her frugality is of little use, if she have one of these inmates to provide for. Many a hundred thousand times has it happened that the butcher and the butterman have been applied to solely because there was a servant to satisfy. You cannot, with this clog everlastingly attached to you, be frugal if you would: you can save nothing against the days of expense, which are, however, pretty sure to come. And why should you bring into your house a trouble like this; an absolute annoyance; a something for your wife to watch; to be a constraint upon her, to thwart her in her best intentions, to make her uneasy, and to sour her temper? Why should you do this foolish thing? Merely to comply with corrupt fashion—merely from false shame, and false and contemptible pride. If a young man were, on his marriage, to find any difficulty in setting this ruinous fashion at defiance, a very good way would be to count down to his wife at the end of every week, the amount of the expense of a servant for that week, and request her to deposit in it her drawer. In a short time, she would find the sum so large, that she would be frightened at the thoughts of a servant; and would never dream of one again, except is case of absolute necessity, and then for as short a time as possible.

159. But the wife may not be able to do all the work to be done in the house. Not able! A young woman not able to cook and wash, and mend and make, and clean the house and make the bed for one young man and herself, and that young man her husband too, who is quite willing (if he be worth a straw) to put up with cold dinner, or with a crust; to get up and light her fire; to do anything that the mind can suggest to spare her labour, and to conduce to her convenience! Not able to do this? Then, if she brought no fortune, and he had none, she ought not to have been able to marry: and, let me tell you, young man, a small fortune would not put a servant-keeping wife upon an equality with one who required no such inmate.

160. If, indeed, the work of a house were harder than a young woman could perform without pain, or great fatigue; if it had a tendency to impair her health or deface her beauty; then you might hesitate; but it is not too hard, and it tends to preserve health, to keep the spirits buoyant, and, of course, to preserve beauty. You often hear girls, while scrubbing or washing, singing till they are out of breath; but never while they are at what they call working at the needle. The American wives are most exemplary in this respect. They have none of that false pride which prevents thousands in England from doing that which interest, reason, and even their own inclination would prompt them to do. They work, not from necessity; not from compulsion of any sort; for their husbands are the most indulgent in the whole world. In the towns they go to the market, and cheerfully

carry home the result: in the country they not only do the work in the house, but extend their labours to the garden, plant and weed and hoe, and gather and preserve the fruits and the herbs; and this, too, in a climate far from being so favourable to labour as that of England; and they are amply repaid for these by those gratifications which their excellent economy enables their husbands to bestow upon them, and which it is their universal habit to do with a liberal hand.

161. But did I practise what I am here preaching? Aye, and to the full extent. Till I had a second child, no servant ever entered my house, though well able to keep one; and never, in my whole life, did I live in a house so clean, in such trim order, and never have I eaten or drunk, or slept or dressed, in a manner so perfectly to my fancy, as I did then. I had a great deal of business to attend to, that took me a great part of the day from home; but whenever I could spare a minute from business, the child was in my arms. I rendered the mother's labour as light as I could; any bit of food satisfied me; when watching was necessary we shared it between us; and that famous Grammar for teaching French people English, which has been for thirty years, and still is, the great work of this kind throughout all America and in every nation in Europe, was written by me in hours not employed in business, and, in great part, during my share of the night watchings over a sick, and then only, child, who, after lingering many months, died in my arms.

162. This was the way that we went on: this was

the way that we began the married life; and surely
that which we did with pleasure, no young couple,
unendowed with fortune, ought to be ashamed to do.
But she may be ill; the time may be near at hand, or
may have actually arrived, when she must encounter
that particular pain and danger of which you have
been the happy cause! Oh! that is quite another
matter! And if you now exceed in care, in watchings
over her, in tender attention to all her wishes, in
anxious efforts to quiet her fears; if you exceed in
pains and expense to procure her relief and secure
her life; if you, in any of these, exceed that which I
would recommend, you must be romantic indeed!
She deserves them all, and more than all, ten
thousand times told. And now it is that you feel the
blessing conferred by her economy. That heap of
money which might have been squandered on, or
by, or in consequence of, a useless servant, you now
have in hand wherewith to procure an abundance of
that skill and that attendance of which she stands in
absolute need; and she, when restored to you in
smiling health, has the just pride to reflect, that she
may have owed her life and your happiness to the
effects of her industry.

163. It is the beginning that is everything in this
important case; and you will have, perhaps, much to
do to convince her, not that what you recommend is
advantageous; not that it is right; but to convince
her that she can do it without sinking below her
station that she ought to maintain. She would cheerfully do it; but there are her next-door neighbours
who do not do it, though, in all other respects, on a

par with her. It is not laziness, but pernicious fashion, that you will have to combat. But the truth is, that there ought to be no combat at all; this important matter ought to be settled and fully agreed on beforehand. If she really love you, and have common sense, she will not hesitate a moment; and if she be deficient in either of these respects, and if you be so mad in love as to be unable to exist without her, it is better to cease to exist at once, than to become the toiling and embarrassed slave of a wasting and pillaging servant.

164. The next thing to be attended to is, your demeanour towards a young wife. As to oldish ones, or widows, time and other things have, in most cases, blunted their feelings, and rendered harsh or stern demeanour in the husband a matter not of heart-breaking consequence. But with a young and in-experienced one the case is very different; and you should bear in mind that the first frown that she receives from you is a dagger to her heart. Nature has so ordered it, that men shall become less ardent in their passion after the wedding-day, and that women shall not. Their ardour increases rather than the contrary; and they are surprisingly quick-sighted and inquisitive on this score. When the child comes, it divides this ardour with the father; but until then, you have it all; and if you have a mind to be happy, repay it with all your soul. Let what may happen to put you out of humour with others, let nothing put you out of humour with her. Let your words and looks and manners be just what they were before you called her wife.

165. But now, and throughout your life, show your affection for her, and your admiration of her, not in nonsensical compliment; not in picking up her handkerchief or her glove, or in carrying her fan or parasol; not, if you have the means, in hanging trinkets and baubles upon her; not in making yourself a fool by winking at, and seeming pleased at, her foibles, or follies, or faults; but show them by acts of real goodness towards her; prove by unequivocal deeds the high value that you set on her health and life and peace of mind; let your praise of her go to the full extent of her deserts; but let it be consistent with truth and with sense, and such as to convince her of your sincerity. He who is the flatterer of his wife only prepares her ears for the hyperbolical stuff of others. The kindest appellation that her Christian name affords is the best you can use, especially before faces. An everlasting " my dear " is but a sorry compensation for a want of that sort of love that makes the husband cheerfully toil by day, break his rest by night, endure all sorts of hardships, if the life or health of his wife demand it. Let your deeds, and not your words, carry to her heart a daily and hourly confirmation of the fact, that you value her health and life and happiness beyond all other things in the world; and let this be manifest to her, particularly at those times when life is always more or less in danger.

166. I began my young marriage days in and near Philadelphia. At one of those times to which I have just alluded, in the middle of the burning hot month of July, I was greatly afraid of fatal consequences to

my wife for want of sleep, she not having, after the great danger was over, had any sleep for more than forty-eight hours. All great cities, in hot countries, are, I believe, full of dogs; and they, in the very hot weather, keep up, during the night, a horrible barking and fighting and howling. Upon the particular occasion to which I am adverting, they made a noise so terrible and so unremitted, that it was next to impossible that even a person in full health and free from pain should obtain a minute's sleep. I was, about nine in the evening, sitting by the bed: " I do think," said she, " that I could go to sleep now, if it were not for the dogs." Downstairs I went, and out I sallied, in my shirt and trousers, and without shoes and stockings; and, going to a heap of stones lying beside the road, set to work upon the dogs, going backward and forward, and keeping them at two or three hundred yards' distance from the house. I walked thus the whole night, barefooted, lest the noise of my shoes might possibly reach her ears; and I remember that the bricks of the causeway were, even in the night, so hot as to be disagreeable to my feet. My exertions produced the desired effect: a sleep of several hours was the consequence; and, at eight o'clock in the morning, off went I to a day's business which was to end at six in the evening.

167. Women are all patriots of the soil; and when her neighbours used to ask my wife whether all English husbands were like hers, she boldly answered in the affirmative. I had business to occupy the whole of my time, Sundays and week-days, except sleeping hours; but I used to make time to

assist her in the taking care of her baby, and in all sorts of things: get up, light her fire, boil her tea-kettle, carry her up warm water in cold weather, take the child while she dressed herself and got the breakfast ready, then breakfast, get her in water and wood for the day, then dress myself neatly, and sally forth to my business. The moment that was over I used to hasten back to her again; and I no more thought of spending a moment away from her, unless business compelled me, than I thought of quitting the country and going to sea. The thunder and lightning are tremendous in America, compared with what they are in England. My wife was, at one time, very much afraid of thunder and lightning; and, as is the feeling of all such women, and, indeed, all men too, she wanted company, and particularly her husband, in those times of danger. I knew well, of course, that my presence would not diminish the danger; but, be I at what I might, if within reach of home, I used to quit my business and hasten to her the moment I perceived a thunder-storm approach-ing. Scores of miles have I, first and last, run on this errand in the streets of Philadelphia! The French-men who were my scholars used to laugh at me exceedingly on this account; and sometimes, when I was making an appointment with them, they would say, with a smile and a bow, " Sauve la tonnerre tou-jours, Monsieur Cobbett."

168. I never dangled about at the heels of my wife; seldom, very seldom, ever walked out, as it is called, with her; I never " went a-walking " in the whole course of my life; never went to walk without

having some object in view other than the walk; and as I never could walk at a slow pace, it would have been hard work for her to keep up with me; so that, in the nearly forty years of our married life, we have not walked out together perhaps twenty times. I hate a dangler, who is more like a footman than a husband. It is very cheap to be kind in trifles; but that which rivets the affections is not to be purchased with money. The great thing of all, however, is to prove your anxiety at those times of peril to her, and for which times you nevertheless wish. Upon those occasions I was never from home, be the necessity for it ever so great: it was my rule that everything must give way to that. In the year 1809 some English local militiamen were flogged in the Isle of Ely, in England, under a guard of Hanoverians, then stationed in England. I, reading an account of this in a London newspaper called the *Courier*, expressed my indignation at it in such terms as became an Englishman to do. The Attorney-General, Gibbs, was set on upon me; he harassed me for nearly a year, then brought me to trial, and I was, by Ellenborough, Grose, Le Blanc, and Bailey, sentenced to two years' imprisonment in Newgate, to pay a fine to the King of a thousand pounds, and to be held in heavy bail for seven years after the expiration of the imprisonment! Every one regarded it as a sentence of death. I lived in the country at the time, seventy miles from London; I had a farm on my hands; I had a family of small children, amongst whom I had constantly lived; I had a most anxious and devoted wife, who was, too, in that state which rendered the separation more painful tenfold. I was put into a place amongst felons, from which I had to rescue myself at the price of twelve guineas a week for the whole of the two years. The king, poor man! was, at the close of my imprisonment, not in a condition to receive the thousand pounds; but his son, the present king, punctually received it " in his name and behalf; " and he keeps it still.

169. The sentence, though it proved not to be one of death, was, in effect, one of ruin, as far as then possessed property went. But this really appeared as nothing compared with the circumstance that I must now have a child born in a felon's jail, or be absent from the scene at the time of birth. My wife, who had come to see me for the last time previous to her lying-in, perceiving my deep dejection at the approach of her departure for Botley, resolved not to go, and actually went and took a lodging as near to Newgate as she could find one, in order that the communication between us might be as speedy as possible, and in order that I might see the doctor, and receive assurances from him relative to her state. The nearest lodging that she could find was in Skinner Street, at the corner of a street leading to Smithfield. So that there she was, amidst the incessant rattle of coaches and butchers' carts, and the noise of cattle, dogs, and bawling men, instead of being in a quiet and commodious country house, with neighbours and servants and everything necessary about her. Yet, so great is the power of the mind in such cases, she, though the circumstances proved uncommonly perilous, and were attended with the

loss of the child, bore her sufferings with the greatest composure, because at any minute she could send a message to, and hear from me. If she had gone to Botley, leaving me in that state of anxiety in which she saw me, I am satisfied that she would have died; and that event taking place at such a distance from me, how was I to contemplate her corpse, surrounded by her distracted children, and to have escaped death or madness myself? If such was not the effect of this merciless act of the Government towards me, that amiable body may be well assured that I have taken and recorded the will for the deed, and that as such it will live in my memory as long as that memory shall last.

170. I make no apology for this account of my own conduct, because example is better than precept, and because I believe that my example may have weight with many thousands, as it has had in respect to early rising, abstinence, sobriety, industry, and mercy towards the poor. It is not, then, dangling about after a wife; it is not the loading her with baubles and trinkets; it is not the jaunting of her about from show to show, and from what is called pleasure to pleasure; it is none of these that endears you to her: it is the adherence to that promise you have made her: " With my body I thee worship; " that is to say, respect and honour by personal attention and acts of affection. And remember, that the greatest possible proof that you can give of real and solid affection is to give her your time, when not wanted in matters of business; when not wanted for the discharge of some duty, either towards the public

or towards private persons. Amongst duties of this
sort we must, of course, in some ranks and circumstances of life, include the intercourse among friends
and neighbours, which may frequently and reasonably call the husband from his home; but what are
we to think of the husband who is in the habit of
leaving his own fireside, after the business of the day
is over, and seeking promiscuous companions in the
ale or the coffee-house? I am told that in France it
is rare to meet with a husband who does not spend
every evening of his life in what is called a café; that
is to say, a place for no other purpose than that of
gossiping, drinking, and gaming. And it is with great
sorrow that I acknowledge that many English husbands indulge too much in a similar habit. Drinking
clubs, smoking clubs, singing clubs, clubs of odd-
fellows, whist clubs, sotting clubs: these are inexcusable, they are censurable, they are at once foolish
and wicked even in single men; what must they be,
then, in husbands; and how are they to answer, not
only to their wives, but to their children, for this
profligate abandonment of their homes; this breach
of their solemn vow made to the former, this evil
example to the latter?

171. Innumerable are the miseries that spring
from this cause. The expense is, in the first place,
very considerable. I much question whether,
amongst tradesmen, a shilling a night pays the
average score; and that, too, for that which is really
worth nothing at all, and cannot, even by possibility,
be attended with any one single advantage, however
small. Fifteen pounds a year thus thrown away would

amount, in the course of a tradesman's life, to a decent fortune for a child. Then there is the injury to health from these night adventures; there are the quarrels; there is the vicious habit of loose and filthy talk; there are the slanders and the backbitings; there are the admiration of contemptible wit; and there are the scoffings at all that is sober and serious.

172. And does the husband who thus abandons his wife and children imagine that she will not, in some degree at least, follow his example? If he do, he is very much deceived. If she imitate him even in drinking, he has no great reason to complain; and then the cost may be two shillings the night instead of one, equal in amount to the cost of all the bread wanted in the family, while the baker's bill is, perhaps, unpaid. Here are the slanderings, too, going on at home; for, while the husbands are assembled, it would be hard if the wives were not to do the same; and the very least that is to be expected is, that the tea-pot should keep pace with the porter-pot or grog-glass. Hence crowds of female acquaintances and intruders, and all the consequent and inevitable squabbles which form no small part of the torment of the life of man.

173. If you have servants, they know to a moment the time of your absence; and they regulate their proceedings accordingly. " Like master like man," is an old and true proverb; and it is natural, if not just, that it should be thus; for it would be unjust if the careless and neglectful sot were served as faithfully as the vigilant, attentive, and sober man. Late hours, cards and dice, are amongst the consequences of the

master's absence; and why not, seeing that he is
setting the example? Fire, candle, profligate visitants,
expenses, losses, children ruined in habits and
morals, and, in short, a train of evils hardly to be
enumerated arise from this most vicious habit of the
master spending his leisure time from home. But
beyond all the rest is the ill treatment of the wife.
When left to ourselves we all seek the company that
we like best; the company in which we take the most
delight: and therefore every husband, be his state of
life what it may, who spends his leisure time, or who,
at least, is in the habit of doing it, in company other
than that of his wife and family, tells her and them,
as plainly by deeds as he could possibly do by words,
that he takes more delight in other company than in
theirs. Children repay this with disregard for their
father; but to a wife of any sensibility, it is either a
dagger to her heart or an incitement to revenge, and
revenge, too, of a species which a young woman will
seldom be long in want of the means to gratify. In
conclusion of these remarks respecting absentee
husbands, I would recommend all those who are
prone to, or likely to fall into, the practice, to remember the words of Mrs. Sullen, in the " Beaux
Stratagem: " " My husband," says she, addressing
a footman whom she had taken as a paramour,
" comes reeling home at midnight, tumbles in
beside me as a salmon flounces in a net, oversets the
economy of my bed, belches the fumes of his drink
in my face, then twists himself round, leaving me
half naked, and listening till morning to that tuneful
nightingale, his nose." It is at least forty-three years

since I read the " Beaux Stratagem," and I now quote
from memory; but the passage has always occurred
to me whenever I have seen a sottish husband; and
though that species of revenge, for the taking of
which the lady made this apology, was carrying the
thing too far, yet I am ready to confess, that if I had
to sit in judgment on her for taking even this revenge,
my sentence would be very lenient; for what right
has such a husband to expect fidelity? He has broken
his vow; and by what rule of right has she to be
bound to hers? She thought that she was marrying
a man, and she finds that she was married to a beast.
He has, indeed, committed no offence that the law
of the land can reach; but he has violated the vow
by which he obtained possession of her person; and,
in the eye of justice, the compact between them is
dissolved.

174. The way to avoid the sad consequences of
which I have been speaking is to begin well: many a
man has become a sottish husband, and brought a
family to ruin, without being sottishly inclined, and
without liking the gossip of the ale or coffee-house.
It is by slow degrees that the mischief is done. He is
first inveigled, and, in time, he really likes the thing;
and, when arrived at that point, he is incurable. Let
him resolve, from the very first, never to spend an
hour from home unless business, or, at least, some
necessary and rational purpose demand it. Where
ought he to be but with the person whom he himself
has chosen to be his partner for life and the mother
of his children? What other company ought he to
deem so good and so fitting as this? With whom else

can he so pleasantly spend his hours of leisure and
relaxation? Besides, if he quit her to seek company
more agreeable, is not she set at large by that act
of his? What justice is there in confining her at
home without any company at all, while he rambles
forth in search of company more gay than he finds
at home?

175. Let the young married man try the thing; let
him resolve not to be seduced from his home; let
him never go, in one single instance, unnecessarily
from his own fire-side. Habit is a powerful thing;
and if he begin right, the pleasure that he will derive
from it will induce him to continue right. That is not
being " tied to the apron-strings," which means quite
another matter, as I shall show by-and-by. It is being
at the husband's place, whether he have children or
not. And is there any want of matter for conversation
between a man and his wife? Why not talk of the
daily occurrences to her as well as to anybody else,
and especially to a company of tippling and noisy
men? If you excuse yourself by saying that you go
to read the newspaper, I answer buy the newspaper,
if you must read it; the cost is not half of what you
spend per day at the pot-house; and then you have
it your own, and may read it at your leisure, and
your wife can read it as well as yourself, if read it
you must. And, in short, what must that man be
made of who does not prefer sitting by his own
fireside with his wife and children, reading to them,
or hearing them read, to hearing the gabble and
balderdash of a club or a pot-house company!

176. Men must frequently be from home at all

hours of the day and night. Sailors, soldiers, merchants, all men out of the common track of labour, and even some in the very lowest walks, are sometimes compelled by their affairs, or by circumstances, to be from their homes. But what I protest against is the habit of spending leisure hours from home, and near to it, and doing this without any necessity, and by choice: liking the next door, or any house in the same street, better than your own. When absent from necessity, there is no wound given to the heart of the wife; she concludes that you would be with her if you could, and that satisfies; she laments the absence, but submits to it without complaining. Yet, in these cases, her feelings ought to be consulted as much as possible; she ought to be fully apprized of the probable duration of the absence, and of the time of return; and if these be dependent on circumstance, those circumstances ought to be fully stated; for you have no right to keep her mind upon the rack, when you have it in your power to put it in a state of ease. Few men have been more frequently taken from home by business, or by a necessity of some sort, than I have; and I can positively assert, that, as to my return, I never once disappointed my wife in the whole course of our married life. If the time of return was contingent I never failed to keep her informed from day to day: if the time was fixed, or when it became fixed, my arrival was as sure as my life. Going from London to Botley once, with Mr. Finnerty, whose name I can never pronounce without an expression of my regard for his memory, we stopped at Alton, to dine with a friend, who, delighted with Finnerty's talk, as everybody else was, kept us till ten or eleven o'clock, and was proceeding to the other bottle, when I put in my protest, saying, " We must go; my wife will be frightened." " Blood, man," said Finnerty, " you do not mean to go home to-night! " I told him I did; and then sent my son, who was with us, to order out the post-chaise. We had twenty-three miles to go, during which we debated the question, whether Mrs. Cobbett would be up to receive us, I contending for the affirmative, and he for the negative. She was up, and had a nice fire for us to sit down at. She had not committed the matter to a servant; her servants and children were all in bed; and she was up, to perform the duty of receiving her husband and his friend. " You did not expect him? " said Finnerty. " To be sure I did," said she; " he never disappointed me in his life."

177. Now, if all young men knew how much value women set upon this species of fidelity, there would be fewer unhappy couples than there are. If men have appointments with lords, they never dream of breaking them; and I can assure them that wives are as sensitive in this respect as lords. I had seen many instances of conjugal unhappiness arising out of that carelessness which left wives in a state of uncertainty as to the movements of their husbands; and I took care, from the very outset, to guard against it. For no man has a right to sport with the feelings of any innocent person whatever, and particularly with those of one who has committed her happiness to his hands. The truth is, that men in general look upon women as having no feelings different from

their own; and they know that they themselves would regard such disappointments as nothing. But this is a great mistake: women feel more acutely than men; their love is more ardent, more pure, more lasting, and they are more frank and sincere in the utterance of their feelings. They ought to be treated with due consideration had for all their amiable qualities and all their weaknesses, and nothing by which their minds are affected ought to be deemed a trifle.

178. When we consider what a young woman gives up on her wedding-day; she makes a surrender, an absolute surrender, of her liberty, for the joint lives of the parties; she gives the husband the absolute right of causing her to live in what place, and in what manner and in what society, he pleases; she gives him the power to take from her, and to use for his own purposes, all her goods, unless reserved by some legal instrument; and, above all, she surrenders to him her person. Then, when we consider the pains which they endure for us, and the large share of all the anxious parental cares that fall to their lot; when we consider their devotion to us, and how unshaken their affection remains in our ailments, even though the most tedious and disgusting; when we consider the offices that they perform, and cheerfully perform, for us, when, were we left to one another, we should perish from neglect; when we consider their devotion to their children, how evidently they love them better, in numerous instances, than their own lives; when we consider these things, how can a just man think anything a trifle that affects their happiness? I was once going, in my gig, up the hill, in the village

of Frankford, near Philadelphia, when a little girl, about two years old, who had toddled away from a small house, was lying basking in the sun, in the middle of the road. About two hundred yards before I got to the child, the teams, five big horses in each, of three waggons, the drivers of which had stopped to drink at a tavern on the brow of the hill, started off, and came, nearly abreast, galloping down the road. I got my gig off the road as speedily as I could, but expected to see the poor child crushed to pieces. A young man, a journeyman carpenter, who was shingling a shed by the side of the road, seeing the child, and seeing the danger, though a stranger to the parents, jumped from the top of the shed, ran into the road, and snatched up the child, from scarcely an inch before the hoof of the leading horse. The horse's leg knocked him down; but he, catching the child by its clothes, flung it back, out of the way of the other horses, and saved himself by rolling back with surprising agility. The mother of the child, who had apparently been washing, seeing the teams coming, and seeing the situation of the child, rushed out, and catching up the child, just as the carpenter had flung it back, and hugging it in her arms, uttered a shriek such as I never heard before, never heard since, and, I hope, shall never hear again, and then she dropped down, as if perfectly dead! By the application of the usual means, she was restored however, in a little while; and I, being about to depart, asked the carpenter if he were a married man, and whether he were a relation of the parents of the child. He said he was neither: " Well, then,"

said I, " you merit the gratitude of every father and
mother in the world, and I will show mine by giving
you what I have," pulling out the nine or ten dollars
that I had in my pocket. " No; I thank you, sir,"
said he: " I have only done what it was my duty to
do."

179. Bravery, disinterestedness, and maternal
affection surpassing these, it is impossible to imagine.
The mother was going right in amongst the feet of
these powerful and wild horses, and amongst the
wheels of the waggons. She had no thought for
herself; no feeling of fear for her own life; her shriek
was the sound of inexpressible joy: joy too great for
her to support herself under. Perhaps ninety-nine
mothers out of every hundred would have acted the
same part, under similar circumstances. There are,
comparatively, very few women not replete with
maternal love; and by-the-by, take you care if you
meet with a girl who " is not fond of children," not
to marry her by any means. Some few there are who
even make a boast that they " cannot bear children,"
that is, cannot endure them. I never knew a man that
was good for much who had a dislike to little children; and I never knew a woman of that taste who
was good for anything at all. I have seen a few such
in the course of my life, and I have never wished
to see one of them a second time.

180. Being fond of little children argues no
effeminacy in a man, but, as far as my observation
has gone, the contrary. A regiment of soldiers presents no bad school wherein to study character.
Soldiers have leisure, too, to play with children, as

well as with " women and dogs," for which the
proverb has made them famed. And I have never
observed that effeminacy was at all the marked
companion of fondness for little children. This
fondness manifestly arises from a compassionate
feeling towards creatures that are helpless, and that
must be innocent. For my own part, how many
days, how many months, all put together, have I
spent with babies in my arms! My time, when at
home, and when babies were going on, was chiefly
divided between the pen and the baby. I have fed
them and put them to sleep hundreds of times,
though there were servants to whom the task might
have been transferred. Yet I have not been effeminate;
I have not been idle; I have not been a waster of
time; but I should have been all these if I had dis-
liked babies, and had liked the porter-pot and the
grog-glass.

181. It is an old saying, " Praise the child, and you
make love to the mother; " and it is surprising how
far this will go. To a fond mother you can do nothing
so pleasing as to praise the baby, and, the younger it
is, the more she values the compliment. Say fine
things to her, and take no notice of her baby, and she
will despise you. I have often beheld this in many
women, with great admiration; and it is a thing that
no husband ought to overlook; for if the wife wish
her child to be admired by others, what must be the
ardour of her wishes with regard to his admiration.
There was a drunken dog of a Norfolk man in our
regiment, who came from Thetford, I recollect, who
used to say, that his wife would forgive him for

spending all the pay, and the washing money into the bargain, " if he would but kiss her ugly brat, and say it was pretty." Now, though this was a very profligate fellow, he had philosophy in him; and certain it is, that there is nothing worthy of the name of conjugal happiness unless the husband clearly evince that he is fond of his children, and that, too, from their very birth.

182. But though all the afore-mentioned considerations demand from us the kindest possible treatment of a wife, the husband is to expect dutiful deportment at her hands. He is not to be her slave; he is not to yield to her against the dictates of his own reason and judgment; it is her duty to obey all his lawful commands; and, if she have sense, she will perceive that it is a disgrace to herself to acknowledge as a husband a thing over which she has an absolute control. It should always be recollected that you are the party whose body must, if any do, lie in jail for debts, and for debts of her contracting, too, as well as of your own contracting. Over her tongue, too, you possess a clear right to exercise, if necessary, some control; for if she use it in an unjustifiable manner, it is against you, and not against her, that the law enables, and justly enables, the slandered party to proceed; which would be monstrously unjust, if the law were not founded on the right which the husband has to control, if necessary, the tongue of the wife, to compel her to keep it within the limits prescribed by the law. A charming, a most enchanting life, indeed, would be that of a husband, if he were bound to cohabit with and to maintain

one for all the debts and all the slanders of whom he was answerable, and over whose conduct he possessed no compulsory control.

183. Of the remedies in the case of really bad wives, squanderers, drunkards, adulteresses, I shall speak further on; it being the habit of us all to put off to the last possible moment the performances of disagreeable duties. But, far short of these vices, there are several faults in a wife that may, if not cured in time, lead to great unhappiness, great injury to the interests as well as character of her husband and children; and which faults it is, therefore, the husband's duty to correct. A wife may be chaste, sober in the full sense of the word, industrious, cleanly, frugal, and may be devoted to her husband and her children to a degree so enchanting as to make them all love her beyond the power of words to express; and yet she may, partly under the influence of her natural disposition, and partly encouraged by the great and constant homage paid to her virtues, and presuming, too, on the pain with which she knows her will would be thwarted; she may, with all her virtues, be thus led to a bold interference in the affairs of her husband; may attempt to dictate to him in matters quite out of her own sphere; and, in the pursuit of the gratification of her love of power and command, may wholly overlook the acts of folly or injustice which she would induce her husband to commit, and overlook, too, the contemptible thing that she is making the man whom it is her duty to honour and obey, and the abasement of whom cannot take place without some portion of

degradation falling upon herself. At the time when
" The Book," came out, relative to the late ill-
treated Queen Caroline, I was talking upon the
subject, one day, with a parson, who had not read
the book, but who, as was the fashion with all those
who were looking up to the Government, condemned
the Queen unheard. " Now," said I, " be not so
shamefully unjust; but get the book, read it, and
then give your judgment." " Indeed," said his wife,
who was sitting by, " but he *sha'n't*," pronouncing
the word sha'n't with an emphasis and a voice tre-
mendously masculine. " Oh! " said I, " if he *sha'n't*,
that is another matter; but if he sha'n't read, if he
sha'n't hear the evidence, he sha'n't be looked upon,
by me, as a just judge; and I sha'n't regard him, in
future, as having any opinion of his own in anything."
All which the husband, the poor hen-pecked thing,
heard without a word escaping his lips.

184. A husband thus under command is the most
contemptible of God's creatures. Nobody can place
reliance on him for anything; whether in the capacity
of employer or employed, you are never sure of him.
No bargain is firm, no engagement sacred, with such
a man. Feeble as a reed before the boisterous she-
commander, he is bold in injustice towards those
whom it pleases her caprice to mark out for ven-
geance. In the eyes of neighbours, for friends such
a man cannot have, in the eyes of servants, in the
eyes of even the beggars at his door, such a man is a
mean and despicable creature, though he may roll in
wealth and possess great talents into the bargain.
Such a man has, in fact, no property; he has nothing

that he can rightly call his own; he is a beggarly dependent under his own roof; and if he have anything of the man left in him, and if there be rope or river near, the sooner he betakes himself to the one or the other the better. How many men, how many families, have I known brought to utter ruin only by the husband suffering himself to be subdued, to be cowed down, to be held in fear, of even a virtuous wife! What, then, must be the lot of him who submits to a commander who, at the same time, sets all virtue at defiance!

185. Women are a sisterhood. They make common cause in behalf of the sex; and, indeed, this is natural enough, when we consider the vast power that the law gives us over them. The law is for us, and they combine, wherever they can, to mitigate its effects. This is perfectly natural, and, to a certain extent, laudable, evincing fellow-feeling and public spirit: but when carried to the length of " he sha'n't," it is despotism on the one side, and slavery on the other. Watch, therefore, the incipient steps of encroachment; and they come on so slowly, so softly, that you must be sharp-sighted if you perceive them; but the moment you do perceive them; your love will blind for too long a time; but the moment you do perceive them, put at once an effectual stop to their progress. Never mind the pain that it may give you: a day of pain at this time will spare you years of pain in time to come. Many a man has been miserable, and made his wife miserable too, for a score or two of years, only for want of resolution to bear one day of pain: and it is a great deal to bear; it is a

great deal to do to thwart the desire of one whom you so dearly love, and whose virtues daily render her more and more dear to you. But (and this is one of the most admirable of the mother's traits) as she herself will, while the tears stream from her eyes, force the nauseous medicine down the throat of her child, whose every cry is a dagger to her heart; as she herself has the courage to do this for the sake of her child, why should you flinch from the performance of a still more important and more sacred duty towards herself, as well as towards you and your children?

186. Am I recommending tyranny? Am I recommending disregard of the wife's opinions and wishes? Am I recommending a reserve towards her that would seem to say that she was not trustworthy, or not a party interested in her husband's affairs? By no means: on the contrary, though I would keep anything disagreeable from her, I should not enjoy the prospect of good without making her a participator. But reason says, and God has said, that it is the duty of wives to be obedient to their husbands; and the very nature of things prescribes that there must be a head of every house, and an undivided authority. And then it is so clearly just that the authority should rest with him on whose head rests the whole responsibility, that a woman, when patiently reasoned with on the subject, must be a virago in her very nature not to submit with docility to the terms of her marriage vow.

187. There are, in almost every considerable neighbourhood, a little squadron of she-commanders,

generally the youngish wives of old or weak-minded men, and generally without children. These are the tutoresses of the young wives of the vicinage; they, in virtue of their experience, not only school the wives, but scold the husbands; they teach the former how to encroach and the latter how to yield: so that if you suffer this to go quietly on, you are soon under the care of a *comité* as completely as if you were insane. You want no *comité*: reason, law, religion, the marriage vow; all these have made you head, have given you full power to rule your family, and if you give up your right, you deserve the contempt that assuredly awaits you, and also the ruin that is, in all probability, your doom.

188. Taking it for granted that you will not suffer more than a second or third session of the female *comité*, let me say a word or two about the conduct of men in deciding between the conflicting opinions of husbands and wives. When a wife has a point to carry, and finds herself hard pushed, or when she thinks it necessary to call to her aid all the force she can possibly muster, one of her resources is, the vote on her side of all her husband's visiting friends. "My husband thinks so and so, and I think so and so; now, Mr. Tomkins, don't you think I am right?" To be sure he does; and so does Mr. Jenkins, and so does Wilkins, and so does Mr. Dickins, and you would swear that they were all her *kins*. Now this is very foolish, to say the least of it. None of these complaisant *kins* would like this in their own case. It is the fashion to say aye to all that a woman asserts, or contends for, especially in contradiction to her

husband; and a very pernicious fashion it is. It is, in fact, not to pay her a compliment worthy of acceptance, but to treat her as an empty and conceited fool; and no sensible woman will, except from mere inadvertence, make the appeal. This fashion, however, foolish and contemptible as it is in itself, is attended very frequently with serious consequences. Backed by the opinion of her husband's friends, the wife returns to the charge with redoubled vigour and obstinacy; and if you do not yield, ten to one but a quarrel is the result; or, at least, something approaching towards it. A gentleman at whose house I was, about five years ago, was about to take a farm for his eldest son, who was a very fine young man, about eighteen years old. The mother, who was as virtuous and as sensible a woman as I have ever known, wished him to be " in the law." There were six or eight intimate friends present, and all unhesitatingly joined the lady, thinking it a pity that Harry, who had had " such a good education," should be buried in a farmhouse. " And don't you think so, too, Mr. Cobbett? " said the lady, with great earnestness. " Indeed, ma'am," said I, " I should think it very great presumption in me to offer any opinion at all, and especially in opposition to the known decision of the father, who is the best judge, and the only rightful judge, in such a case." This was a very sensible and well-behaved woman, and I still respect her very highly; but I could perceive that I instantly dropped out of her good graces. Harry, however, I was glad to hear, went " to be buried in the farmhouse."

189. "A house divided against itself," or, rather, in itself, "cannot stand;" and it is divided against itself if there be a divided authority. The wife ought to be heard, and patiently heard; she ought to be reasoned with, and, if possible, convinced; but if, after all endeavours in this way, she remain opposed to the husband's opinion, his will must be obeyed, or he at once becomes nothing; she is, in fact, the master, and he is nothing but an insignificant inmate. As to matters of little comparative moment; as to what shall be for dinner; as to how the house shall be furnished; as to the management of the house and of menial servants: as to those matters, and many others, the wife may have her way without any danger; but when the questions are, what is to be the calling to be pursued; what is to be the place of residence; what is to be the style of living and scale of expense; what is to be done with property; what the manner and place of educating children; what is to be their calling or state of life; who are to be employed or entrusted by the husband; what are the principles that he is to adopt as to public matters; whom he is to have for coadjutors or friends; all these must be left solely to the husband; in all these he must have his will; or there never can be any harmony in the family.

190. Nevertheless, in some of these concerns, wives should be heard with a great deal of attention, especially in the affairs of choosing your male acquaintances and friends and associates. Women are more quick-sighted than men; they are less disposed to confide in persons upon a first acquaintance;

they are more suspicious as to motives; they are less liable to be deceived by professions and protestations; they watch words with a more scrutinizing ear, and looks with a keener eye; and, making due allowance for their prejudices in particular cases, their opinions and remonstrances, with regard to matters of this sort, ought not to be set at naught without great deliberation. Louvet, one of the Brissotins who fled for their lives in the time of Robespierre; this Louvet, in his narrative, entitled " Mes Perils," and which I read, for the first time, to divert my mind from the perils of the yellow-fever, in Philadelphia, but with which I was so captivated as to have read it many times since; this writer, giving an account of his wonderful dangers and escapes, relates, that being on his way to Paris from the vicinity of Bordeaux, and having no regular passport, he fell lame, but finally crept on to a miserable pot-house, in a small town in the Limosin. The landlord questioned him with regard to who and what he was, and whence he came; and was satisfied with his answers. But the landlady, who had looked sharply at him on his arrival, whispered a little boy, who ran away, and quickly returned with the mayor of the town. Louvet soon discovered that there was no danger in the mayor, who could not decipher his forged passport, and who, being well plied with wine, wanted to hear no more of the matter. The landlady perceiving this, slipped out and brought a couple of aldermen, who asked to see the passport. " Oh yes; but drink first." Then there was a laughing story to tell over again, at the request of the half-drunken mayor; then a laughing and more drinking; the passport in Louvet's hand, but never opened, and, while another toast was drinking, the passport slid back quietly into the pocket; the woman looking furious all the while. At last, the mayor, the aldermen, and the landlord, all nearly drunk, shook hands with Louvet, and wished him a good journey, swore he was a true *sans culotte;* but he says that the " sharp-sighted woman, who was to be deceived by none of his stories or professions, saw him get off with deep and manifest disappointment and chagrin." I have thought of this many times since, when I have had occasion to witness the quick-sightedness and penetration of women. The same quality that makes them, as they notoriously are, more quick in discovering expedients in cases of difficulty, makes them more apt to penetrate into motives and character.

191. I now come to a matter of the greatest possible importance; namely, that great troubler of the married state, that great bane of families, jealousy; and I shall first speak of jealousy in the wife. This is always an unfortunate thing, and sometimes fatal. Yet, if there be a great propensity towards it, it is very difficult to be prevented. One thing, however, every husband can do in the way of prevention; and that is, to give no ground for it. And here, it is not sufficient that he strictly adhere to his marriage vow; he ought further to abstain from every act, however free from guilt, calculated to awaken the slightest degree of suspicion in a mind, the peace of which he is bound by every tie of justice and humanity not to disturb, or, if he can avoid it, to

suffer it to be disturbed by others. A woman that is very fond of her husband, and this is the case with nine-tenths of English and American women, does not like to share with another any, even the smallest portion, not only of his affection, but of his assiduities and applause; and, as the bestowing of them on another, and receiving payment in kind, can serve no purpose other than of gratifying one's vanity, they ought to be abstained from, and especially if the gratification be to be purchased with even the chance of exciting uneasiness in her, whom it is your sacred duty to make as happy as you can.

192. For about two or three years after I was married, I, retaining some of my military manners, used, both in France and America, to romp most famously with the girls that came in my way; till one day, at Philadelphia, my wife said to me, in a very gentle manner, " Don't do that: I do not like it." That was quite enough: I had never thought on the subject before: one hair of her head was more dear to me than all the other women in the world, and this I knew that she knew; but I now saw that this was not all that she had a right to from me; I saw that she had the further claim upon me that I should abstain from everything that might induce others to believe that there was any other woman for whom, even if I were at liberty, I had any affection. I beseech young married men to bear this in mind; for, on some trifle of this sort, the happiness or misery of a long life frequently turns. If the mind of a wife be disturbed on this score, every possible means ought to be used to restore it to peace; and

though her suspicions be perfectly groundless; though they be wild as the dreams of madmen; though they may present a mixture of the furious and the ridiculous, still they are to be treated with the greatest lenity and tenderness; and if, after all, you fail, the frailty is to be lamented as a misfortune, and not punished as a fault, seeing that it must have its foundation in a feeling towards you, which it would be the basest of ingratitude, and the most ferocious of cruelty, to repay by harshness of any description.

193. As to those husbands who make the unjust suspicions of their wives a justification for making those suspicions just; as to such as can make a sport of such suspicions, rather brag of them than otherwise, and endeavour to aggravate rather than assuage them; as to such I have nothing to say, they being far without the scope of any advice that I can offer. But to such as are not of this description, I have a remark or two to offer with respect to measures of prevention.

194. And, first, I never could see the sense of its being a piece of etiquette, a sort of mark of good-breeding, to make it a rule that man and wife are not to sit side by side in a mixed company; that if a party walk out, the wife is to give her arm to some other than her husband; that if there be any other hand near, his is not to help to a seat or into a carriage. I never could see the sense of this; but I have always seen the nonsense of it plainly enough: it is, in short, amongst many other foolish and mischievous things that we do in aping the manners of those whose riches (frequently ill-gotten) and whose power embolden

them to set, with impunity, pernicious examples; and to their example this nation owes more of its degradation in morals than to any other source. The truth is, that this is a piece of false refinement: it, being interpreted, means, that so free are the parties from a liability to suspicion, so innately virtuous and pure are they, that each man can safely trust his wife with another man, and each woman her husband with another woman. But this piece of false refinement, like all others, overshoots its mark; it says too much; for it says that the parties have lewd thoughts in their minds. This is not the fact, with regard to people in general; but it must have been the origin of this set of consummately ridiculous and contemptible rules.

195. Now I would advise a young man, especially if he have a pretty wife, not to commit her unnecessarily to the care of any other man; not to be separated from her in this studious and ceremonious manner; and not to be ashamed to prefer her company and conversation to that of any other woman. I never could discover any good-breeding in setting another man, almost expressly, to poke his nose up in the face of my wife, and talk nonsense to her; for, in such cases, nonsense it generally is. It is not a thing of much consequence, to be sure; but when the wife is young, especially, it is not seemly, at any rate, and it cannot possibly lead to any good, though it may not lead to any great evil. And, on the other hand, you may be quite sure that, whatever she may seem to think of the matter, she will not like you the better for your attentions of this sort to other women, especially if they be young and handsome; and as

this species of fashionable nonsense can do you no good, why gratify your love of talk, or the vanity of any woman, at even the risk of exciting uneasiness in that mind of which it is your most sacred duty to preserve, if you can, the uninterrupted tranquillity.

196. The truth is, that the greatest security of all against jealousy in a wife is to show, to prove by your acts, by your words also, but more especially by your acts, that you prefer her to all the world; and, as I said before, I know of no act that is, in this respect, equal to spending in her company every moment of your leisure time. Everybody knows, and young wives better than anybody else, that people who can choose will be where they like best to be, and that they will be along with those whose company they best like. The matter is very plain, then, and I do beseech you to bear it in mind. Nor do I see the use, or sense, of keeping a great deal of company, as it is called. What company can a young man and woman want more than their two selves, and their children, if they have any? If here be not company enough, it is but a sad affair. The pernicious cards are brought forth by the company-keeping, the rival expenses, the sittings up late at night, the seeing of " the ladies home," and a thousand squabbles and disagreeable consequences. But the great thing of all is, that this hankering after company proves, clearly proves, that you want something beyond the society of your wife; and that she is sure to feel most acutely: the bare fact contains an imputation against her, and it is pretty sure to lay the foundation of jealousy, or of something still worse.

197. If acts of kindness in you are necessary in all cases, they are especially so in cases of her illness, from whatever cause arising. I will not suppose myself to be addressing any husband capable of being unconcerned while his wife's life is in the most distant danger from illness, though it has been my very great mortification to know, in my lifetime, two or three brutes of this description; but, far short of this degree of brutality, a great dealt of fault may be committed. When men are ill, they feel every neglect with double anguish, and what then must be, in such cases, the feelings of women, whose ordinary feelings are so much more acute than those of men; what must be their feelings in case of neglect in illness, and especially if the neglect come from the husband! Your own heart will, I hope, tell you what those feelings must be, and will spare me the vain attempt to describe them; and, if it do thus instruct you, you will want no arguments from me to induce you, at such a season, to prove the sincerity of your affection by every kind word and kind act that your mind can suggest. This is the time to try you; and, be you assured, that the impression left on her mind now will be the true and lasting impression; and, if it be good, will be a better preservative against her being jealous, than ten thousand of your professions ten thousand times repeated. In such a case, you ought to spare no expense that you can possibly afford; you ought to neglect nothing that your means will enable you to do; for, what is the use of money if it be not to be expended in this case? But, more than all the rest, is your own personal attention. This is the valuable

thing; this is the great balm to the sufferer, and it is efficacious in proportion as it is proved to be sincere. Leave nothing to other hands that you can do yourself; the mind has a great deal to do in all the ailments of the body; and, bear in mind, that, whatever be the event, you have a more than ample reward. I cannot press this point too strongly upon you; the bed of sickness presents no charms, no allurements, and women know this well; they watch, in such a case, your every word and every look; and now it is that their confidence is secured, or their suspicions excited, for life.

198. In conclusion of these remarks, as to jealousy in a wife, I cannot help expressing my abhorrence of those husbands who treat it as a matter for ridicule. To be sure, infidelity in a man is less heinous than infidelity in the wife; but still, is the marriage vow nothing? Is a promise solemnly made before God, and in the face of the world, nothing? Is a violation of a contract, and that, too, with a feebler party, nothing of which a man ought to be ashamed? But, besides all these, there is the cruelty. First, you win, by great pains, perhaps, a woman's affections; then, in order to get possession of her person, you marry her; then, after enjoyment, you break your vow, you bring upon her the mixed pity and jeers of the world, and thus you leave her to weep out her life. Murder is more horrible than this, to be sure, and the criminal law, which punishes divers other crimes, does not reach this; but, in the eye of reason and of moral justice, it is surpassed by very few of those crimes. Passion may be pleaded, and so it may for almost

every other crime of which man can be guilty. It is not a crime against nature; nor are any of these which men commit in consequence of their necessities. The temptation is great; and is not the temptation great when men thieve or rob? In short, there is no excuse for an act so unjust and so cruel, and the world is just as to this matter; for, I have always observed, that however men are disposed to laugh at these breaches of vows in men, the act seldom fails to produce injury to the whole character; it leaves, after all the joking, a stain, and, amongst those who depend on character for a livelihood, it often produces ruin. At the very least, it makes an unhappy and wrangling family; it makes children despise or hate their fathers; and it affords an example at the thought of the ultimate consequences of which a father ought to shudder. In such a case children will take part, and they ought to take part, with the mother: she is the injured party; the shame brought upon her attaches in part to them; they feel the injustice done them; and if such a man, when the gray hairs, and tottering knees, and piping voice come, look round him in vain for a prop, let him, at last, be just, and acknowledge that he has now the due reward of his own wanton cruelty to one whom he had solemnly sworn to love and to cherish to the last hour of his or her life.

199. But, bad as is conjugal infidelity in the husband, it is much worse in the wife: a proposition that it is necessary to maintain by the force of reason, because the women, as a sisterhood, are prone to deny the truth of it. They say that adultery is

adultery, in men as well as in them; and that, therefore, the offence is as great in the one case as in the
other. As a crime, abstractedly considered, it certainly is; but, as to the consequences, there is a wide
difference. In both cases there is the breach of a
solemn vow, but there is this great distinction, that
the husband, by his breach of that vow, only brings
shame upon his wife and family; whereas the wife,
by a breach of her vow, may bring the husband a
spurious offspring to maintain, and may bring that
spurious offspring to rob of their fortunes, and in
some cases of their bread, her legitimate children.
So that here is a great and evident wrong done to
numerous parties, besides the deeper disgrace inflicted in this case than in the other.

200. And why is the disgrace deeper? Because here
is a total want of delicacy; here is, in fact, prostitution; here is grossness and filthiness of mind; here is
everything that argues baseness of character. Women
should be, and they are, except in few instances, far
more reserved and more delicate than men: nature
bids them be such; the habits and manners of the
world confirm this precept of nature; and therefore,
when they commit this offence, they excite loathing,
as well as call for reprobation. In the countries where
a plurality of wives in permitted, there is no plurality
of husbands. It is there thought not at all indelicate
for a man to have several wives; but the bare thought
of a woman having two husbands would excite horror.
The widows of the Hindoos burn themselves in the
pile that consumes their husbands; but the Hindoo
widowers do not dispose of themselves in this way.

The widows devote their bodies to complete destruction, lest, even after the death of their husbands, they
should be tempted to connect themselves with other
men; and though this is carrying delicacy far indeed,
it reads to Christian wives a lesson not unworthy of
their attention; for, though it is not desirable that
their bodies should be turned into handfuls of ashes,
even that transmutation were preferable to that infidelity which fixes the brand of shame on the cheeks
of their parents, their children, and on those of all
who ever called them friend.

201. For these plain and forcible reasons it is that
this species of offence is far more heinous in the wife
than in the husband; and the people of all civilized
countries act upon this settled distinction. Men who
have been guilty of the offence are not cut off from
society, but women who have been guilty of it are;
for, as we all know well, no woman, married or
single, of fair reputation, will risk that reputation by
being ever seen, if she can avoid it, with a woman
who has ever, at any time, committed this offence,
which contains in itself, and by universal award, a
sentence of social excommunication for life.

202. If, therefore, it be the duty of the husband to
adhere strictly to his marriage vow: if his breach of
that vow be naturally attended with the fatal consequences above described: how much more imperative
is the duty on the wife to avoid even the semblance
of a deviation from that vow! If the man's misconduct, in this respect, bring shame on so many
innocent parties, what shame, what dishonour, what
misery follow such misconduct in the wife! Her

parents, those of her husband, all her relations, and all her friends, share in her dishonour. And her children! how is she to make atonement to them! They are commanded to honour their father and their mother; but not such a mother as this, who, on the contrary, has no claim to anything from them but hatred, abhorrence, and execration. It is she who has broken the ties of nature; she has dishonoured her own offspring; she has fixed a mark of reproach on those who once made a part of her own body: nature shuts her out of the pale of its influence, and condemns her to the just detestation of those whom it formerly bade love her as their own life.

203. But as the crime is so much more heinous, and the punishment so much more severe, in the case of the wife than it is in the case of the husband, so that caution ought to be greater in making the accusation, or entertaining the suspicion. Men ought to be very slow in entertaining such suspicions: they ought to have clear proof before they can suspect; a proneness to such suspicions is a very unfortunate turn of the mind; and, indeed, few characters are more despicable than that of a jealous-headed husband; rather than be tied to the whims of one of whom, an innocent woman of spirit would earn her bread over the washing-tub, or with a hay-fork, or a reap-hook. With such a man there can be no peace; and, as far as children are concerned, the false accusation is nearly equal to the reality. When a wife discovers her jealousy, she merely imputes to her husband inconstancy and breach of his marriage vow: but jealousy in him imputes to her a willingness

to palm a spurious offspring upon him, and upon her legitimate children, as robbers of their birthright; and, besides this, grossness, filthiness, and prostitution. She imputes to him injustice and cruelty: but he imputes to her that which banishes her from society; that which cuts her off for life from everything connected with female purity; that which brands her with infamy to her latest breath.

204. Very slow, therefore, ought a husband to be in entertaining even the thought of this crime in his wife. He ought to be quite sure before he take the smallest step in the way of accusation; but if unhappily he have the proof, no consideration on earth ought to induce him to cohabit with her one moment longer. Jealous husbands are not despicable because they have grounds; but because they have not grounds; and this is generally the case. When they have grounds, their own honour commands them to cast off the object, as they would cut out a corn or a cancer. It is not the jealousy in itself which is despicable; but the continuing to live in that state. It is no dishonour to be a slave in Algiers, for instance; the dishonour begins only where you remain a slave voluntarily; it begins the moment you can escape from slavery, and do not. It is despicable unjustly to be jealous of your wife; but it is infamy to cohabit with her if you know her to be guilty.

205. I shall be told that the law compels you to live with her, unless you be rich enough to disengage yourself from her; but the law does not compel you to remain in the same country with her; and, if a man have no other means of ridding himself of such

a curse, what are mountains or seas to traverse? And what is the risk (if such there be) of exchanging a life of bodily ease for a life of labour? What are these, and numerous other ills (if they happen) superadded? Nay, what is death itself, compared with the baseness, the infamy, the never-ceasing shame and reproach of living under the same roof with a prostituted woman, and calling her your wife? But there are children, and what are to become of these? To be taken away from the prostitute, to be sure; and this is a duty which you owe to them: the sooner they forget her the better, and the farther they are from her the sooner that will be. There is no excuse for continuing to live with an adulteress: no inconvenience, no loss, no suffering, ought to deter a man from delivering himself from such a state of filthy infamy; and to suffer his children to remain in such a state is a crime that hardly admits of adequate description; a jail is paradise compared with such a life, and he who can endure this latter, from the fear of encountering hardship, is a wretch too despicable to go by the name of man.

206. But, now, all this supposes, that the husband has well and truly acted his part! It supposes, not only that he has been faithful; but that he has not, in any way, been the cause of temptation to the wife to be unfaithful. If he have been cold and neglectful; if he have led a life of irregularity; if he have proved to her that home was not his delight; if he have made his house the place of resort for loose companions; if he have given rise to a taste for visiting, junketing, parties of pleasure and gaiety; if he have introduced

the habit of indulging in what are called " innocent freedoms; " if these, or any of these, the fault is his, he must take the consequences, and he has no right to inflict punishment on the offender, the offence being, in fact, of his own creating. The laws of God, as well as the laws of man, have given him all power in this respect: it is for him to use that power for the honour of his wife as well as for that of himself: if he neglects to use it, all the conseqences ought to fall on him; and, as far as my observation has gone, in nineteen out of twenty cases of infidelity in wives, the crimes have been fairly ascribable to the husbands. Folly or misconduct in the husband cannot, indeed, justify or even palliate infidelity in the wife, whose very nature ought to make her recoil at the thought of the offence; but it may, at the same time, deprive him of the right of inflicting punishment on her: her kindred, her children, and the world, will justly hold her in abhorrence; but the husband must hold his peace.

207. " Innocent freedoms! " I know of none that a wife can indulge in. The words, as applied to the demeanour of a married woman, or even a single one, imply a contradiction. For freedom, thus used, means an exemption or departure from the strict rules of female reserve; and I do not see how this can be innocent. It may not amount to crime, indeed; but still it is not innocent; and the use of the phrase is dangerous. If it had been my fortune to be yoked to a person who liked " innocent freedoms," I should have unyoked myself in a very short time. But, to say the truth, it is all a man's own fault. If

he have not sense, and influence enough to prevent " innocent freedoms," even before marriage, he will do well to let the thing alone, and leave wives to be managed by those who have. But men will talk to your wife, and flatter her. To be sure they will, if she be young and pretty; and would you go and pull her away from them? Oh no, by no means; but you must have very little sense, or must have made very little use of it, if her manner do not soon convince them that they employ their flattery in vain.

208. So much of a man's happiness and of his efficiency through life depends upon his mind being quite free from all anxieties of this sort, that too much care cannot be taken to guard against them; and, I repeat, that the great preservation of all is, the young couple living as much as possible at home, and having as few visitors as possible. If they do not prefer the company of each other to that of all the world besides; if either of them be weary of the company of the other; if they do not, when separated by business or any other cause, think with pleasure of the time of meeting again, it is a bad omen. Pursue this course when young, and the very thought of jealousy will never come into your mind; and if you do pursue it, and show by your deeds that you value your wife as you do your own life, you must be pretty nearly an idiot if she do not think you to be the wisest man in the world. The best man she will be sure to think you, and she will never forgive any one that calls your talents or your wisdom in question.

209. Now, will you say that, if to be happy, nay,

if to avoid misery and ruin in the married state, requires all these precautions, all these cares, to fail to any extent in any of which is to bring down on a man's head such fearful consequences; will you say that, if this be the case, it is better to remain single? If you should say this, it is my business to show that you are in error. For, in the first place, it is against nature to suppose that children can cease to be born; they must and will come; and then it follows that they must come by promiscuous intercourse or by particular connection. The former nobody will contend for, seeing that it would put us in this respect on a level with the brute creation. Then, as the connection is to be particular, it must be during pleasure, or for the joint lives of the parties. The former would seldom hold for any length of time: the tie would seldom be durable, and it would be feeble on account of its uncertain duration. Therefore, to be a father, with all the lasting and delightful ties attached to the name, you must first be a husband; and there are very few men in the world who do not, first or last, desire to be fathers. If it be said that marriage ought not to be for life, but that its duration ought to be subject to the will, the mutual will at least, of the parties; the answer is, that it would seldom be of long duration. Every trifling dispute would lead to a separation; a hasty word would be enough. Knowing that the engagement is for life prevents disputes too; it checks anger in its beginnings. Put a rigging horse into a field with a weak fence, and with captivating pasture on the other side, and he is continually trying to get out; but let the field be walled round, he makes the best of his hard fare, and divides his time between grazing and sleeping. Besides, there could be no families, no assemblages of persons worthy of that name; all would be confusion and indiscribable intermixture: the names of brother and sister would hardly have a meaning; and, therefore, there must be marriage, or there can be nothing worthy of the name of family or of father.

210. The cares and troubles of the married life are many; but are those of the single life few? Take the farmer, and it is nearly the same with the tradesman; but take the farmer, for instance, and let him, at the age of twenty-five, go into business unmarried. See his maid-servants, probably rivals for his smiles, but certainly rivals in the charitable distribution of his victuals and drink amongst those of their own rank: behold their guardianship of his pork-tub, his bacon-rack, his butter, cheese, milk, poultry, eggs, and all the rest of it: look at their care of all his household stuff, his blankets, sheets, pillow-cases, towels, knives and forks, and particularly of his crockery-ware, of which last they will hardly exceed a single cart-load of broken bits in the year. And how nicely they will get up and take care of his linen and other wearing apparel, and always have it ready for him without his thinking about it! If absent at market, or especially at a distant fair, how scrupulously they will keep all their cronies out of his house, and what special care they will take of his cellar, more particularly that which holds the strong beer! And his groceries, and his spirits, and his wine (for a bachelor can afford it), how safe these

will all be! Bachelors have not, indeed, any more than married men, a security for health; but if our young farmer be sick, there are his couple of maids to take care of him, to administer his medicine, and to perform for him all other nameless offices, which in such a case are required; and, what is more, take care of everything downstairs at the same time, especially his desk with the money in it! Never will they, good-humoured girls as they are, scold him for coming home too late; but, on the contrary, like him the better for it; and if he have drunk a little too much, so much the better, for then he will sleep late in the morning, and when he comes out at last, he will find that his men have been so hard at work, and that all his animals have been taken such good care of!

211. Nonsense! a bare glance at the thing shows that a farmer, above all men living, can never carry on his affairs with profit without a wife, or a mother, or a daughter, or some such person; and mother and daughter imply matrimony. To be sure a wife would cause some trouble, perhaps, to this young man. There might be the midwife and nurse to gallop after at midnight: there might be, and there ought to be, if called for, a little complaining of late hours: but, good God! what are these, and all the other troubles that could attend a married life; what are they compared to the one single circumstance of the want of a wife at your bedside during one single night of illness! A nurse! what is a nurse to do for you? Will she do the things that a wife will do? Will she watch your looks and your half-uttered wishes? Will she use the urgent persuasions so often necessary to save

life in such cases? Will she, by her acts, convince you that it is not a toil, but a delight, to break her rest for your sake? In short, now it is that you find that what the women themselves say is strictly true, namely, that without wives, men are poor helpless mortals.

212. As to the expense, there is no comparison between that of a woman-servant and a wife in the house of a farmer or a tradesman. The wages of the former is not the expense; it is the want of a common interest with you, and this you can obtain in no one but a wife. But there are the children. I, for my part, firmly believe that a farmer, married at twenty-five, and having ten children during the first ten years, would be able to save more money during these years than a bachelor, of the same age, would be able to save on the same farm in a like space of time, he keeping only one maid-servant. One single fit of illness, of two months' duration, might sweep away more than all the children would cost in the whole ten years, to say nothing of the continual waste and pillage, and the idleness going on from the first day of the ten years to the last.

213. Besides, is the money all? What a life to lead! No one to talk to without going from home, or without getting some one to come to you; no friend to sit and talk to: pleasant evenings to pass! Nobody to share with you your sorrows or your pleasures: no soul having a common interest with you: all around you taking care of themselves, and no care of you: no one to cheer you in moments of depression: to say all in a word, no one to love you, and no prospect

of ever seeing any such one to the end of your days. For, as to parents and brethren, if you have them, they have other and very different ties; and, however laudable your feelings are of son and brother, those feelings are of a different character. Then as to gratifications, from which you will hardly abstain altogether, are they generally of little expense? and are they attended with no trouble, no vexation, no disappointment, no jealousy even, are they never followed by shame or remorse?

214. It does very well in bantering songs, to say that the bachelor's life is " devoid of care." My observation tells me the contrary, and reason concurs, in this regard, with experience. The bachelor has no one on whom he can in all cases rely. When he quits his home, he carries with him cares that are unknown to the married man. If, indeed, like the common soldier, he have merely a lodging-place, and a bundle of clothes, given in charge to some one, he may be at his ease; but, if he possess anything of a home, he is never sure of its safety; and this uncertainty is a great enemy to cheerfulness. And as to efficiency in life, how is the bachelor to equal the married man? In the case of farmers and tradesmen, the latter have so clearly the advantage over the former, that one need hardly insist upon the point; but it is, and must be, the same in all the situations of life. To provide for a wife and children is the greatest of all possible spurs to exertion. Many a man, naturally prone to idleness, has become active and industrious when he saw children growing up about him; many a dull sluggard has become, if not

a bright man, at least a bustling man, when roused to exertion by his love. Dryden's account of the change wrought in Cymon is only a strong case of the kind. And, indeed, if a man will not exert himself for the sake of a wife and children, he can have no exertion in him; or he must be deaf to all the dictates of nature.

215. Perhaps the world never exhibited a more striking proof of the truth of this doctrine than that which is exhibited in me; and I am sure that every one will say, without any hesitation, that a fourth part of the labours I have performed never would have been performed if I had not been a married man. In the first place, they could not; for I should, all the early part of my life, have been rambling and roving about as most bachelors are. I should have had no home that I cared a straw about, and should have wasted the far greater part of my time. The great affair of home being settled, having the home secured, I had leisure to employ my mind on things which it delighted in. I got rid at once of all cares, all anxieties, and had only to provide for the very moderate wants of that home. But the children began to come. They sharpened my industry: they spurred me on. To be sure, I had other and strong motives: I wrote for fame, and was urged forward by ill-treatment, and by the desire to triumph over my enemies; but, after all, a very large part of my nearly a hundred volumes may be fairly ascribed to the wife and children.

216. I might have done something; but, perhaps, not a thousandth part of what I have done; not even

a thousandth part; for the chances are, that I being fond of a military life, should have ended my days ten or twenty years ago in consequence of wounds, or fatigue, or, more likely, in consequence of the persecutions of some haughty and insolent fool, whom nature had formed to black my shoes, and whom a system of corruption had made my commander. Love came and rescued me from this state of horrible slavery; placed the whole of my time at my own disposal; made me as free as air; removed every restraint upon the operations of my mind, naturally disposed to communicate its thoughts to others; and gave me for my leisure hours a companion, who, though deprived of all opportunity of acquiring what is called learning, had so much good sense, so much useful knowledge, was so innocent, so just in all her ways, so pure in thought, word, and deed, so disinterested, so generous, so devoted to me and her children, so free from all disguise, and, withal, so beautiful and so talkative, and in a voice so sweet, so cheering, that I must, seeing the health and the capacity which it had pleased God to give me, have been a criminal, if I had done much less than that which I have done; and I have always said, that if my country feel any gratitude for my labours, that gratitude is due to her as full as much as to me.

217. " Care! " What care have I known! I have been buffeted about by this powerful and vindictive Government; I have repeatedly had the fruit of my labour snatched away from me by it; but I had a partner that never frowned, that was never melancholy, that never was subdued in spirit, that never

abated a smile on these occasions, that fortified me, and sustained me by her courageous example, and that was just as busy and as zealous in taking care of the remnant as she had been in taking care of the whole; just as cheerful, and just as full of caresses, when brought down to a mean hired lodging, as when the mistress of a fine country-house with all its accompaniments; and, whether from her words or her looks, no one could gather that she regretted the change. What " cares " have I had, then? What have I had worthy of the name of " cares? "

218. And, how is it now? How is it when the sixty-fourth year has come? And how should I have been without this wife and these children? I might have amassed a tolerable heap of money; but what would that have done for me? It might have bought me plenty of professions of attachments; plenty of persons impatient for my exit from the world; but not one single grain of sorrow for any anguish that might have attended my approaching end. To me, no being in this world appears so wretched as an old bachelor. Those circumstances, those changes in his person and in his mind, which, in the husband, increase rather than diminish the attentions to him, produce all the want of feeling attendant on disgust; and he beholds, in the conduct of the mercenary crowd that generally surround him, little besides an eager desire to profit from that event, the approach of which nature makes a subject of sorrow with him.

219. Before I quit this part of my work I cannot refrain from offering my opinion with regard to what is due from husband to wife, when the disposal of

his property comes to be thought of. When marriage is an affair settled by deeds, contracts, lawyers, the husband being bound beforehand, has really no will to make. But where he has a will to make, and a faithful wife to leave behind him, it is his first duty to provide for her future well-being to the utmost of his power. If she brought him no money, she brought him her person; and by delivering that up to him she established a claim to his careful protection of her to the end of her life. Some men think, or act as if they thought, that, if a wife bring no money, and if the husband gain money by his business or profession, that money is his, and not hers, because she had not been doing any of those things for which the money has been received. But is this way of thinking just? By the marriage vow the husband endows the wife with all his wordly goods; and not a bit too much is this, when she is giving him the command and possession of her person. But does she not help to acquire the money? Speaking, for instance, of the farmer, or the merchant, the wife does not, indeed, go to plough, or to look after the ploughing and sowing; she does not purchase or sell the stock; she does not go to the fair or the market; but she enables him to do all these without injury to his affairs at home; she is the guardian of his property; she preserves what would otherwise be lost to him. The barn and the granary, though they create nothing, have, in the bringing of food to our mouths, as much merit as the fields themselves. The wife does not, indeed, assist in the merchant's counting-house; she does not go upon the Exchange; she does not even know what he is doing; but she keeps his house in order; she rears up his children; she provides a scene of suitable resort for his friends; she ensures him a constant retreat from the fatigues of his affairs; she makes his home pleasant, and is the guardian of his income.

220. In both these cases the wife helps to gain the money; and in cases where there is no gain, where the income is by descent, or is fixed, she helps to prevent it from being squandered away. It is, therefore, as much hers as it is the husband's; and though the law gives him, in many cases, the power of keeping her share from her, no just man will ever avail himself of that power. With regard to the tying up of widows from marrying again, I will relate what took place in a case of this kind in America. A merchant who had, during his married state, risen from poverty to very great riches, and who had, nevertheless, died at about forty years of age, left the whole of his property to his wife for her life, and at her disposal at her death, provided that she did not marry. The consequence was, that she took a husband without marrying, and, at her death (she having no children), gave the whole of the property to the second husband. So much for posthumous jealousy!

221. Where there are children, indeed, it is the duty of the husband to provide, in certain cases, against stepfathers, who are very prone not to be the most just and affectionate parents. It is an unhappy circumstance when a dying father is compelled to have fears of this sort. There is seldom an apology to

be offered for a mother that will hazard the happiness of her children by a second marriage. The law allows it, to be sure; but there is, as Prior says, " something beyond the letter of the law." I know what ticklish ground I am treading on here; but, though it is as lawful for a woman to take a second husband as for a man to take a second wife, the cases are different, and widely different, in the eye of morality and of reason; for, as adultery in the wife is a greater offence than adultery in the husband; as it is more gross, as it includes prostitution; so a second marriage in the woman is more gross than in the man, argues great deficiency in that delicacy, that innate modesty which, after all, is the great charm, the charm of charms in the female sex. I do not like to hear a man talk of his first wife, especially in the presence of a second; but to hear a woman thus talk of her first husband, has never, however beautiful and good she might be, failed to sink her in my estimation. I have, in such cases, never been able to keep out of my mind that concatenation of ideas which, in spite of custom, in spite of the frequency of the occurrence, leaves an impression deeply disadvantageous to the party; for, after the greatest of ingenuity has exhausted itself in the way of apology, it comes to this at last, that the person has a second time undergone that surrender, to which nothing but the most ardent affection could ever reconcile a chaste and delicate woman.

222. The usual apologies, that " a lone woman wants a protector; that she cannot manage her estate; that she cannot carry on her business; that she wants

a home for her children;" all these apologies are not
worth a straw; for what is the amount of them? Why,
that she surrenders her person to secure these ends!
And if we admit the validity of such apologies, are
we far from apologizing for the kept-mistress, and
even the prostitute? Nay, the former of these may
(if she confine herself to one man) plead more boldly
in her defence; and even the latter may plead that
hunger which knows no law, and no decorum, and
no delicacy. These unhappy, but justly reprobated
and despised parties are allowed no apology at all:
though reduced to the begging of their bread, the
world grants them no excuse. The sentence on them
is: " You shall suffer every hardship; you shall submit to hunger and nakedness; you shall perish by the
wayside rather than you shall surrender your person
to the dishonour of the female sex." But can we,
without crying injustice, pass this sentence upon
them, and, at the same time, hold it to be proper,
decorous, and delicate, that widows shall surrender
their persons for worldly gain, for the sake of ease, or
for any consideration whatsoever?

223. It is disagreeable to contemplate the possibility of cases of separation; but amongst the evils of
life such have occurred, and will occur; and the
injured parties, while they are sure to meet with the
pity of all just persons, must console themselves that
they have not merited their fate. In the making one's
choice, no human foresight or prudence can, in all
cases, guard against an unhappy result. There is one
species of husbands to be occasionally met with in
all countries meriting particular reprobation, and

causing us to lament that there is no law to punish offenders so enormous. There was a man in Pennsylvania, apparently a very amiable young man, having a good estate of his own, and marrying a most beautiful woman of his own age, of rich parents, and of virtue perfectly spotless. He very soon took to both gaming and drinking (the last being the most fashionable vice of the country); he neglected his affairs and his family; in about four years spent his estate and became a dependent on his wife's father, together with his wife and three children. Even this would have been of little consequence as far as related to expense; but he led the most scandalous life, and was incessant in his demands of money for the purposes of that infamous life. All sorts of means were resorted to to reclaim him, and all in vain; and the wretch, availing himself of the pleading of his wife's affection, and of his power over the children more especially, continued for ten or twelve years to plunder the parents, and to disgrace those whom it was his bounden duty to assist in making happy. At last, going out in the dark, in a boat, and being partly drunk, he went to the bottom of the Delaware, and became food for otters or fishes, to the great joy of all who knew him, excepting only his amiable wife. I can form an idea of no baseness equal to this. There is more of baseness in this character than in that of the robber. The man who obtains the means of indulging in vice by robbery, exposes himself to the inflictions of the law; but though he merits punishment, he merits it less than the base miscreant who obtains his means by his threats to disgrace his own

wife, children, and the wife's parents. The short way
in such a case is the best: set the wretch at defiance;
resort to the strong arm of the law wherever it will
avail you; drive him from your house like a mad dog;
for, be assured, that a being so base and cruel is never
to be reclaimed; all your efforts at persuasion are
useless; his promises and vows are made but to be
broken; all your endeavours to keep the thing from
the knowledge of the world only prolong his plunder-
ing of you; and many a tender father and mother
have been ruined by such endeavours; the whole
story must come out at last, and it is better to come
out before you be ruined, than after your ruin is
completed.

224. However, let me hope that those who read
this work will always be secure against evils like
these; let me hope that the young men who read it
will abstain from those vices which lead to such
fatal results; that they will, before they utter the
marriage vow, duly reflect on the great duties that
that vow imposes on them; that they will repel from
the outset every temptation to anything tending to
give pain to the defenceless persons whose love for
them has placed them at their mercy; and that they
will imprint on their own minds this truth, that a bad
husband was never yet a happy man.

LETTER V

ADVICE TO A FATHER

225. " LITTLE children," says the Scripture, " are like arrows in the hands of the giant, and blessed is the man that hath his quiver full of them "; a beautiful figure to describe in forcible terms the support, the power which a father derives from being surrounded by a family. And what father thus blessed is there who does not feel, in this sort of support, a reliance which he feels in no other? In regard to this sort of support there is no uncertainty, no doubts, no misgivings; it is yourself that you see in your children: their bosoms are the safe repository of even the whispers of your mind: they are the great and unspeakable delight of your youth, the pride of your prime of life, and the props of your old age. They proceed from that love, the pleasures of which no tongue or pen can adequately describe, and the various blessings which they bring are equally incapable of description.

226. But, to make them blessings, you must act your part well; for they may, by your neglect, your ill-treatment, your evil example, be made to be the contrary of blessings; instead of pleasure, they may bring you pain; instead of making your heart glad, the sight of them may make it sorrowful; instead of

215

being the staff of your old age, they may bring your grey hairs in grief to the grave.

227. It is, therefore, of the greatest importance that you here act well your part, omitting nothing, even from the very beginning, tending to give you great and unceasing influence over their minds; and, above all things, to ensure, if possible, an ardent love of their mother. Your first duty towards them is resolutely to prevent their drawing the means of life from any breast but hers. That is their own; it is their birthright; and if that fail from any natural cause, the place of it ought to be supplied by those means which are frequently resorted to without employing a hireling breast. I am aware of the too frequent practice of the contrary; I am well aware of the offence which I shall here give to many; but it is for me to do my duty and to set, with regard to myself, consequences at defiance.

228. In the first place, no food is so congenial to the child as the milk of its own mother; its quality is made by nature to suit the age of the child; it comes with the child, and is calculated precisely for its stomach. And, then, what sort of a mother must that be who can endure the thought of seeing her child at another breast! The suckling may be attended with great pain, and it is so attended in many cases: but this pain is a necessary consequence of pleasures foregone; and, besides, it has its accompanying pleasures too. No mother ever suffered more than my wife did from suckling her children. How many times have I seen her, when the child was beginning to draw, bite her lips while the tears ran down her

cheeks! Yet, having endured this, the smiles came and dried up the tears; and the little thing that had caused the pain received abundant kisses as its punishment.

229. Why, now, did I not love her the more for this? Did not this tend to rivet her to my heart? She was enduring this for me; and would not this endearing thought have been wanting if I had seen the baby at a breast that I had hired and paid for; if I had had two women, one to bear the child and another to give it milk? Of all the sights that this world affords, the most delightful in my eyes, even to an unconcerned spectator, is a mother with her clean and fat baby lugging at her breast, leaving off now and then and smiling, and she occasionally half smothering it with kisses. What must that sight be, then, to the father of the child!

230. Besides, are we to overlook the great and wonderful effect that this has on the minds of children. As they succeed each other, they see with their own eyes the pain, the care, the caresses which their mother has endured for, or bestowed on, them; and nature bids them love her accordingly. To love her ardently becomes part of their very nature; and when the time comes that her advice to them is necessary as a guide for their conduct, this deep and early impression has all its natural weight, which must be wholly wanting if the child be banished to a hireling breast, and only brought at times into the presence of the mother, who is, in fact, no mother, or, at least, but half a one. The children who are thus banished, love (as is natural and just) the foster-

mother better than the real mother as long as they are at the breast. When this ceases, they are taught to love their own mother most; but this teaching is of a cold and formal kind. They may, and generally do, in a short time care little about the foster-mother; the teaching weans all their affection from her, but it does not transfer it to the other.

231. I had the pleasure to know, in Hampshire, a lady who had brought up a family of ten children by hand, as they call it. Owing to some defect she could not suckle her children; but she wisely and heroically resolved that her children should hang upon no other breast, and that she would not participate in the crime of robbing another child of its birthright, and, is as mostly the case, of its life. Who has not seen these banished children, when brought and put into the arms of their mothers, screaming to get from them, and stretching out their little hands to get back into the arms of the nurse, and when safely got there hugging the hireling as if her bosom were a place of refuge? Why, such a sight is, one would think, enough to strike a mother dead. And what sort of a husband and father, I want to know, must that be who can endure the thought of his child loving another woman more than its own mother and his wife?

232. And besides all these considerations, is there no crime in robbing the child of the nurse, and in exposing it to perish? It will not do to say that the child of the nurse may be dead, and thereby leave her breast for the use of some other. Such cases must happen too seldom to be at all relied on; and,

indeed, every one must see that, generally speaking, there must be a child cast off for every one that is put to a hireling breast. Now, without supposing it possible that the hireling will in any case contrive to get rid of her own child; every man who employs such hireling must know that he is exposing such child to destruction; that he is assisting to rob it of the means of life; and, of course, assisting to procure its death as completely as a man can in any case assist in causing death by starvation; a consideration which will make every just man in the world recoil at the thought of employing a hireling breast. For he is not to think of pacifying his conscience by saying that he knows nothing about the hireling's child. He does know: for he must know that she has a child, and that he is a principal in robbing it of the means of life. He does not cast it off and leave it to perish himself, but he causes the thing to be done; and to all intents and purposes he is a principal in the cruel and cowardly crime.

233. And if an argument could possibly be yet wanting to the husband; if his feelings were so stiff as still to remain unmoved, must not the wife be aware that whatever face the world may put upon it, however custom may seem to bear her out; must she not be aware that every one must see the main motive which induces her to banish from her arms that which has formed part of her own body? All the pretences about her sore breasts and her want of strength are vain: nature says that she is to endure the pains as well as the pleasures: whoever has heard the bleating of the ewe for her lamb, and has seen

her reconciled, or at least pacified, by having presented to her the skin or some of the blood of her dead lamb; whoever has witnessed the difficulty of inducing either ewe or cow to give her milk to an alien young one: whoever has seen the valour of the timid hen in defending her brood, and has observed that she never swallows a morsel that is fit for her young, until they be amply satisfied: whoever has seen the wild birds, though at other times shunning even the distant approach of man, flying and screaming round his head, and exposing themselves to almost certain death in defence of their nests: whoever has seen these things, or any one of them, must question the motive that can induce a mother to banish a child from her own breast to that of one who has already been so unnatural as to banish hers. And, in seeking for a motive sufficiently powerful to lead to such an act, women must excuse men if they be not satisfied with the ordinary pretences; they must excuse me at any rate if I do not stop even at love of ease and want of maternal affection, and if I express my fear that, superadded to the unjustifiable motives, there is one which is calculated to excite disgust; namely a desire to be quickly freed from that restraint which the child imposes, and to hasten back, unbridled and undisfigured, to those enjoyments, to have an eagerness for which, or to wish to excite a desire for which, a really delicate woman will shudder at the thought of being suspected.

234. I am well aware of the hostility that I have here been exciting; but there is another, and still more furious bull to take by the horns, and which

would have been encountered some pages back (that being the proper place), had I not hesitated between my duty and my desire to avoid giving offence; I mean the employment of male operators on those occasions where females used to be employed. And here I have everything against me; the now general custom, even amongst the most chaste and delicate women; the ridicule continually cast on old mid-wives; the interest of a profession for the members of which I entertain more respect and regard than for those of any other; and, above all the rest, my own example to the contrary, and my knowledge that every husband has the same apology that I had. But because I acted wrong myself, it is not less, but rather more, my duty to endeavour to dissuade others from doing the same. My wife had suffered very severely with her second child, which at last was still-born. The next time I pleaded for the doctor; and, after every argument that I could think of, obtained a reluctant consent. Her life was so dear to me that everything else appeared as nothing. Every husband has the same apology to make; and thus from the good, and not from the bad feelings of men, the practice has become far too general for me to hope even to narrow it; but, nevertheless, I cannot refrain from giving my opinion on the subject.

235. We are apt to talk in a very unceremonious style of our rude ancestors, of their gross habits, their want of delicacy in their language. No man shall ever make me believe that those who reared the cathedral of Ely (which I saw the other day) were rude, either in their manners, or in their minds and

words. No man shall make me believe that our
ancestors were a rude and beggarly race, when I read
in an Act of Parliament passed in the reign of
Edward the Fourth, regulating the dresses of the
different ranks of the people, and forbidding the
labourers to wear coats of cloth that cost more than
two shillings a yard (equal to forty shillings of our
present money), and forbidding their wives and
daughters to wear sashes or girdles trimmed with
gold or silver. No man shall make me believe that
this was a rude and beggarly race compared with
those who now shirk and shiver about in canvas
frocks and rotten cottons. Nor shall any man persuade me that that was a rude and beggarly state of
things, in which (reign of Edward the Third) an Act
was passed regulating the wages of labour, and
ordering that a woman for weeding in the corn should
receive a penny a day, while a quart of red wine was
sold for a penny, and a pair of men's shoes for twopence. No man shall make me believe that agriculture
was in a rude state when an Act like this was passed,
or that our ancestors of that day were rude in their
minds or in their thoughts. Indeed, there are a
thousand proofs that, whether in regard to domestic
or foreign affairs, whether in regard to internal freedom and happiness, or to weight in the world, England
was at her zenith about the reign of Edward the Third.
The Reformation, as it is called, gave her a complete
pull down. She revived again in the reigns of the
Stuarts as far as related to internal affairs; but the
" Glorious Revolution " and its debt and taxes have,
amidst the false glare of new palaces, roads, and

canals, brought her down until she has become the land of domestic misery and of foreign impotence and contempt; and until she, amidst all her boasted improvements and refinements, tremblingly awaits her fall.

236. However, to return from this digression, rude and unrefined as our mothers might be, plain and unvarnished as they might be in their language, accustomed as they might be to call things by their names, though they were not so very delicate as to use the word small-clothes; and to be quite unable in speaking of horn-cattle, horses, sheep, the canine race, and poultry, to designate them by their sexual appellations; though they might not absolutely faint at hearing these appellations used by others; rude and unrefined and indelicate as they might be, they did not suffer, in the cases alluded to, the approaches of men, which approaches are unceremoniously suffered and even sought by their polished and refined and delicate daughters; and of unmarried men, too, in many cases; and of very young men.

237. From all antiquity this office was allotted to woman. Moses's life was saved by the humanity of the Egyptian midwife; and to the employment of females in this memorable case the world is probably indebted for that which has been left it by that greatest of all lawgivers, whose institutes, rude as they were, have been the foundation of all the wisest and most just laws in all the countries of Europe and America. It was the fellow-feeling of the midwife for the poor mother that saved Moses. And none but a mother can, in such cases, feel to the full and effectual

extent that which the operator ought to feel. She has been in the same state herself; she knows more about the matter, except in cases of very rare occurrence, than any man, however great his learning and experience, can ever know. She knows all the previous symptoms; she can judge more correctly than any man can judge in such a case; she can put questions to the party which a man cannot put; the communication between the two is wholly without reserve; the person of the one is given up to the other as completely as her own is under her command. This never can be the case with a man operator; for, after all that can be said or done, the native feeling of woman, in whatever rank of life, will, in these cases, restrain them from saying and doing before a man, even before a husband, many things which they ought to say and do. So that, perhaps, even with regard to the bare question of comparative safety to life, the midwife is the preferable person.

238. But safety to life is not all. The preservation of life is not to be preferred to everything. Ought not a man to prefer death to the commission of treason against his country? Ought not a man to die rather than save his life by the prostitution of his wife to a tyrant who insists upon the one or the other? Every man and every woman will answer in the affirmative to both these questions. These are, then, cases when people ought to submit to certain death. Surely, then, the mere chance, the mere possibility of it, ought not to outweigh the mighty considerations on the other side; ought not to overcome that inborn modesty, that sacred reserve as to their persons, which, as I

said before, is the charm of charms of the female sex, and which our mothers, rude as they are called by us, took, we may be satisfied, the best and most effectual means of preserving.

239. But is there, after all, anything real in this greater security for the life of either mother or child? If, then, risk were so great as to call upon women to overcome this natural repugnance to suffer the approaches of a man, that risk must be general; it must apply to all women; and, further, it must, ever since the creation of man, always have so applied. Now, resorting to the employment of men operators has not been in vogue in Europe more than about seventy years, and has not been general in England more than about thirty or forty years. So that the risk in employing midwives must, of late years, have become vastly greater than it was even when I was a boy, or the whole race must have been extinguished long ago. And, then, how puzzled we should be to account for the building of all the cathedrals, and all the churches, and the draining of all the marshes, and all the fens, more than a thousand years before the word " accoucheur " ever came from the lips of woman, and before the thought came into her mind? And here, even in the use of this word, we have a specimen of the refined delicacy of the present age; here we have, varnish the matter over how we may, modesty in the word and grossness in the thought. Farmers' wives, daughters, and maids cannot now allude to, or hear named, without blushing, those affairs of the homestead which they, within my memory, used to talk about as freely as of

milking or spinning; but have they become more really modest than their mothers were? Has this refinement made them more continent than those rude mothers? A jury at Westminster gave, about six years ago, damages to a man, calling himself a gentleman, against a farmer, because the latter, for the purpose for which such animals are kept, had a bull in his yard on which the windows of the gentleman looked! The plaintiff alleged that this was so offensive to his wife and daughters that, if the defendant were not compelled to desist, he should be obliged to brick up his windows, or to quit the house! If I had been the father of these at once delicate and curious daughters, I would not have been the herald of their purity of mind; and if I had been the suitor of one of them I would have taken care to give up the suit with all convenient speed; for how could I reasonably have hoped ever to be able to prevail on delicacy so exquisite to commit itself to a pair of bridal sheets? In spite, however, of all this " refinement in the human mind," which is everlastingly dinned in our ears; in spite of the " small-clothes," and of all the other affected stuff, we have this conclusion, this indubitable proof, of the falling off in real delicacy; namely, that common prostitutes, formerly unknown, now swarm in our towns, and are seldom wanting even in our villages; and where there was one illegitimate child (including those coming before the time) only fifty years ago there are now twenty.

240. And who can say how far the employment of men, in the cases alluded to, may have assisted in producing this change, so disgraceful to the present

age and so injurious to the female sex? The prostitution and the swarms of illegitimate children have a
natural and inevitable tendency to lessen that respect
and that kind and indulgent feeling which is due
from all men to virtuous women. It is well known
that the unworthy members of any profession,
calling, or rank in life, cause, by their acts, the whole
body to sink in the general esteem; it is well known
that the habitual dishonesty of merchants trading
abroad, the habitual profligate behaviour of travellers
from home, the frequent proofs of abject submission
to tyrants; it is well known that these may give the
character of dishonesty, profligacy, or cowardice to
a whole nation. There are, doubtless, many men in
Switzerland who abhor the infamous practices of men
selling themselves by whole regiments to fight for
any foreign State that will pay them, no matter in
what cause, and no matter whether against their own
parents or brethren; but the censure falls upon the
whole nation: and " no money no Swiss," is a
proverb throughout the world. It is, amidst those
scenes of prostitution and bastardy, impossible for
men in general to respect the female sex to the degree
that they formerly did; while numbers will be apt to
adopt the unjust sentiment of the old bachelor, Pope,
that " every woman is at heart a rake."

241. Who knows, I say, in what degree the employment of men operators may have tended to
produce this change so injurious to the female sex?
Aye, and to encourage unfeeling and brutal men to
propose that the dead bodies of females, if poor,
should be sold for the purpose of exhibition and

dissection before an audience of men; a proposition that our " rude ancestors " would have answered not by words, but by blows! Alas! our women may talk of " small-clothes " as long as they please; they may blush to scarlet at hearing animals designated by their sexual appellations; it may, to give the world a proof of our excessive modesty and delicacy, even pass a law (indeed we have done it) to punish " an exposure of the person "; but as long as our streets swarm with prostitutes, our asylums and private houses with bastards; as long as we have men operators in the delicate cases alluded to, and as long as the exhibiting of the dead body of a virtuous female before an audience of men shall not be punished by the law, and even with death; as long as we shall appear to be satisfied in this state of things, it becomes us at any rate to be silent about purity of mind, improvement of manners, and an increase of refinement and delicacy.

242. This practice has brought the " doctor " into every family in the kingdom, which is of itself no small evil. I am not thinking of the expense; for, in cases like these, nothing in that way ought to be spared. If necessary to the safety of his wife, a man ought not only to part with his last shilling, but to pledge his future labour. But we all know that there are imaginary ailments, many of which are absolutely created by the habit of talking with or about the " doctor." Read the " Domestic Medicine," and by the time that you have done, you will imagine that you have at times all the diseases of which it treats. This practice has added to, has doubled, aye, has

augmented, I verily believe, tenfold the number of
the gentlemen who are in common parlance called
" doctors "; at which, indeed, I, on my own private
account, ought to rejoice; for invariably I have, even
in the worst of times, found them everywhere among
my staunchest and kindest friends. But though these
gentlemen are not to blame for this any more than
attorneys are for their increase in number; and
amongst these gentlemen, too, I have, with very few
exceptions, always found sensible men and zealous
friends; though the parties pursuing these professions
are not to blame; though the increase of attorneys has
risen from the endless number and the complexity of
the laws, and from the tenfold mass of crimes caused
by poverty arising from oppresive taxation; and though
the increase of " doctors " has arisen from the diseases
and the imaginary ailments arising from that
effeminate luxury which has been created by the
drawing of wealth from the many and giving it to
the few; and as the lower classes will always endeavour to imitate the higher, so the " accoucheur "
has, along with the " small-clothes," descended from
the loan-monger's palace down to the hovel of the
pauper, there to take his fee out of the poor-rates;
though these parties are not to blame, the thing is
not less an evil. Both professions have lost in character
in proportion to the increase in the number of its
members; peaches, if they grew on hedges, would
rank but little above the berries of the bramble.

243. But to return once more to the matter of risk
of life; can it be that nature has so ordered it, that,
as a general thing, the life of either mother or child

shall be in danger, even if there were no attendant at all? Can this be? Certainly it cannot: safety must be the rule, and danger the exception; this must be the case, or the world never could have been peopled; and, perhaps, in ninety-nine cases out of every hundred, if nature were left wholly to herself, all would be right. The great doctor, in these cases, is comforting, consoling, cheering up. And who can perform this office like women? who have for these occasions a language and sentiments which seem to have been invented for the purpose; and be they what they may as to general demeanour and character, they have all, upon these occasions, one common feeling, and that so amiable, so excellent, as to admit of no adequate description. They completely forget, for the time, all rivalships, all squabbles, all animosities, all hatred even; every one feels as if it were her own particular concern.

244. These, we may be well assured, are the proper attendants on these occasions; the mother, the aunt, the sister, the cousin, and the female neighbour; these are the suitable attendants, having some experienced women to afford extraordinary aid, if such be necessary; and in the few cases where the preservation of life demands the surgeon's skill, he is always at hand. The contrary practice, which we got from the French, is not, however, so general in France as in England. We have outstripped all the world in this, as we have in everything which proceeds from luxury and effeminacy on the one hand, and from poverty on the other; the millions have been stripped of their means to heap wealth on the

thousands, and have been corrupted in manners, as well as in morals, by vicious examples set them by the possessors of that wealth. As reason says that the practice of which I complain cannot be cured without a total change in society, it would be presumption in me to expect such cure from any efforts of mine. I therefore must content myself with hoping that such change will come, and with declaring, that if I had to live my life over again, I would act upon the opinions which I have thought it my bounden duty here to state and endeavour to maintain.

245. Having gotten over these thorny places as quickly as possible, I gladly come back to the babies; with regard to whom I shall have no prejudices, no affectation, no false pride, no sham fears to encounter; every heart (except there be one made of flint) being with me here. " Then were there brought unto Him little children, that He should put His hands on them and pray: and the disciples rebuked them. But Jesus said, Suffer little children, and forbid them not, to come unto me; for of such is the kingdom of heaven." A figure most forcibly expressive of the character and beauty of innocence, and, at the same time, most aptly illustrative of the doctrine of re-generation. And where is the man; the woman who is not fond of babies is not worthy the name; but where is the man who does not feel his heart softened; who does not feel himself become gentler; who does not lose all the hardness of his temper; when, in any way, for any purpose, or by anybody, an appeal is made to him in behalf of these so helpless and so perfectly innocent little creatures?

246. Shakspeare, who is cried up as the great interpreter of the human heart, has said, that the man in whose soul there is no music, or love of music, is " fit for murders, treasons, stratagems, and spoils." " Our immortal bard," as the profligate Sheridan used to call him in public, while he laughed at him in private; our " immortal bard " seems to have forgotten that Shadrach, Meshach, and Abednego, were flung into the fiery furnace (made seven times hotter than usual) amidst the sound of the cornet, flute, harp, sackbut, and dulcimer, and all kinds of music; he seems to have forgotten that it was a music and a dance-loving damsel that chose, as a recompense for her elegant performance, the bloody head of John the Baptist, brought to her in a charger; he seems to have forgotten that, while Rome burned, Nero fiddled. He did not know, perhaps, that cannibals always dance and sing while their victims are roasting; but he might have known, and he must have known, that England's greatest tyrant, Henry VIII, had, as his agent in blood, Thomas Cromwell, expressed it, " his sweet soul enwrapped in the celestial sounds of music; " and this was just at the time when the ferocious tyrant was ordering Catholics and Protestants to be tied back to back on the same hurdle, dragged to Smithfield on that hurdle, and there tied to, and burnt from, the same stake. Shakspeare must have known these things, for he lived immediately after their date; and if he had lived in our day, he would have seen instances enough of " sweet souls " enwrapped in the same manner, and capable, if not of deeds

equally bloody, of others, discovering a total want of feeling for sufferings not unfrequently occasioned by their own wanton waste, and waste arising, too, in part, from their taste for these " celestial sounds."

247. Oh no! the heart of man is not to be known by this test: a great fondness for music is a mark of great weakness, great vacuity of mind: not of hardness of heart; not of vice; not of downright folly; but of a want of capacity, or inclination, for sober thought. This is not always the case: accidental circumstances almost force the taste upon people: but, generally speaking, it is a preference of sound to sense. But the man, and especially the father, who is not fond of babies; who does not feel his heart softened when he touches their almost boneless limbs; when he sees their little eyes first begin to discern; when he hears their tender accents; the man whose heart does not beat truly to this test, is, to say the best of him, an object of compassion.

248. But the mother's feelings are here to be thought of too; for, of all gratifications, the very greatest that a mother can receive, is notice taken of, and praise bestowed on, her baby. The moment that gets into her arms, everything else diminishes in value, the father only excepted. Her own personal charms, notwithstanding all that men say and have written on the subject, become, at most, a secondary object as soon as the baby arrives. A saying of the old, profligate King of Prussia is frequently quoted in proof of the truth of the maxim, that a woman will forgive anything but calling her ugly: a very true maxim, perhaps, as applied to prostitutes, whether

in high or low life; but a pretty long life of observation has told me, that a mother, worthy of the name,
will care little about what you say of her person, so
that you will but extol the beauty of her baby. Her
baby is always the very prettiest that ever was born!
It is always an eighth wonder of the world! And thus
it ought to be, or there would be a want of that
wondrous attachment to it which is necessary to bear
her up through all those cares and pains and toils
inseparable from the preservation of its life and
health.

249. It is, however, of the part which the husband
has to act in participating in these cares and toils
that I am now to speak. Let no man imagine that the
world will despise him for helping to take care of his
own child: thoughtless fools may attempt to ridicule;
the unfeeling few may join in the attempt; but all
whose good opinion is worth having will applaud
his conduct, and will, in many cases, be disposed
to repose confidence in him on that very account.
To say of a man that he is fond of his family is, of
itself, to say that, in private life at least, he is a
good and trustworthy man; aye, and in public life,
too, pretty much; for it is no easy matter to separate
the two characters; and it is naturally concluded that
he who has been flagrantly wanting in feeling for his
own flesh and blood will not be very sensitive towards
the rest of mankind. There is nothing more amiable,
nothing more delightful to behold, than a young man
especially taking part in the work of nursing the
children; and how often have I admired this in the
labouring men in Hampshire! It is, indeed, generally

the same all over England; and as to America, it
would be deemed brutal for a man not to take his
full share of these cares and labours.

250. The man who is to gain a living by his labour
must be drawn away from home, or at least from the
cradle-side, in order to perform that labour; but this
will not, if he be made of good stuff, prevent him
from doing his share of the duty due to his children.
There are still many hours in the twenty-four that
he will have to spare for this duty; and there ought
to be no toils, no watchings, no breaking of rest
imposed by this duty, of which he ought not to
perform his full share, and that, too, without
grudging. This is strictly due from him in payment
for the pleasures of the married state. What right
has he to the sole possession of a woman's person;
what right to a husband's vast authority; what right
to the honourable title and the boundless power of
father: what right has he to all, or any of these,
unless he can found his claim on the faithful performance of all the duties which these titles imply?

251. One great source of the unhappiness amongst
mankind arises, however, from a neglect of these
duties; but, as if by way of compensation for their
privations, they are much more duly performed by
the poor than by the rich. The fashion of the labouring people is this: the husband, when free from his
toil in the fields, takes his share in the nursing, which
he manifestly looks upon as a sort of reward for his
labour. However distant from his cottage, his heart
is always at that home towards which he is carried at
night by limbs that feel not their weariness, being

urged on by a heart anticipating the welcome of those who attend him there. Those who have, as I so many hundreds of times have, seen the labourers in the woodland parts of Hampshire and Sussex coming at nightfall towards their cottage wickets laden with fuel for a day or two; whoever has seen three or four little creatures looking out for the father's approach, running in to announce the glad tidings, and then scampering out to meet him, clinging round his knees or hanging on his skirts; whoever has witnessed scenes like this, to witness which has formed one of the greatest delights of my life, will hesitate long before he prefer a life of ease to a life of labour; before he prefer a communication with children intercepted by servants and teachers to that communication which is here direct, and which admits not of any division of affection.

252. Then comes the Sunday; and amongst all those who keep no servants a great deal depends on the manner in which the father employs that day. When there are two or three children, or even one child, the first thing after the breakfast (which is late on this day of rest) is to wash and dress the child or children. Then, while the mother is dressing the dinner, the father, being in his Sunday-clothes himself, takes care of the child or children. When dinner is over, the mother puts on her best; and then all go to church, or, if that cannot be, whether from distance or other cause, all pass the afternoon together. This used to be the way of life amongst the labouring people; and from this way of life arose the most able and most moral people that the world ever

saw, until grinding taxation took from them the means of obtaining a sufficiency of food and of raiment; plunged the whole, good and bad, into one indiscriminate mass, under the degrading and hateful name of paupers.

253. The working man, in whatever line, and whether in town or country, who spends his day of rest, or any part of it, except in case of absolute necessity, away from his wife and children, is not worthy of the name of father, and is seldom worthy of the trust of any employer. Such absence argues a want of fatherly and of conjugal affection, which want is generally duly repaid by a similar want in the neglected parties; and though stern authority may command and enforce obedience for awhile, the time soon comes when it will be set at defiance; and when such a father, having no example, no proofs of love to plead, complains of filial ingratitude, the silent indifference of his neighbours, and, which is more poignant, his own heart will tell him that his complaint is unjust.

254. Thus far with regard to working people; but much more necessary is it to inculcate these principles in the minds of young men in the middle rank of life, and to be more particular in their case with regard to the care due to very young children, for here servants come in; and many are but too prone to think that when they have handed their children over to well-paid and able servants they have done their duty by them, than which there can hardly be a more mischievous error. The children of the poorer people are in general much fonder of their parents

than those of the rich are of theirs: this fondness is
reciprocal; and the cause is that the children of the
former have, from the very birth, had a greater share
than those of the latter of the personal attention and
of the never-ceasing endearments of their parents.

255. I have before urged upon young married
men in the middle walks of life to keep the servants
out of the house as long as possible; and when they
must come at last, when they must be had even to
assist in taking care of children, let them be assistants
in the most strict sense of the word; let them not be
confided in; let children never be left to them alone;
and the younger the child the more necessary a rigid
adherence to this rule. I shall be told, perhaps, by
some careless father, or some play-hunting mother,
that female servants are women, and have the tender
feelings of women. Very true; and in general as good
and kind in their nature as the mother herself. But
they are not the mothers of your children, and it is
not in nature that they should have the care and
anxiety adequate to the necessity of the case. Out of
the immediate care and personal superintendence of
one or the other of the parents, or of some trusty
relation, no young child ought to be suffered to be,
if there be, at whatever sacrifice of ease or of property, any possibility of preventing it: because, to
insure, if possible, the perfect form, the straight
limbs, the sound body, and the sane mind of your
children, is the very first of all your duties. To provide fortunes for them; to make provision for their
future fame; to give them the learning necessary to
the calling for which you destine them: all these may

be duties, and the last is a duty; but a duty far greater than, and prior to, all these, is the duty of neglecting nothing within your power to insure them a sane mind in a sound and undeformed body. And, good God! how many are the instances of deformed bodies, of crooked limbs, of idiocy, or of deplorable imbecility proceeding solely from young children being left to the care of servants! One would imagine that one single sight of this kind to be seen or heard of in a whole nation would be sufficient to deter parents from the practice. And what, then, must those parents feel who have brought this life-long sorrow on themselves! When once the thing is done, to repent is unavailing. And what is now the worth of all the ease and all the pleasures, to enjoy which the poor sufferer was abandoned to the care of servants!

256. What! can I plead example, then, in support of this rigid precept? Did we, who have bred up a family of children, and have had servants during the greater part of the time, never leave a young child to the care of servants? Never; no, not for one single hour. Were we, then, tied constantly to the house with them? No; for we sometimes took them out; but one or the other of us was always with them, until, in succession, they were able to take good care of themselves; or until the elder ones were able to take care of the younger, and then they sometimes stood sentinel in our stead. How could we visit, then? Why, if both went, we bargained beforehand to take the children with us; and if this were a thing not to be proposed, one of us went, and the other stayed at home, the latter being very frequently my lot. From

this we never once deviated. We cast aside all consideration of convenience; all calculations of expense; all thoughts of pleasure of every sort. And what could have equalled the reward that we have received for our care and for our unshaken resolution in this respect?

257. In the rearing of children there is resolution wanting as well as tenderness. That parent is not truly affectionate who wants the courage to do that which is sure to give the child temporary pain. A great deal in providing for the health and strength of children depends upon their being duly and daily washed, when well, in cold water from head to foot. Their cries testify to what a degree they dislike this. They squall and kick and twist about at a fine rate; and many mothers, too many, neglect this, partly from reluctance to encounter the squalling, and partly, and much too often, from what I will not call idleness, but to which I cannot apply a milder term than neglect. Well and duly performed, it is an hour's good tight work; for, besides the bodily labour, which is not very slight when the child gets to be five or six months old, there is the singing to overpower the voice of the child. The moment the stripping of the child used to begin, the singing used to begin, and the latter never ceased till the former had ceased. After having heard this go on with all my children, Rousseau taught me the philosophy of it. I happened, by accident, to look into his " Emile," and there I found him saying that the nurse subdued the voice of the child and made it quiet by drowning its voice in hers, and thereby making it perceive that

it could not be heard, and that to continue to cry was of no avail. " Here, Nancy," said I (going to her with the book in my hand), " you have been a great philosopher all your life without either of us knowing it." A silent nurse is a poor soul. It is a great disadvantage to the child if the mother be of a very silent, placid, quiet turn. The singing, the talking to, the tossing and rolling about that mothers in general practise, are very beneficial to the children: they give them exercise, awaken their attention, animate them, and rouse them to action. It is very bad to have a child even carried about by a dull, inanimate, silent servant, who will never talk, sing, or chirrup to it; who will but just carry it about, always kept in the same attitude, and seeing and hearing nothing to give it life and spirit. It requires nothing but a dull creature like this, and the washing and dressing left to her, to give a child the rickets, and make it, instead of being a strong, straight person, tup-shinned, bow-kneed, or hump-backed; besides other ailments not visible to the eye. By-and-by, when the deformity begins to appear, the doctor is called in, but it is too late: the mischief is done; and a few months of neglect are punished by a life of mortification and sorrow not wholly unaccompanied with shame.

258. It is, therefore, a very spurious kind of tenderness that prevents a mother from doing the things which, though disagreeable to the child, are so necessary to its lasting well-being. The washing daily in the morning is a great thing; cold water, winter or summer, and this never left to a servant who has not, in such a case, either the patience or the

courage that is necessary for the task. When the washing is over, and the child dressed in its day-clothes, how gay and cheerful it looks! The exercise gives it appetite, and then disposes it to rest; and it sucks and sleeps and grows, the delight of all eyes, and particularly those of the parents. " I can't bear that squalling! " I have heard men say; and to which I answer, that " I can't bear such men ! " There are, I thank God, very few of them; for, if they do not always reason about the matter, honest nature teaches them to be considerate and indulgent towards little creatures so innocent and so helpless and so un-conscious of what they do. And the noise: after all, why should it disturb a man? He knows the exact cause of it: he knows that it is the unavoidable con-sequence of a great good to his child, and of course to him: it lasts but an hour, and the recompense in-stantly comes in the looks of the rosy child, and in the new hopes which every look excites. It never disturbed me, and my occupation was one of those most liable to disturbance by noise. Many a score papers have I written amidst the noise of children, and in my whole life never bade them be still. When they grew up to be big enough to gallop about the house, I have, in wet weather, when they could not go out, written the whole day amidst noise that would have made some authors half mad. It never annoyed me at all. But a Scotch piper, whom an old lady, who lived beside us at Brompton, used to pay to come and play a long tune every day, I was obliged to bribe into a breach of contract. That which you are pleased with, however noisy, does not disturb you.

That which is indifferent to you has not more effect. The rattle of coaches, the clapper of a mill, the fall of water, leave your mind undisturbed. But the sound of the pipe, awakening the idea of the lazy life of the piper, better paid than the labouring man, drew the mind aside from its pursuit; and, as it really was a nuisance, occasioned by the money of my neighbour, I thought myself justified in abating it by the same sort of means.

259. The cradle is in poor families necessary; because necessity compels the mother to get as much time as she can for her work, and a child can rock the cradle. At first we had a cradle; and I rocked the cradle, in great part, during the time that I was writing my first work, that famous " Maître d'Anglois," which has long been the first book in Europe, as well as in America, for the teaching of French people the English language. But we left off the use of the cradle as soon as possible. It causes sleep more, and oftener, than necessary: it saves trouble; but to take trouble was our duty. After the second child, we had no cradle, however difficult at first to do without it. When I was not at my business, it was generally my affair to put the child to sleep: sometimes by sitting with it in my arms, and sometimes by lying down on a bed with it, till it fell asleep. We soon found the good of this method. The children did not sleep so much, but they slept more soundly. The cradle produces a sort of dozing, or dreaming sleep. This is a matter of great importance, as everything must be that has any influence on the health of the children. The poor must use the cradle,

at least until they have other children big enough to hold the baby, and to put it to sleep; and it is truly wonderful at how early an age they, either girls or boys, will do this business faithfully and well. You see them in the lanes, and on the skirts of woods and commons, lugging a baby about, when it sometimes weighs half as much as the nurse. The poor mother is frequently compelled, in order to help to get bread for her children, to go to a distance from home, and leave the group, baby and all, to take care of the house and of themselves, the eldest of four or five, not, perhaps, above six or seven years old; and it is quite surprising, that, considering the millions of instances in which this is done in England, in the course of a year, so very, very few accidents or injuries arise from the practice; and not a hundredth part so many as arise in the comparatively few instances in which children are left to the care of servants. In summer-time you see these little groups rolling about up the green, or amongst the heath, not far from the cottage, and at a mile, perhaps, from any other dwelling, the dog their only protector. And what fine and straight and healthy and fearless and acute persons they become! It used to be remarked in Philadelphia, when I lived there, that there was not a single man of any eminence, whether doctor, lawyer, merchant, trader, or anything else, that had not been born and bred in the country, and of parents in a low state of life. Examine London, and you will find it much about the same. From this very childhood they are from necessity entrusted with the care of something valuable. They practically learn to think, and to calculate as to consequences. They are thus taught to remember things; and it is quite surprising what memories they have, and how scrupulously a little carter-boy will deliver half a dozen messages, each of a different purport from the rest, to as many persons, all the messages committed to him at one and the same time, and he not knowing one letter of the alphabet from another. When I want to remember something, and am out in the field, and cannot write it down, I say to one of the men, or boys, come to me at such a time, and tell me so and so. He is sure to do it; and I therefore look upon the memorandum as written down. One of these children, boy or girl, is much more worthy of being entrusted with the care of a baby, anybody's baby, than a servant-maid with curled locks and with eyes rolling about for admirers. The locks and the rolling eyes, very nice, and, for aught I know, very proper things in themselves; but incompatible with the care of your baby, Ma'am; her mind being absorbed in contemplating the interesting circumstances which are to precede her having a sweet baby of her own; and a sweeter than yours, if you please, Ma'am; or, at least, such will be her anticipations. And this is all right enough; it is natural that she should think and feel thus; and knowing this, you are admonished that it is your bounden duty not to delegate this sacred trust to anybody.

260. The courage of which I have spoken, so necessary in the case of washing the children in spite of their screaming remonstrances, is, if possible, more necessary in cases of illness, requiring the

application of medicine, or of surgical means of cure. Here the heart is put to the test indeed! Here is anguish to be endured by a mother, who has to force down the nauseous physic, or to apply the tormenting plaster! Yet it is the mother, or the father, and more properly the former, who is to perform this duty of exquisite pain. To no nurse, to no hireling, to no alien hand, ought, if possible to avoid it, this task to be committed. I do not admire those mothers who are too tender-hearted to inflict this pain on their children, and who, therefore, leave it to be inflicted by others. Give me the mother who, while the tears stream down her face, has the resolution scrupulously to execute, with her own hands, the doctor's commands. Will a servant, will any hireling do this? Committed to such hands, the least trouble will be preferred to the greater: the thing will, in general, not be half done; and if done, the suffering from such hands is far greater in the mind of the child than if it came from the hands of the mother. In this case, above all others, there ought to be no delegation of the parental office. Here life or limb is at stake; and the parent, man or woman, who, in any one point, can neglect his or her duty here, is unworthy of the name of parent. And here, as in all the other instances, where goodness in the parents towards the children gives such weight to their advice when the children grow up, what a motive to filial gratitude! The children who are old enough to discern and remember, will witness this proof of love and self-devotion in their mother. Each of them feels that she has done the same towards them all; and they love her and admire and revere her accordingly.

261. This is the place to state my opinions, and the result of my experience, with regard to that fearful disease the small-pox; a subject, too, to which I have paid great attention. I was always, from the very first mention of the thing, opposed to the cow-pox scheme. If efficacious in preventing the small-pox, I objected to it merely on the score of its beastliness. There are some things, surely, more hideous than death, and more resolutely to be avoided than the mere risk of suffering death. And, amongst other things, I always reckoned that of a parent causing the blood, and the diseased blood too, of a beast to be put into the veins of human beings, and those beings the children of that parent. I, therefore, as will be seen in the pages of the *Register* of that day, most strenuously opposed the giving of twenty thousand pounds to Jenner out of the taxes, paid in great part by the working-people, which I deemed and asserted to be a scandalous waste of the public money.

262. I contended that this beastly application could not, in nature, be efficacious in preventing the small-pox; and that, even if efficacious for that purpose, it was wholly unnecessary. The truth of the former of these assertions has now been proved in thousands upon thousands of instances. For a long time, for ten years, the contrary was boldly and bravely asserted. This nation is fond of quackery of all sorts; and this particular quackery having been sanctioned by King, Lords, and Commons, it spread

over the country like a pestilence borne by the winds.
Speedily sprang up the " *Royal* Jennerian Institu-
tion," and branch institutions, issuing from the
parent trunk, set instantly to work, impregnating the
veins of the rising and enlightened generation with
the beastly matter. " Gentlemen and ladies " made
the commodity a pocket-companion; and if a cot-
tager's child (in Hampshire at least), ever seen by
them, on a common, were not pretty quick in taking
to its heels, it had to carry off more or less of the
disease of the cow. One would have thought that
one-half of the cows in England must have been
tapped to get at such a quantity of the stuff.

263. In the midst of all this mad work, to which
the doctors, after having found it in vain to resist,
had yielded, the real small-pox, in its worst form,
broke out in the town of Ringwood, in Hampshire,
and carried off, I believe (I have not the account at
hand), more than a hundred persons, young and old,
every one of whom had had the cox-pox " so nicely! "
And what was now said? Was the quackery exploded,
and were the granters of the twenty thousand pounds
ashamed of what they had done? Not at all: the
failure was imputed to unskilful operators; to the
staleness of the matter: to its not being of the
genuine quality. Admitting all this, the scheme
stood condemned; for the great advantages held
forth were, that anybody might perform the operation, and that the matter was everywhere abundant,
and cost free. But these were paltry excuses; the
mere shuffles of quackery; for what do we know now?
Why, that in hundreds of instances, persons cow-

poxed by Jenner himself have taken the real small-pox afterwards, and have either died from the disorder, or narrowly escaped with their lives! I will mention two instances, the parties concerned being living and well known, one of them to the whole nation, and the other to a very numerous circle in the higher walks of life. The first is Sir Richard Phillips, so well known by his able writings, and equally well known by his exemplary conduct as Sheriff of London, and by his life-long labours in the cause of real charity and humanity. Sir Richard had, I think, two sons, whose veins were impregnated by the grantee himself. At any rate he had one, who had, several years after Jenner had given him the insuring matter, a very hard struggle for his life, under the hands of the good, old-fashioned, seam-giving, and dimple-dipping small-pox. The second is Philip Codd, Esq., formerly of Kensington, and now of Rumsted Court, near Maidstone, in Kent, who has a son that had a very narrow escape under the real small-pox, about four years ago, and who also had been cow-poxed by Jenner himself. This last-mentioned gentleman I have known, and most sincerely respected, from the time of our both being about eighteen years of age. When the young gentleman, of whom I am now speaking, was very young, I having him upon my knee one day, asked his kind and excellent mother whether he had been inoculated. " Oh, no! " said she, " we are going to have him vaccinated." Whereupon I, going into the garden to the father, said, " I do hope, Codd, that you are not going to have that beastly cow-stuff put into that

fine boy." " Why," said he, " you see, Cobbett, it is to
be done by Jenner himself." What answer I gave, what
names and epithets I bestowed upon Jenner and his
quackery, I will leave the reader to imagine.

264. Now, here are instances enough; but every
reader has heard of, if not seen, scores of others.
Young Mr. Codd caught the small-pox at a school;
and, if I recollect rightly, there were several other
" vaccinated " youths who did the same at the same
time. Quackery, however, has always a shuffle left.
Now that the cow-pox has been proved to be no
guarantee against the small-pox, it makes it " milder"
when it comes! A pretty shuffle, indeed, this! You
are to be all your life in fear of it, having as your sole
consolation, that when it comes (and it may overtake
you in a camp or on the seas), it will be " milder! "
It was not too mild to kill at Ringwood, and its
mildness, in the case of young Mr. Codd, did not
restrain it from blinding him for a suitable number
of days. I shall not easily forget the alarm and
anxiety of the father and mother upon this occasion;
both of them the best of parents, and both of them
now punished for having yielded to this fashionable
quackery. I will not say, justly punished; for affection
for their children, in which respect they were never
surpassed by any parents on earth, was the cause of
their listening to the danger-obviating quackery.
This, too, is the case with other parents; but parents
should be under the influence of reason and experience as well as under that of affection; and now, at
any rate, they ought to set this really dangerous
quackery at naught.

265. And what does my own experience say on the other side? There are my seven children, the sons as tall, or nearly so, as their father, and the daughters as tall as their mother; all, in due succession, inoculated with the good old-fashioned face-tearing small-pox; neither of them with a single mark of that disease on their skins; neither of them having been, that we could perceive, ill for a single hour in consequence of the inoculation. When we were in the United States, we observed that the Americans were never marked with the small-pox; or, if such a thing were seen, it was very rarely. The cause we found to be, the universal practice of having the children inoculated at the breast, and, generally, at a month or six weeks old. When we came to have children we did the same. I believe that some of ours have been a few months old when the operation has been performed, but always while at the breast, and as early as possible after the expiration of six weeks from the birth; sometimes put off a little while by some slight disorder in the child, or on account of some circumstance or other; but, with these exceptions, done at, or before, the end of six weeks from the birth, and always at the breast. All is then pure: there is nothing in either body or mind to favour the natural fury of the disease. We always took particular care about the source from which the infectious matter came. We employed medical men, in whom we could place perfect confidence: we had their solemn word for the matter coming from some healthy child: and, at last, we had sometimes to wait for this, the cow-affair having rendered patients of this sort rather rare.

266. While the child has the small-pox, the mother should abstain from food and drink, which she may require at other times, but which might be too gross just now. To suckle a hearty child requires good living; for, besides that this is necessary to the mother, it is also necessary to the child. A little forbearance, just at this time, is prudent; making the diet as simple as possible, and avoiding all violent agitation either of the body or the spirits; avoiding too, if you can, very hot or very cold weather.

267. There is now, however, this inconvenience, that the greater part of the present young women have been be-Jennered; so that they may catch the beauty-killing disease from their babies! To hearten them up, however, and more especially, I confess, to record a trait of maternal affection and of female heroism, which I have never heard of anything to surpass, I have the pride to say that my wife had eight children inoculated at her breast, and never had the small-pox in her life, I, at first, objected to the inoculating of the child, but she insisted upon it, and with so much pertinacity that I gave way on condition that she would be inoculated too. This was done with three or four of the children, I think, she always being reluctant to have it done, saying that it looked like distrusting the goodness of God. There was, to be sure, very little in this argument; but the long experience wore away the alarm; and there she is now, having had eight children hanging at her breast with that desolating disease in them, and she never having been affected by it from first to last. All her children know, of course, the risk

that she voluntarily incurred for them. They all have this indubitable proof that she valued their lives above her own; and is it in nature that they should ever wilfully do anything to wound the heart of that mother; and must not her bright example have great effect on their character and conduct! Now, my opinion is, that the far greater part of English or American women, if placed in the above circumstances, would do just the same thing; and I do hope that those who have yet to be mothers will seriously think of putting an end, as they have the power to do, to the disgraceful and dangerous quackery, the evils of which I have so fully proved.

268. But there is, in the management of babies, something besides life, health, strength and beauty and something too, without which all these put together are nothing worth; and that is sanity of mind. There are, owing to various causes, some who are born idiots; but a great many more become insane from the misconduct, or neglect, of parents; and, generally, from the children being committed to the care of servants. I knew, in Pennsylvania, a child, as fine, and as sprightly, and as intelligent a child as ever was born, made an idiot for life by being, when about three years old, shut into a dark closet, by a maid-servant, in order to terrify it into silence. The thoughtless creature first menaced it with sending it to " the bad place," as the phrase is there; and, at last, to reduce it to silence, put it into the closet, shut the door, and went out of the room. She went back, in a few minutes, and found the child in a fit. It recovered from that, but was for life an idiot.

When the parents, who had been out two days and two nights on a visit of pleasure, came home, they were told that the child had had a fit; but they were not told the cause. The girl, however, who was a neighbour's daughter, being on her death-bed about ten years afterwards, could not die in peace without sending for the mother of the child (now become a young man) and asking forgiveness of her. The mother herself was, however, the greatest offender of the two: a whole lifetime of sorrow and of mortification was a punishment too light for her and her husband. Thousands upon thousands of human beings have been deprived of their senses by these and similar means.

269. It is not long since that we read, in the newspapers, of a child being absolutely killed, at Birmingham, I think it was, by being thus frightened. The parents had gone out into what is called an evening party. The servants, naturally enough, had their party at home; and the mistress, who, by some unexpected accident, had been brought home at an early hour, finding the parlour full of company, ran up stairs to see about her child, about two or three years old. She found it with its eyes open, but fixed; touching it, she found it inanimate. The doctor was sent for in vain: it was quite dead. The maid affected to know nothing of the cause; but some one of the parties assembled discovered, pinned up to the curtains of the bed, a horrid figure, made up partly of a frightful mask! This, as the wretched girl confessed, had been done to keep the child quiet, while she was with her company below. When one

reflects on the anguish that the poor little thing must have endured, before the life was quite frightened out of it, one can find no terms sufficiently strong to express the abhorrence due to the perpetrator of this crime, which was, in fact, a cruel murder; and, if it was beyond the reach of the law, it was so and is so because, as in the cases of parricide, the law, in making no provision for punishment peculiarly severe, has, out of respect to human nature, supposed such crimes to be impossible. But if the girl was criminal; if death, or a life of remorse, was her due, what was the due of the parents, and especially of the mother! And what was the due of the father, who suffered that mother, and who, perhaps, tempted her to neglect her most sacred duty!

270. If this poor child had been deprived of its mental faculties, instead of being deprived of its life, the cause would, in all likelihood, never have been discovered. The insanity would have been ascribed to " brain-fever," or to some other of the usual causes of insanity; or, as in thousands upon thousands of instances, to some unaccountable cause. When I was, in paragraphs from 227 to 233, both inclusive, maintaining with all my might, the unalienable right of the child to the milk of its mother, I omitted, amongst the evils arising from banishing the child from the mother's breast, to mention, or, rather, it had never occurred to me to mention, the loss of reason to the poor, innocent creatures thus banished. And now, as connected with this measure, I have an argument of experience, enough to terrify every young man and woman upon earth from the

thought of committing this offence against nature. I
wrote those paragraphs at Cambridge, on Sunday,
the 28th of March; and before I quitted Shrewsbury,
on the 14th of May, the following facts reached my
ears. A very respectable tradesman, who, with his
wife, had led a most industrious life, in a town that
it is not necessary to name, said to a gentleman that
told it to me: " I wish to God I had read Mr.
Cobbett's ' Advice to Young Men ' fifteen years
ago! " He then related that he had had ten children,
all put out to be suckled, in consequence of the
necessity of his having the mother's assistance to
carry on his business; and that two out of the ten
had come home idiots; though the rest were all sane,
and though insanity had never been known in the
family of either father or mother! These parents,
whom I myself saw, are very clever people, and the
wife singularly industrious and expert in her affairs.

271. Now the motive, in this case, unquestionably
was good; it was that the mother's valuable time
might, as much as possible, be devoted to the earning
of a competence for her children. But, alas! what is
this competence to these two unfortunate beings!
and what is the competence to the rest, when put in
the scale against the mortification that they must,
all their lives, suffer on account of the insanity of
their brother and sister, exciting as it must, in
all their circle, and even in themselves, suspicious of
their own perfect soundness of mind! When weighed
against this consideration, what is all the wealth in
the world! And as to the parents, where are they to
find compensation for such a calamity, embittered

additionally too, by the reflection, that it was in their power to prevent it, and that nature, with loud voice, cried out to them to prevent it? Money! Wealth acquired in consequence of this banishment of these poor children; these victims of this, I will not call it avarice, but over-eager love of gain! wealth, thus acquired! What wealth can console these parents for the loss of reason in these children! Where is the father and the mother, who would not rather see their children ploughing in other men's fields, and sweeping other men's houses, than led about parks or houses of their own, objects of pity even of the menials procured by their wealth?

272. If what I have now said be not sufficient to deter a man from suffering any consideration, no matter what, to induce him to delegate the care of his children, when very young, to anybody whomsoever, nothing that I can say can possibly have that effect; and I will, therefore, now proceed to offer my advice with regard to the management of children when they get beyond the danger of being crazed or killed by nurses or servants.

273. We here come to the subject of education in the true sense of that word, which is rearing up, seeing that the word comes from the Latin *educo*, which means to breed up, or to rear up. I shall, afterwards, have to speak of education in the now common acceptation of the word, which makes it mean book-learning. At present, I am to speak of education in its true sense, as the French (who, as well as we, take the word from the Latin) always use it. They, in their agricultural works, talk of the

" education du Cochon, de l'Allouette," &c., that is, of the hog, the lark, and so of other animals; that is to say, of the manner of breeding them, or rearing them up, from their being little things till they be of full size.

274. The first thing in the rearing of children, who have passed from the baby-state, is, as to the body, plenty of good food; and, as to the mind, constant good example in the parents. Of the latter, I shall speak more by-and-by. With regard to the former, it is of the greatest importance that children be well fed; and there never was a greater error than to believe that they do not need good food. Every one knows that, to have fine horses, the colts must be kept well, and that it is the same with regard to all animals of every sort and kind. The fine horses and cattle and sheep all come from the rich pastures. To have them fine, it is not sufficient that they have plenty of food when young, but that they have rich food. Were there no land, no pasture, in England, but such as is found in Middlesex, Essex, and Surrey, we should see none of those coach-horses and dray-horses, whose height and size make us stare. It is the keep when young that makes the fine animal.

275. There is no other reason for the people in the American States being generally so much taller and stronger than the people in England are. Their forefathers went, for the greater part, from England. In the four Northern States they went wholly from England, and then, on their landing, they founded a new London, a new Falmouth, a new Plymouth, a new Portsmouth, a new Dover, a new Yarmouth, a

new Lynn, a new Boston, and a new Hull, and the country itself they called, and their descendants still call it, New England. This country of the best and boldest of seamen, and of the most moral and happy people in the world, is also the country of the tallest and ablest-bodied men in the world. And why? Because, from their very birth, they have an abundance of good food; not only of food, but of rich food. Even when the child is at the breast, a strip of beef-steak, or something of that description, as big and as long as one's finger, is put into its hand. When a baby gets a thing in its hand, the first thing it does is to poke some part of it into its mouth. It cannot bite the meat, but its gums squeeze out the juice. When it has done with the breast, it eats meat constantly twice, if not thrice a day. And this abundance of good food is the cause, to be sure, of the superior size and strength of the people of that country.

276. Nor is this, in any point of view, an unimportant matter. A tall man is, whether as labourer, carpenter, bricklayer, soldier, or sailor, or almost anything else, worth more than a short man: he can look over a higher thing; he can reach higher and wider; he can move on from place to place faster; in mowing grass or corn he takes a wider swarth; in pitching he wants a shorter prong; in making buildings, he does not so soon want a ladder or a scaffold; in fighting he keeps his body farther from the point of his sword. To be sure, a man may be tall and weak: but this is the exception and not the rule: height and weight and strength, in men, as in speechless animals, generally go together. Aye, and

in enterprise and courage too, the powers of the body have a great deal to do. Doubtless there are, have been, and always will be, great numbers of small and enterprising and brave men; but it is not in nature, that, generally speaking, those who are conscious of their inferiority in point of bodily strength, should possess the boldness of those who have a contrary description.

277. To what but this difference in the size and strength of the opposing combatants are we to ascribe the ever-to-be-blushed-at events of our last war against the United States! The hearts of our seamen and soldiers were as good as those of the Yankees: on both sides they had sprung from the same stock: on both sides equally well supplied with all the materials of war: if on either side, the superior skill was on ours: French, Dutch, Spaniards, all had confessed our superior prowess: yet when, with our whole undivided strength, and to that strength adding the flush and pride of victory and conquest, crowned even in the capital of France; when, with all these tremendous advantages, and with all the nations of the earth looking on, we came foot to foot and yard-arm to yard-arm with the Americans, the result was such as an English pen refuses to describe. What, then, was the great cause of this result, which filled us with shame, and the world with astonishment? Not the want of courage in our men. There were, indeed, some moral causes at work; but the main cause was the great superiority of size and of bodily strength on the part of the enemy's soldiers and sailors. It was so many men on each side; but it

was men of a different size and strength; and, on the side of the foe, men accustomed to daring enterprise from a consciousness of that strength.

278. Why are abstinence and fasting enjoined by the Catholic Church? Why, to make men humble, meek, and tame; and they have this effect too: this is visible in whole nations as well as in individuals. So that good food, and plenty of it, is not more necessary to the forming of a stout and able body than to the forming of an active and enterprising spirit. Poor food, short allowance, while they check the growth of the child's body, check also the daring of the mind; and, therefore, the starving or pinching system ought to be avoided by all means. Children should eat often, and as much as they like at a time. They will, if at full heap, never take, of plain food, more than it is good for them to take. They may, indeed, be stuffed with cakes and sweet things till they be ill, and, indeed, until they bring on dangerous disorders: but, of meat plainly and well cooked, and of bread, they will never swallow the tenth part of an ounce more than it is necessary for them to swallow. Ripe fruit, or cooked fruit, if no sweetening take place, will never hurt them; but, when they once get a taste for sugary stuff, and to cram down loads of garden vegetables; when ices, creams, tarts, raisins, almonds, all the endless pamperings come, the doctor must soon follow with his drugs. The blowing out of the bodies of children with tea, coffee, soup, or warm liquids of any kind, is very bad: these have an effect precisely like that which is produced by feeding young rabbits, or pigs, or other young animals, upon

watery vegetables: it makes them big-bellied and bare-boned at the same time; and it effectually prevents the frame from becoming strong. Children in health want no drink other than skim milk, or buttermilk, or whey; and, if none of those be at hand, water will do very well, provided they have plenty of good meat. Cheese and butter do very well for part of the day. Puddings and pies; but always without sugar, which, say what people will about the wholesomeness of it, is not only of no use in the rearing of children, but injurious: it forces an appetite: like strong drink, it makes daily encroachments on the taste: it wheedles down that which the stomach does not want: it finally produces illness: it is one of the curses of the country; for it, by taking off the bitter taste of the tea and coffee, is the great cause of sending down into the stomach those quantities of warm water by which the body is debilitated and deformed, and the mind enfeebled. I am addressing myself to persons in the middle walk of life; but no parent can be sure that his child will not be compelled to labour hard for its daily bread: and then, how vast is the difference between one who has been pampered with sweets, and one who has been reared on plain food and simple drink!

279. The next thing after good and plentiful and plain food is good air. This is not within the reach of every one; but, to obtain it is worth great sacrifices in other respects. We know that there are smells which will cause instant death; we know, that there are others which will cause death in a few years; and, therefore, we know that it is the duty of

parents to provide, if possible, against this danger to the health of their offspring. To be sure, when a man is so situated, that he cannot give his children sweet air without putting himself into a jail for debt; when, in short, he has the dire choice of sickly children, children with big heads, small limbs, and rickety joints: or children sent to the poor-house: when this is his hard lot, he must decide for the former sad alternative: but before he will convince me that this is his lot, he must prove to me, that he and his wife expend not a penny in the decoration of their persons; that on his table, morning, noon, or night, nothing ever comes that is not the produce of English soil; that of his time not one hour is wasted in what is called pleasure; that down his throat not one drop or morsel ever goes, unless necessary to sustain life and health. How many scores and how many hundreds of men have I seen; how many thousands could I go and point out, to-morrow, in London, the money expended on whose guzzlings in porter, grog, and wine, would keep, and keep well, in the country, a considerable part of the year, a wife surrounded by healthy children, instead of being stewed up in some alley, or back room, with a parcel of poor creatures about her, whom she, though their fond mother, is almost ashamed to call hers! Compared with the life of such a woman, that of the labourer, however poor, is paradise. Tell me not of the necessity of providing money for them, even if you waste not a farthing: you can provide them with no money equal in value to health and straight limbs and good looks: these it is, if within your power, your bounden duty to provide for them: as to providing them with money, you deceive yourself; it is your own avarice, or vanity, that you are seeking to gratify, and not to insure the good of your children. Their most precious possession is health and strength; and you have no right to run the risk of depriving them of these for the sake of heaping together money to bestow on them: you have the desire to see them rich: it is to gratify yourself that you act in such a case; and you, however you may deceive yourself, are guilty of injustice towards them. You would be ashamed to see them without fortune; but not at all ashamed to see them without straight limbs, without colour in their cheeks, without strength, without activity, and with only half their due portion of reason.

280. Besides sweet air, children want exercise. Even when they are babies in arms, they want tossing and pulling about, and want talking and singing to. They should be put upon their feet by slow degrees, according to the strength of their legs; and this is a matter which a good mother will attend to with incessant care. If they appear to be likely to squint, she will, always when they wake up, and frequently in the day, take care to present some pleasing object right before, and never on the side of their face. If they appear, when they begin to talk, to indicate a propensity to stammer, she will stop them, repeat the word or words slowly herself, and get them to do the same. These precautions are amongst the most sacred of the duties of parents; for, remember, the deformity is for life; a thought which will fill every good parent's heart with solicitude. All swaddling

and tight-covering are mischievous. They produce distortions of some sort or other. To let children creep and roll about till they get upon their legs of themselves is a very good way. I never saw a native American with crooked limbs or hump-back, and never heard any man say that he had seen one. And the reason is, doubtless, the loose dress in which children, from the moment of their birth, are kept, the good food that they always have, and the sweet air that they breathe in consequence of the absence of all dread of poverty on the part of the parents.

281. As to bodily exercise, they will, when they begin to get about, take, if you let them alone, just as much of it as nature bids them, and no more. That is a pretty deal, indeed, if they be in health; and, it it your duty, now, to provide for their taking of that exercise, when they begin to be what are called boys and girls, in a way that shall tend to give them the greatest degree of pleasure, accompanied with the smallest risk of pain: in other words, to make their lives as pleasant as you possibly can. I have always admired the sentiment of Rousseau upon this subject. " The boy dies, perhaps, at the age of ten or twelve. Of what use, then, all the restraints, all the privations, all the pain, that you have inflicted upon him? He falls, and leaves your mind to brood over the possibility of your having abridged a life so dear to you." I do not recollect the very words; but the passage made a deep impression upon my mind, just at the time, too, when I was about to become a father; and I was resolved never to bring upon myself remorse from such a cause; a resolution from

which no importunities, coming from what quarter they might, ever induced me, in one single instance, or for one single moment, to depart. I was resolved to forego all the means of making money, all the means of living in anything like fashion, all the means of obtaining fame or distinction, to give up everything, to become a common labourer rather than make my children lead a life of restraint and rebuke; I could not be sure that my children would love me as they loved their own lives; but I was, at any rate, resolved to deserve such love at their hands; and, in possession of that, I felt that I could set calamity, of whatever description, at defiance.

282. Now, proceeding to relate what was, in this respect, my line of conduct, I am not pretending that every man, and particularly every man living in a town, can, in all respects, do as I did, in the rearing up of children. But, in many respects, any man may, whatever may be his state of life. For I did not lead an idle life; I had to work constantly for the means of living; my occupation required unremitted attention; I had nothing but my labour to rely on; and I had no friend, to whom, in case of need, I could fly for assistance: I always saw the possibility, and even the probability, of being totally ruined by the hand of power; but happen what would, I was resolved, that, as long as I could cause them to do it, my children should lead happy lives; and happy lives they did lead, if ever children did in this whole world.

283. The first thing that I did, when the fourth child had come, was to get into the country, and so far as to render a going backward and forward to

London, at short intervals, quite out of the question. Thus was health, the greatest of all things, provided for, as far as I was able to make the provision. Next, my being always at home was secured as far as possible; always with them to set an example of early rising, sobriety, and application to something or other. Children, and especially boys, will have some out-of-doors pursuits; and it was my duty to lead them to choose such pursuits as combined future utility with present innocence. Each his flower bed, little garden, plantation of trees; rabbits, dogs, asses, horses, pheasants and hares; hoes, spades, whips, guns; always some object of lively interest, and as much earnestness and bustle about the various objects as if our living had solely depended upon them. I made everything give way to the great object of making their lives happy and innocent. I did not know what they might be in time, or what might be my lot; but I was resolved not to be the cause of their being unhappy then, let what might become of us afterwards. I was, as I am, of opinion, that it is injurious to the mind to press book-learning upon it at an early age: I always felt pain for poor little things, set up, before " company," to repeat verses, or bits of plays, at six or eight years old. I have sometimes not known which way to look, when a mother (and, too often, a father), whom I could not but respect on account of her fondness for her child, has forced the feeble-voiced eighth wonder of the world, to stand with its little hand stretched out, spouting the soliloquy of Hamlet, or some such thing. I remember, on one occasion, a little pale-faced creature, only five years old, was brought in, after the feeding part of the dinner was over, first to take his regular half-glass of vintner's brewings, commonly called wine, and then to treat us to a display of his wonderful genius. The subject was a speech of a robust and bold youth, in a Scotch play, the title of which I have forgotten, but the speech began with, " My name is Norval: on the Grampian hills my father fed his flocks . . ." And this in a voice so weak and distressing as to put me in mind of the plaintive squeaking of little pigs when the sow is lying on them. As we were going home (one of my boys and I), he, after a silence of half a mile perhaps, rode up close to the side of my horse, and said, " Papa, where be the Grampian hills? " " Oh," said I, " they are in Scotland; poor, barren, beggarly places, covered with heath and rushes, ten times as barren as Sherrit Heath." " But," said he, " how could that little boy's father feed his flocks there, then? " I was ready to tumble off the horse with laughing.

284. I do not know anything much more distressing to the spectators than exhibitions of this sort. Every one feels, not for the child, for it is insensible to the uneasiness it excites, but for the parents, whose amiable fondness displays itself in this ridiculous manner. Upon these occasions, no one knows what to say, or whither to direct his looks. The parents, and especially the fond mother, looks sharply round for the so evidently merited applause, as an actor of the name of Munden, whom I recollect thirty years ago, used, when he had treated us to a witty shrug

of his shoulders, or twist of his chin, to turn his face up to the gallery for a clap. If I had to declare on my oath, which have been the most disagreeable moments of my life, I verily believe, that, after due consideration, I should fix upon those, in which parents, whom I have respected, have made me endure exhibitions like these; for, this is your choice, to be insincere, or to give offence.

285. And, as towards the child, it is to be unjust, thus to teach it to set a high value on trifling, not to say mischievous attainments; to make it, whether it be in its natural disposition or not, vain and conceited. The plaudits which it receives, in such cases, puffs it up in its own thoughts, sends it out into the world stuffed with pride and insolence, which must and will be extracted out of it by one means or another; and none but those who have had to endure the drawing of firmly-fixed teeth, can, I take it, have an adequate idea of the painfulness of this operation. Now, parents have no right thus to indulge their own feelings at the risk of the happiness of their children.

286. The greater matter is, however, the spoiling of the mind by forcing on it thoughts which it is not fit to receive. We know well, we daily see, that in men, as well as in other animals, the body is rendered comparatively small and feeble by being heavily loaded, or hard-worked, before it arrive at size and strength proportioned to such load and such work. It is just so with the mind: the attempt to put old heads upon young shoulders is just as unreasonable as it would be to expect a colt six months old to be

able to carry a man. The mind, as well as the body, requires time to come to its strength; and the way to have it possess, at last, its natural strength, is not to attempt to load it too soon; and to favour it in its progress by giving to the body good and plentiful food, sweet air, and abundant exercise, accompanied with as little discontent or uneasiness as possible. It is universally known, that ailments of the body are, in many cases, sufficient to destroy the mind, and to debilitate it in innumerable instances. It is equally well known, that the torments of the mind, are, in many cases, sufficient to destroy the body. This, then, being so well known, is it not the first duty of a father to secure to his children, if possible, sound and strong bodies? Lord Bacon says, that " a sound mind in a sound body is the greatest of God's blessings." To see his children possess these, there-fore, ought to be the first object with every father; an object which I cannot too often endeavour to fix in his mind.

287. I am to speak presently of that sort of learning which is derived from books, and which is a matter by no means to be neglected, or to be thought little of, seeing that it is the road, not only to fame, but to the means of doing great good to one's neighbours and to one's country, and, thereby, of adding to those pleasant feelings which are, in other words, our happiness. But, notwithstanding this, I must here insist, and endeavour to impress my opinion upon the mind of every father, that his children's happi-ness ought to be his first object; that book-learning, if it tend to militate against this, ought to be disre-

garded; and that, as to money, as to fortune, as to
rank and title, that father who can, in the destination
of his children, think of them more than of the
happiness of those children, is, if he be of sane mind,
a great criminal. Who is there, having lived to the
age of thirty, or even twenty, years, and having the
ordinary capacity for observation; who is there, being
of this description, who must not be convinced of the
inadequacy of riches and what are called honours to
insure happiness? Who, amongst all the classes of
men, experience, on an average, so little of real
pleasure and so much of real pain as the rich and
lofty? Pope gives us, as the materials for happiness,
" health, peace, and competence." Aye, but what is
peace, and what is competence? If by peace, he
mean that tranquillity of mind which innocence and
good deeds produce, he is right and clear so far; for
we all know that, without health, which has a well-
known positive meaning, there can be no happiness.
But, competence is a word of unfixed meaning. It
may, with some, mean enough to eat, drink, wear
and be lodged and warmed with; but with others, it
may include horses, carriages, and footmen laced
over from top to toe. So that, here, we have no
guide; no standard; and, indeed, there can be none.
But as every sensible father must know that the
possession of riches do not, never did, and never
can, afford even a chance of additional happiness,
it is his duty to inculcate in the minds of his children
to make no sacrifice of principle, of moral obligation
of any sort, in order to obtain riches, or distinction;
and it is a duty still more imperative on him, not to

expose them to the risk of loss of health, or diminu-
tion of strength, for purposes which have, either
directly, or indirectly, the acquiring of riches in view,
whether for himself or for them.

288. With these principles immovably implanted
in my mind, I became the father of a family, and on
these principles I have reared that family. Being
myself fond of book-learning, and knowing well its
powers, I naturally wished them to possess it too;
but never did I impose it upon any one of them.
My first duty was to make them healthy and strong,
if I could, and to give them as much enjoyment of
life as possible. Born and bred up in the sweet air
myself, I was resolved that they should be bred up
in it too. Enjoying rural scenes and sports, as I had
done, when a boy, as much as any one that ever was
born, I was resolved that they should have the same
enjoyments tendered to them. When I was a very
little boy, I was, in the barley-sowing season, going
along by the side of a field, near Waverly Abbey; the
primroses and blue-bells bespangling the banks on
both sides of me; a thousand linnets singing in a
spreading oak over my head; while the jingle of the
traces and the whistling of the ploughboys saluted
my ear from over the hedge; and, as it were to
snatch me from the enchantment, the hounds, at that
instant, having started a hare in the hanger on the
other side of the field, came up scampering over it in
full cry, taking me after them many a mile. I was not
more than eight years old; but this particular scene
has presented itself to my mind many times every
year from that day to this. I always enjoy it over

again; and I was resolved to give, if possible, the same enjoyments to my children.

289. Men's circumstances are so various; there is such a great variety in their situations in life, their business, the extent of their pecuniary means, the local state in which they are placed, their internal resources; the variety in all these respects is so great, that, as applicable to every family, it would be impossible to lay down any set of rules, or maxims, touching every matter relating to the management and rearing up of children. In giving an account, therefore, of my own conduct, in this respect, I am not to be understood as supposing that every father can, or ought to attempt to do the same; but while it will be seen, that there are many, and these the most important parts of that conduct, and that all fathers may imitate, if they choose, there is no part of it which thousands and thousands of fathers might not adopt and pursue, and adhere to, to the very letter.

290. I effected everything without scolding, and even without command. My children are a family of scholars, each sex its appropriate species of learning; and, I could safely take my oath, that I never ordered a child of mine, son or daughter, to look into a book, in my life. My two eldest sons, when about eight years old, were, for the sake of their health, placed, for a short time, at a clergyman's at Micheldever, and my eldest daughter, a little older, at a school a few miles from Botley, to avoid taking them to London in the winter. But, with these exceptions, never had they, while children, teacher of any description; and

I never, and nobody else ever, taught any one of them to read, write, or anything else, except in conversation; and yet no man was ever more anxious to be the father of a family of clever and learned persons.

291. I accomplished my purpose indirectly. The first thing of all was health, which was secured by the deeply interesting and never-ending sports of the field and pleasures of the garden. Luckily these things were treated of in books and pictures of endless variety; so that, on wet days, in long evenings, these came into play. A large, strong table, in the middle of the room, their mother sitting at her work, used to be surrounded with them, the baby, if big enough, set up in a high chair. Here were inkstands, pens, pencils, india-rubber, and paper, all in abundance, and every one scrabbled about as he or she pleased. There were prints of animals of all sorts; books treating of them; others treating of gardening, of flowers, of husbandry, of hunting, coursing, shooting, fishing, planting, and, in short, of everything with regard to which we had something to do. One would be trying to imitate a bit of my writing, another drawing the pictures of some of our dogs or horses, a third poking over Bewick's " Quadrupeds," and picking out what he said about them; but our book of never-failing resource was the French " Maison Rustique," or Farm-house, which, it is said, was the book that first tempted Duquesnois (I think that was the name), the famous physician, in the reign of Louis XIV, to learn to read. Here are all the four-legged animals, from the horse down to the mouse, portraits and all; all the birds, reptiles, insects; all

the modes of rearing, managing, and using the tame ones; all the modes of taking the wild ones, and of destroying those that are mischievous; all the various traps, springs, nets; all the implements of husbandry and gardening; all the labours of the field and the garden exhibited, as well as the rest, in plates; and, there was I, in my leisure moments, to join this inquisitive group, to read the French, and tell them what it meaned in English, when the picture did not sufficiently explain itself. I never have been without a copy of this book for forty years, except during the time that I was fleeing from the dungeons of Castlereagh and Sidmouth, in 1817; and, when I got to Long Island, the first book I bought was another " Maison Rustique."

292. What need had we of schools? What need of teachers? What need of scolding and force, to induce children to read, write, and love books? What need of cards, dice, or of any games, to " kill time; " but, in fact, to implant in the infant heart a love of gaming, one of the most destructive of all human vices? We did not want to " kill time; " we were always busy, wet weather or dry weather, winter or summer. There was no force, in any case; no command; no authority; none of these was ever wanted. To teach the children the habit of early rising was a great object; and every one knows how young people cling to their beds, and how loth they are to go to those beds. This was a capital matter; because here were industry and health both at stake. Yet, I avoided command even here; and merely offered a reward. The child that was downstairs first, was called the lark for that day;

and, further, sat at my right hand at dinner. They soon discovered, that to rise early, they must go to bed early; and thus was this most important object secured, with regard to girls as well as boys. Nothing is more inconvenient, and, indeed, more disgusting, than to have to do with girls, or young women, who lounge in bed: " A little more sleep, a little more slumber, a little more folding of the hands to sleep." Solomon knew them well: he had, I dare say, seen the breakfast cooling, carriages and horses and servants waiting, the sun coming burning on, the day wasting, the night growing dark too early, appointments broken, and the objects of journeys defeated; and all this from the lolloping in bed of persons who ought to have risen with the sun. No beauty, no modesty, no accomplishments, are a compensation for the effects of laziness in women; and, of all the proofs of laziness, none is so unequivocal as that of lying late in bed. Love makes men overlook this vice (for it is a vice), for awhile; but, this does not last for life. Besides, health demands early rising: the management of a house imperiously demands it; but health, that most precious possession without which there is nothing else worth possessing, demands it too. The morning air is the most wholesome and strengthening: even in crowded cities, men might do pretty well with the aid of the morning air; but, how are they to rise early, if they go to bed late?

293. But, to do the things I did, you must love home yourself; to rear up children in this manner, you must live with them; you must make them, too, feel by your conduct, that you prefer this to any

other mode of passing your time. All men cannot lead this sort of life, but many may; and all much more than many do. My occupation, to be sure, was chiefly carried on at home; but, I had always enough to do; I never spent an idle week, or even day, in my whole life. Yet I found time to talk with them, to walk, or ride, about with them; and when forced to go from home, always took one or more with me. You must be good-tempered too with them; they must like your company better than any other person's; they must not wish you away, not fear your coming back, not look upon your departure as a holiday. When my business kept me away from the scrabbling-table, a petition often came, that I would go and talk with the group, and the bearer generally was the youngest, being the most likely to succeed. When I went from home, all followed me to the outer-gate, and looked after me, till the carriage, or horse, was out of sight. At the time appointed for my return, all were prepared to meet me; and if it were late at night, they sat up as long as they were able to keep their eyes open. This love of parents, and this constant pleasure at home, made them not even think of seeking pleasure abroad; and they, thus, were kept from vicious playmates and early corruption.

294. This is the age, too, to teach children to be trustworthy, and to be merciful and humane. We lived in a garden of about two acres, partly kitchen-garden with walls, partly shrubbery and trees, and partly grass. There were the peaches, as tempting as any that ever grew, and yet as safe from fingers as if

no child were ever in the garden. It was not necessary
to forbid. The blackbirds, the thrushes, the white-
throats, and even that very shy bird the goldfinch,
had their nests and bred up their young ones, in great
abundance, all about this little spot, constantly the
play-place of six children; and one of the latter had
its nest, and brought up its young ones, in a raspberry
bush, within two yards of a walk, and at the time
that we were gathering the ripe raspberries. We give
dogs, and justly, great credit for sagacity and
memory; but the following two most curious instances, which I should not venture to state, if there
were not so many witnesses to the facts, in my
neighbours at Botley, as well as in my own family,
will show, that birds are not, in this respect, inferior
to the canine race. All country people know that the
skylark is a very shy bird; that its abode is the open
fields: that it settles on the ground only; that it seeks
safety in the wideness of space; that it avoids en-
closures and is never seen in gardens. A part of our
ground was a grass-plat of about forty rods, or a
quarter of an acre, which, one year, was left to be
mowed for hay. A pair of larks, coming out of the
fields into the middle of a pretty populous village,
chose to make their nest in the middle of this little
spot, and at not more than about thirty-five yards
from one of the doors of the house, in which there
were about twelve persons living, and six of those
children, who had constant access to all parts of the
ground. There we saw the cock rising up and singing,
then taking his turn upon the eggs; and by-and-by
we observed him cease to sing, and saw them both

constantly engaged in bringing food to the young
ones. No unintelligible hint to fathers and mothers
of the human race, who have, before marriage, taken
delight in music. But the time came for mowing the
grass! I waited a good many days for the brood to
get away; but, at last, I determined on the day; and
if the larks were there still, to leave a patch of grass
standing round them. In order not to keep them in
dread longer than necessary, I brought three able
mowers, who would cut the whole in about an hour;
and as the plat was nearly circular, set them to mow
round, beginning at the outside. And now for
sagacity indeed! The moment the men began to whet
their scythes, the two old larks began to flutter over
the nest, and to make a great clamour. When the
men began to mow, they flew round and round,
stooping so low, when near the men, as almost to
touch their bodies, making a great chattering at the
same time; but before the men had got round with
the second swarth, they flew to the nest, and away
they went, young ones and all, across the river, at
the foot of the ground, and settled in the long grass
in my neighbour's orchard.

295. The other instance relates to a house-marten.
It is well known that these birds build their nests
under the eaves of inhabited houses, and sometimes
under those of door-porches; but we had one that
built its nest in the house, and upon the top of a
common door-case, the door of which opened into a
room out of the main passage into the house. Perceiving the marten had begun to build its nest here,
we kept the front door open in the daytime; but were

obliged to fasten it at night. It went on, had eggs, young ones, and the young ones flew. I used to open the door in the morning early, and then the birds carried on their affairs till night. The next year the marten came again, and had another brood in the same place. It found its old nest; and having repaired it, and put it in order, went on again in the former way; and it would, I dare say, have continued to come to the end of its life, if we had remained there so long, notwithstanding there were six healthy children in the house, making just as much noise as they pleased.

296. Now, what sagacity in these birds, to discover that those were places of safety! And how happy must it have made us, the parents, to be sure that our children had thus deeply imbibed habits the contrary of cruelty! For, be it engraven on your heart, young man, that whatever appearances may say to the contrary, cruelty is always accompanied with cowardice, and also with perfidy, when that is called for by the circumstances of the case; and that habitual acts of cruelty to other creatures, will, nine times out of ten, produce, when the power is possessed, cruelty to human beings. The ill-usage of horses, and particularly asses, is a grave and a just charge against this nation. No other nation on earth is guilty of it to the same extent. Not only by blows, but by privation, are we cruel towards these useful, docile, and patient creatures; and especially towards the last, which is the most docile and patient and laborious of the two, while the food that satisfies it is of the coarsest and least costly kind, and in quantity

so small! In the habitual ill-treatment of this animal, which, in addition to all its labours, has the milk taken from its young ones to administer a remedy for our ailments, there is something that bespeaks ingratitude hardly to be described. In a *Register* that I wrote from Long Island, I said, that amongst all the things of which I had been bereft, I regretted no one so much as a very diminutive mare, on which my children had all, in succession, learnt to ride. She was become useless for them, and, indeed, for any other purpose; but the recollection of her was so entwined with so many past circumstances, which, at that distance, my mind conjured up, that I really was very uneasy, lest she should fall into cruel hands. By good luck, she was, after awhile, turned out on the wide world to shift for herself; and when we got back, and had a place for her to stand in, from her native forest we brought her to Kensington, and she is now at Barn Elm, about twenty-six years old, and I dare say, as fat as a mole. Now, not only have I no moral right (considering my ability to pay for keep) to deprive her of life; but it would be unjust, and ungrateful in me, to withhold from her sufficient food and lodging to make life as pleasant as possible while that life last.

297. In the meanwhile the book-learning crept in of its own accord, by imperceptible degrees. Children naturally want to be like their parents, and to do what they do: the boys following their father, and the girls their mother; and as I was always writing or reading, mine naturally desired to do something in the same way. But, at the same time, they heard no

talk from fools or drinkers; saw me with no idle, gabbling, empty companions; saw no vain and affected coxcombs, and no tawdry and extravagant women; saw no nasty gormandizing; and heard no gabble about play-houses and romances and the other nonsense that fit boys to be lobby-loungers, and girls to be the ruin of industrious and frugal young men.

298. We wanted no stimulants of this sort to keep up our spirits: our various pleasing pursuits were quite sufficient for that; and the book-learning came amongst the rest of the pleasures, to which it was, in some sort, necessary. I remember that, one year, I raised a prodigious crop of fine melons, under hand-glasses; and I learned how to do it from a gardening book; or, at least, that book was necessary to remind me of the details. Having passed part of an evening in talking to the boys about getting this crop, " Come," said I, " now, let us read the book." Then the book came forth, and to work we went, following very strictly the precepts of the book. I read the thing but once, but the eldest boy read it, perhaps, twenty times, over; and explained all about the matter to the others. Why here was a motive! Then he had to tell the garden labourer what to do to the melons. Now, I will engage, that more was really learned by this single lesson, than would have been learned by spending, at this son's age, a year at school; and he happy and delighted all the while. When any dispute arose amongst them about hunting or shooting, or any other of their pursuits, they, by degrees, found out the way of settling it by reference to some book; and when any difficulty occurred as to

the meaning, they referred to me, who, if at home, always instantly attended to them, in these matters.

299. They began writing by taking words out of printed books; finding out which letter was which, by asking me, or asking those who knew the letters one from another; and by imitating bits of my writing, it is surprising how soon they began to write a hand like mine, very small, very faint-stroked, and nearly plain as print. The first use that any one of them made of the pen, was to write to me, though in the same house with them. They began doing this in mere scratches, before they knew how to make any one letter; and as I was always folding up letters and directing them, so were they; and they were sure to receive a prompt answer, with most encouraging compliments. All the meddlings and teazings of friends, and, what was more serious, the pressing prayers of their anxious mother, about sending them to school, I withstood without the slightest effect on my resolution. As to friends, preferring my own judgment to theirs, I did not care much; but an expression of anxiety, implying a doubt of the soundness of my own judgment, coming, perhaps, twenty times a day from her whose care they were as well as mine, was not a matter to smile at, and very great trouble it did give me. My answer at last was, as to the boys, I want them to be like me; and as to the girls, in whose hands can they be so safe as in yours? Therefore my resolution is taken: go to school they shall not.

300. Nothing is much more annoying than the intermeddling of friends, in a case like this. The wife

appeals to them, and " good breeding," that is to say, nonsense, is sure to put them on her side. Then, they, particularly the women, when describing the surprising progress made by their own sons at school, used, if one of mine were present, to turn to him, and ask to what school he went, and what he was learning? I leave any one to judge of his opinion of her; and whether he would like her the better for that! " Bless me, so tall, and not learned anything yet! " " Oh, yes, he has," I used to say, " he has learned to ride, and hunt, and shoot, and fish, and look after cattle and sheep, and to work in the garden, and to feed his dogs, and to go from village to village in the dark." This was the way I used to manage with troublesome customers of this sort. And how glad the children used to be when they got clear of such criticising people! And how grateful they felt to me for the protection which they saw that I gave them against that state of restraint, of which other people's boys complained! Go whither they might, they found no place so pleasant as home, and no soul that came near them affording them so many means of gratification as they received from me.

301. In this happy state we lived, until the year 1810, when the Government laid its merciless fangs upon me, dragged from me these delights, and crammed me into a jail amongst felons; of which I shall have to speak more fully, when, in the last Letter, I come to speak of the duties of the Citizen. This added to the difficulties of my task of teaching; for now I was snatched away from the only scene in which it could, as I thought, properly be executed.

But even these difficulties were got over. The blow was, to be sure, a terrible one; and, O God! how was it felt by these poor children! It was in the month of July when the horrible sentence was passed upon me. My wife, having left her children in the care of her good and affectionate sister, was in London, waiting to know the doom of her husband. When the news arrived at Botley, the three boys, one eleven, another nine, and the other seven, years old, were hoeing cabbages in that garden which had been the source of so much delight. When the account of the savage sentence was brought to them, the youngest could not, for some time, be made to understand what a jail was; and, when he did, he, all in a tremor, exclaimed, " Now, I'm sure, William, that papa is not in a place like that! " The other, in order to disguise his tears and smother his sobs, fell to work with the hoe, and chopped about like a blind person. This account, when it reached me, affected me more, filled me with deeper resentment, than any other circumstance. And, oh! how I despise the wretches who talk of my vindictiveness; of my exultation at the confusion of those who inflicted those sufferings! How I despise the base creatures, the crawling slaves, the callous and cowardly hypocrites, who affect to be " shocked " (tender souls!) at my expressions of joy, and at the death of Gibbs, Ellenborough, Perceval, Liverpool, Canning, and the rest of the tribe that I have already seen out, and at the fatal workings of that system, for endeavouring to check which I was thus punished! How I despise these wretches, and how I, above all things, enjoy their ruin, and anticipate their utter beggary! What! I am to forgive, am I, injuries like this; and that, too, without any atonement? Oh, no! I have not so read the Holy Scriptures; I have not, from them, learned that I am not to rejoice at the fall of unjust foes; and it makes a part of my happiness to be able to tell millions of men that I do thus rejoice, and that I have the means of calling on so many just and merciful men to rejoice along with me.

302. Now, then, the book-learning was forced upon us. I had a farm in hand. It was necessary that I should be constantly informed of what was doing. I gave all the orders, whether as to purchases, sales, ploughing, sowing, breeding; in short, with regard to everything, and the things were endless in number and variety, and always full of interest. My eldest son and daughter could now write well and fast. One or the other of them was always at Botley; and I had with me (having hired the best part of the keeper's house) one or two, besides either this brother or sister; the mother coming up to town about once in two or three months, leaving the house and children in the care of her sister. We had a hamper, with a lock and two keys, which came up once a week, or oftener, bringing me fruit and all sorts of country fare, for the carriage of which, cost free, I was indebted to as good a man as ever God created, the late Mr. George Rogers, of Southampton, who, in the prime of life, died deeply lamented by thousands, but by none more deeply than by me and my family, who have to thank him, and the whole of his excellent family, for benefits and marks of kindness without number.

303. This hamper, which was always, at both ends of the line, looked for with the most lively feelings, became our school. It brought me a journal of labours, proceedings, and occurrences, written on paper of shape and size uniform, and so contrived, as to margins, as to admit of binding. The journal used, when my son was the writer, to be interspersed with drawings of our dogs, colts, or anything that he wanted me to have a correct idea of. The hamper brought me plants, bulbs, and the like, that I might see the size of them; and always every one sent his or her most beautiful flowers; the earliest violets, and primroses, and cowslips, and blue-bells; the earliest twigs of trees; and, in short, everything that they thought calculated to delight me. The moment the hamper arrived, I, casting aside everything else, set to work to answer every question, to give new directions, and to add anything likely to give pleasure at Botley. Every hamper brought one " letter," as they called it, if not more, from every child; and to every letter I wrote an answer, sealed up and sent to the party, being sure that that was the way to produce other and better letters; for, though they could not read what I wrote, and though their own consisted at first of mere scratches, and afterwards, for awhile, of a few words written down for them to imitate, I always thanked them for their " pretty letter," and never expressed any wish to see them write better; but took care to write in a very neat and plain hand myself, and to do up my letter in a very neat manner.

304. Thus, while the ferocious tigers thought I

was doomed to incessant mortification, and to rage
that must extinguish my mental powers, I found in
my children, and in their spotless and courageous
and most affectionate mother, delights to which the
callous hearts of those tigers were strangers. " Heaven
first taught letters for some wretch's aid." How often
did this line of Pope occur to me when I opened the
little spuddling " letters " from Botley! This corre-
spondence occupied a good part of my time: I had
all the children with me, turn and turn about; and,
in order to give the boys exercise, and to give the two
eldest an opportunity of beginning to learn French,
I used, for a part of the two years, to send them a
few hours in the day to an Abbé, who lived in Castle
Street, Holborn. All this was a great relaxation to my
mind; and, when I had to return to my literary
labours, I returned fresh and cheerful, full of vigour,
and full of hope, of finally seeing my unjust and
merciless foes at my feet, and that, too, without
caring a straw on whom their fall might bring
calamity, so that my own family were safe; because,
say what any one might, the community, taken as a
whole, had suffered this thing to be done unto us.

305. The paying of the work-people, the keeping
of the accounts, the referring to books, the writing
and reading of letters; this everlasting mixture of
amusement with book-learning, made me, almost
to my own surprise, find, at the end of two years,
that I had a parcel of scholars growing up about me;
and, long before the end of the time, I had dictated
many *Registers* to my two eldest children. Then,
there was copying out of books, which taught spelling

correctly. The calculations about the farming affairs forced arithmetic upon us: the use, the necessity, of the thing, led to the study. By-and-by, we had to look into the laws, to know what to do about the highways, about the game, about the poor, and all rural and parochial affairs. I was, indeed, by the fangs of Government, defeated in my fondly cherished project of making my sons farmers on their own land, and keeping them from all temptation to seek vicious and enervating enjoyments; but those fangs, merciless as they had been, had not been able to prevent me from laying in for their lives a store of useful information, habits of industry, care, sobriety, and a taste for innocent, healthful, and manly pleasures: the fangs had made me and them penniless; but, they had not been able to take from us our health or our mental possessions; and these were ready for application as circumstance might ordain.

306. After the age that I have now been speaking of, fourteen, I suppose every one became a reader and writer according to fancy. As to books, with the exception of the poets, I never bought, in my whole life, any one that I did not want for some purpose of utility, and of practical utility too. I have two or three times had the whole collection snatched away from me; and have begun again to get them together as they are wanted. Go and kick an ants' nest about, and you will see the little laborious, courageous creatures instantly set to work to get it together again; and if you do this ten times over, ten times over they will do the same. Here is the sort of stuff that men must be made of to oppose, with success, those who, by

whatever means, get possession of great and mischievous power.

307. Now, I am aware, that that which I did, cannot be done by every one of hundreds of thousands of fathers, each of whom loves his children with all his soul: I am aware that the attorney, the surgeon, the physician, the trader, and even the farmer, cannot, generally speaking, do what I did, and that they must, in most cases, send their sons to school, if it be necessary for them to have book-learning. But while I say this, I know that there are many things, which I did, which many fathers might do, and which, nevertheless, they do not. It is in the power of every father to live at home with his family, when not compelled by business, or by public duty, to be absent: it is in his power to set an example of industry and sobriety and frugality, and to prevent a taste for gaming, dissipation, extravagance, from getting root in the minds of his children: it is in his power to continue to make his children hearers, when he is reproving servants for idleness, or commending them for industry and care: it is in his power to keep all dissolute and idly-talking companions from his house; it is in his power to teach them, by his uniform example, justice, and mercy towards the inferior animals: it is in his power to do many other things, and something in the way of book-learning too, however busy his life may be. It is completely within his power to teach them early rising and early going to bed; and, if many a man, who says that he has not time to teach his children, were to sit down, in sincerity, with a pen and a bit

of paper, and put down all the minutes, which he, in every twenty-four hours, wastes over the bottle, or over cheese and oranges and raisins and biscuits, after he has dined; how many he lounges away, either at the coffee-house or at home, over the useless part of newspapers; how many he spends in waiting for the coming and the managing of the tea-table; how many he passes by candle-light, wearied of his existence, when he might be in bed; how many he passes in the morning in bed, while the sun and dew shine and sparkle for him in vain: if he were to put all these together, and were to add those which he passes in the reading of books for his mere personal amusement, and without the smallest chance of acquiring from them any useful practical knowledge: if he were to sum up the whole of these, and add to them the time worse than wasted in the contemptible work of dressing off his person, he would be frightened at the result; would send for his boys from school, and if greater book-learning than he possessed were necessary, he would choose for the purpose some man of ability, and see the teaching carried on under his own roof, with safety as to morals, and with the best chance as to health.

308. If after all, however, a school must be resorted to, let it, if in your power, be as little populous as possible. As " evil communications corrupt good manners," so the more numerous the assemblage, and the more extensive the communication, the greater the chance of corruption. Jails, barracks, factories, do not corrupt by their walls, but by their condensed numbers. Populous cities corrupt from

the same cause; and it is, because it must be, the same with regard to schools, out of which children come not what they were when they went in. The master is, in some sort, their enemy; he is their over-looker; he is a spy upon them; his authority is maintained by his absolute power of punishment; the parent commits them to that power; to be taught is to be held in restraint; and, as the sparks fly up-wards, the teaching and the restraint will not be divided in the estimation of the boy. Besides all this, there is the great disadvantage of tardiness in arriving at years of discretion. If boys live only with boys, their ideas will continue to be boyish; if they see and hear and converse with nobody but boys, how are they to have the thoughts and the character of men? It is, at last, only by hearing men talk and see men act, that they learn to talk and act like men; and, therefore, to confine them to the society of boys, is to retard their arrival at the years of discretion; and in case of adverse circumstances in the pecuniary way, where, in all the creation, is there so helpless a mortal as a boy who has always been at school! But if, as I said before, a school there must be, let the con-gregation, be as small as possible; and, do not expect too much from the master; for, if it be irksome to you to teach your own sons, what must that teaching be to him? If he have great numbers, he must delegate his authority; and, like all other delegated authority, it will either be abused or neglected.

309. With regard to girls, one would think that mothers would want no argument to make them shudder at the thought of committing the care of

their daughters to other hands than their own. If fortune have so favoured them as to make them rationally desirous that their daughters should have more of what are called accomplishments than they themselves have, it has also favoured them with the means of having teachers under their own eye. If it have not favoured them so highly as this (and it seldom has in the middle rank of life), what duty so sacred as that imposed on a mother to be the teacher of her daughters! And is she, from love of ease or of pleasure or of anything else, to neglect this duty; is she to commit her daughters to the care of persons, with whose manners and morals it is impossible for her to be thoroughly acquainted; is she to send them into the promiscuous society of girls who belong to nobody knows whom, and come from nobody knows whither, and some of whom, for aught she can know to the contrary, may have been corrupted before, and sent thither to be hidden from their former circle; is she to send her daughters to be shut up within walls, the bare sight of which awaken the idea of intrigue and invite to seduction and surrender; is she to leave the health of her daughters to chance, to shut them up with a motley bevy of strangers, some of whom, as is frequently the case, are proclaimed bastards, by the undeniable testimony given by the colour of their skin; is she to do all this, and still put forward pretensions to the authority and the affection due to a mother! And, are you to permit all this, and still call yourself a father!

310. Well, then, having resolved to teach your own children, or, to have them taught, at home, let us see

now how they ought to proceed as to books for learning. It is evident, speaking of boys, that, at last, they must study the art, or science, that you intend them to pursue; if they be to be surgeons, they must read books on surgery; and the like in other cases. But, there are certain elementary studies; certain books to be used by all persons, who are destined to acquire any book-learning at all. Then there are departments or branches of knowledge, that every man in the middle rank of life, ought, if he can, to acquire, they being, in some sort, necessary to his reputation as a well-informed man, a character to which the farmer and the shopkeeper ought to aspire as well as the lawyer and the surgeon. Let me now, then, offer my advice as to the course of reading, and the manner of reading, for a boy, arrived at his fourteenth year, that being, in my opinion, early enough for him to begin.

311. And, first of all, whether as to boys or girls, I deprecate romances of every description. It is impossible that they can do any good, and they may do a great deal of harm. They excite passions that ought to lie dormant; they give the mind a taste for highly-seasoned matter, they make matters of real life insipid; every girl, addicted to them, sighs to be a Sophia Western, and every boy, a Tom Jones. What girl is not in love with the wild youth, and what boy does not find a justification for his wildness? What can be more pernicious than the teachings of this celebrated romance? Here are two young men put before us, both sons of the same mother; the one a bastard (and by a parson too), the other a legitimate

child; the former wild, disobedient, and squandering; the latter steady, sober, obedient, and frugal; the former everything that is frank and generous in his nature, the latter a greedy hypocrite; the former rewarded with the most beautiful and virtuous of women and a double estate, the latter punished by being made an outcast. How is it possible for young people to read such a book, and to look upon orderliness, sobriety, obedience, and frugality, as virtues? And this is the tenor of almost every romance, and of almost every play, in our language. In the " School for Scandal," for instance, we see two brothers; the one a prudent and frugal man, and, to all appearance, a moral man, the other a hare-brained squanderer, laughing at the morality of his brother; the former turns out to be a base hypocrite and seducer, and is brought to shame and disgrace; while the latter is found to be full of generous sentiment, and Heaven itself seems to interfere to give him fortune and fame. In short, the direct tendency of the far greater part of these books, is, to cause young people to despise all those virtues, without the practice of which they must be a curse to their parents, a burden to the community, and must, except by mere accident, lead wretched lives. I do not recollect one romance nor one play, in our language, which has not this tendency. How is it possible for young princes to read the historical plays of the punning and smutty Shakspeare, and not think, that to be drunkards, blackguards, the companions of debauchees and robbers, is the suitable beginning of a glorious reign?

312. There is, too, another most abominable principle that runs through them all, namely, that there is in high birth something of superior nature, instinctive courage, honour, and talent. Who can look at the two royal youths in " Cymbeline," or at the noble youth in " Douglas," without detesting the base parasites who wrote those plays? Here are youths, brought up by shepherds, never told of their origin, believing themselves the sons of these humble parents, but discovering, when grown up, the highest notions of valour and honour, and thirsting for military renown, even while tending their reputed fathers' flocks and herds? And why this species of falsehood? To cheat the mass of the people; to keep them in abject subjection; to make them quietly submit to despotic sway. And the infamous authors are guilty of the cheat, because they are, in one shape or another, paid by oppressors out of means squeezed from the people. A true picture would give us just the reverse; would show us that " high birth " is the enemy of virtue, of valour, and of talent; would show us, that with all their incalculable advantages, royal and noble families have, only by mere accident, produced a great man; that, in general, they have been amongst the most effeminate, unprincipled, cowardly, stupid, and, at the very least, amongst the most useless persons, considered as individuals, and not in connection with the prerogatives and powers bestowed on them solely by the law.

313. It is impossible for me, by any words that I can use, to express, to the extent of my thoughts, the danger of suffering young people to form their

opinions from the writings of poets and romances.
Nine times out of ten, the morality they teach is bad,
and must have a bad tendency. Their wit is employed
to ridicule virtue, as you will almost always find, if
you examine the matter to the bottom. The world
owes a very large part of its suffering to tyrants; but
what tyrant was there amongst the ancients, whom
the poets did not place amongst the gods? Can you
open an English poet, without, in some part or other
of his works, finding the grossest flatteries of royal
and noble persons? How are young people not to think
that the praises bestowed on these persons are just?
Dryden, Parnell, Gay, Thomson, in short, what poet
have we had, or have we, Pope only excepted, who
was not, or is not, a pensioner, or a sinecure placeman, or the wretched dependent of some part of the
aristocracy? Of the extent of the powers of writers
in producing mischief to a nation, we have two most
striking instances in the cases of Dr. Johnson and
Burke. The former, at a time when it was a question
whether war should be made on America to compel
her to submit to be taxed by the English Parliament,
wrote a pamphlet, entitled " Taxation no Tyranny,"
to urge the nation into that war. The latter, when it
was a question, whether England should wage war
against the people of France, to prevent them from
reforming their government, wrote a pamphlet to
urge the nation into that war. The first war lost us
America, the last cost us six hundred millions of
money, and has loaded us with forty millions a year
as taxes. Johnson, however, got a pension for his life,
and Burke a pension for his life and for three lives

after his own! Cumberland and Murphy, the play-
writers, were pensioners; and, in short, of the whole
mass, where has there been one, whom the people
were not compelled to pay for labours, having for
their principal object the deceiving and enslaving
of that same people? It is, therefore, the duty of
every father, when he puts a book into the hands of
his son or daughter, to give the reader a true account
of who and what the writer of the book was, or is.

314. If a boy be intended for any particular
calling, he ought, of course, to be induced to read
books relating to that calling, if such books there be;
and, therefore, I shall not be more particular on that
head. But, there are certain things, that all men in
the middle rank of life, ought to know something of,
because the knowledge will be a source of pleasure;
and because the want of it must, very frequently,
give them pain, by making them appear inferior, in
point of mind, to many who are, in fact, their inferiors in that respect. These things are grammar,
arithmetic, history, accompanied with geography.
Without these, a man, in the middle rank of life,
however able he may be in his calling, makes but an
awkward figure. Without grammar he cannot, with
safety to his character as a well-informed man, put
his thoughts upon paper; nor can he be sure, that
he is speaking with propriety. How many clever men
have I known, full of natural talent, eloquent by
nature, replete with everything calculated to give
them weight in society; and yet having little or no
weight, merely because unable to put correctly upon
paper that which they have in their minds! For me

not to say that I deem my " English Grammar " the best book for teaching this science, would be affectation, and neglect of duty besides; because I know that it is the best; because I wrote it for the purpose; and because, hundreds and hundreds of men and women have told me, some verbally, and some by letter, that, though (many of them) at grammar-schools for years, they really never knew anything of grammar until they studied my book. I, who know well all the difficulties that I experienced when I read books upon this subject, can easily believe this, and especially when I think of the numerous instances in which I have seen university scholars unable to write English with any tolerable degree of correctness. In this book, the principles are so clearly explained, that the disgust arising from intricacy is avoided; and it is this disgust that is the great and mortal enemy of acquiring knowledge.

315. With regard to arithmetic, it is a branch of learning absolutely necessary to every one, who has any pecuniary transactions beyond those arising out of the expenditure of his week's wages. All the books on this subject that I had ever seen, were so bad, so destitute of everything calculated to lead the mind into a knowledge of the matter, so void of principles, and so evidently tending to puzzle and disgust the learner, by their sententious, and crabbed, and quaint, and almost hieroglyphical definitions, that I, at one time, had the intention of writing a little work on the subject myself. It was put off, from one cause or another; but a little work on the subject has been, partly at my suggestion, written and published by

Mr. Thomas Smith of Liverpool, and is sold by
Messrs. Longman & Co., in London. The author
has great ability, and a perfect knowledge of his
subject. It is a book of principles; and any young
person of common capacity will learn more from it
in a week, than from all the other books, that I ever
saw on the subject, in a twelvemonth.

316. While the foregoing studies are proceeding,
though they very well afford a relief to each other,
history may serve as a relaxation, particularly during
the study of grammar, which is an undertaking requiring patience and time. Of all history, that of our
own country is of the most importance; because, for
want of a thorough knowledge of what has been, we
are, in many cases, at a loss to account for what is,
and still more at a loss, to be able to show what
ought to be. The difference between history and
romance is this; that that which is narrated in the
latter leaves in the mind nothing which it can apply
to present or future circumstances and events; while
the former, when it is what it ought to be, leaves the
mind stored with arguments for experience, applicable, at all times, to the actual affairs of life. The
history of a country ought to show the origin and
progress of its institutions, political, civil, and
ecclesiastical; it ought to show the effects of those
institutions upon the state of the people; it ought to
delineate the measures of the government at the
several epochs; and, having clearly described the
state of the people at the several periods, it ought to
show the cause of their freedom, good morals, and
happiness; or of their misery, immorality, and

slavery; and this, too, by the production of indubitable facts, and of inferences so manifestly fair, as to
leave not the smallest doubt upon the mind.

317. Do the histories of England, which we have,
answer this description? They are very little better
than romances. Their contents are generally confined to narrations relating to battles, negotiations,
intrigues, contests between rival sovereignties, rival
nobles, and to the character of kings, queens,
mistresses, bishops, ministers, and the like; from
scarcely any of which can the reader draw any
knowledge which is at all applicable to the circumstances of the present day.

318. Besides this, there is the falsehood; and the
falsehoods contained in these histories where shall
we find anything to surpass? Let us take one instance. They all tell us that William the Conqueror
knocked down twenty-six parish churches, and laid
waste the parishes in order to make the New Forest;
and this in a tract of the very poorest land in England,
where the churches must then have stood at about
one mile and two hundred yards from each other.
The truth is, that all the churches are still standing
that were there when William landed, and the whole
story is a sheer falsehood from the beginning to the
end.

319. But, this is a mere specimen of these romances; and that, too, with regard to a matter comparatively unimportant to us. The important falsehoods are, those which misguide us by statement or by
inference, with regard to the state of the people at
the several epochs, as produced by the institutions

of the country, or the measures of the government.
It is always the object of those who have power in
their hands, to persuade the people that they are
better off than their forefathers were: it is the great
business of history to show how this matter stands;
and, with respect to this great matter, what are we
to learn from anything that has hitherto been called
a history of England! I remember, that, about a
dozen years ago, I was talking with a very clever
young man, who had read twice or thrice over the
History of England, by different authors; and that
I gave the conversation a turn that drew from him,
unperceived by himself, that he did not know how
tithes, parishes, poor-rates, church-rates, and the
abolition of trial by jury in hundreds of cases, came
to be in England; and, that he had not the smallest
idea of the manner in which the Duke of Bedford
came to possess the power of taxing our cabbages
in Covent Garden. Yet, this is history. I have done
a great deal, with regard to matters of this sort, in
my famous " History of the Protestant Reformation; " for I may truly call that famous, which has
been translated and published in all the modern
languages.

320. But, it is reserved for me to write a complete
history of the country from the earliest times to the
present day; and this, God giving me life and health,
I shall begin to do in monthly numbers, beginning
on the first of September, and in which I shall endeavour to combine brevity with clearness. We do
not want to consume our time over a dozen pages
about Edward the Third dancing at a ball, picking

up a lady's garter, and making that garter the foundation of an order of knighthood, bearing the motto of " Honi soit qui mal y pense." It is not stuff like this; but we want to know what was the state of the people; what were a labourer's wages; what were the prices of the food, and how the labourers were dressed in the reign of that great king. What is a young person to imbibe from a history of England, as it is called, like that of Goldsmith? It is a little romance to amuse children; and the other historians have given us larger romances to amuse lazy persons who are grown up. To destroy the effects of these, and to make the people know what their country has been, will be my object; and this, I trust, I shall effect. We are, it is said, to have a history of England from Sir James Mackintosh; a History of Scotland from Sir Walter Scott; and a History of Ireland from Tommy Moore, the luscious poet. A Scotch lawyer, who is a pensioner, and a member for Knaresborough, which is well known to the Duke of Devonshire, who has the great tithes of twenty parishes in Ireland, will, doubtless, write a most impartial History of England, and particularly as far as relates to boroughs and tithes. A Scotch romance-writer, who, under the name of Malagrowther, wrote a pamphlet to prove that one-pound notes were the cause of riches to Scotland, will write, to be sure, a most instructive History of Scotland. And, from the pen of an Irish poet, who is a sinecure placeman, and a protégé of an English peer that has immense parcels of Irish confiscated estates, what a beautiful history shall we not then have of unfortunate Ireland! Oh, no! We are not going to be content with stuff such as these men will bring out. Hume and Smollett and Robertson have cheated us long enough. We are not in a humour to be cheated any longer.

321. Geography is taught at schools, if we believe the school cards. The scholars can tell you all about the divisions of the earth, and this is very well for persons who have leisure to indulge their curiosity; but it does seem to me monstrous that a young person's time should be spent in ascertaining the boundaries of Persia or China, knowing nothing all the while about the boundaries, the rivers, the soil, the products, or of the anything else of Yorkshire or Devonshire. The first thing in geography is to know that of the country in which we live, especially that in which we were born: I have now seen almost every hill and valley in it with my own eyes; nearly every city and every town, and no small part of the whole of the villages. I am therefore qualified to give an account of the country; and that account, under the title of " Geographical Dictionary of England and Wales," I am now having printed as a companion to my history.

322. When a young man well understands the geography of his own country; when he has referred to maps on this smaller scale; when, in short, he knows all about his own country, and is able to apply his knowledge to useful purposes, he may look at other countries, and particularly at those, the powers or measures of which are likely to affect his own country. It is of great importance to us to be well acquainted with the extent of France, the United

States, Portugal, Spain, Mexico, Turkey and Russia; but what need we care about the tribes of Asia and Africa, the condition of which can affect us no more than we would be affected by anything that is passing in the moon?

323. When people have nothing useful to do, they may indulge their curiosity; but, merely to read books, is not to be industrious, is not to study, and is not the way to become learned. Perhaps there are none more lazy, or more truly ignorant, than your everlasting readers. A book is an admirable excuse for sitting still; and a man who has constantly a newspaper, a magazine, a review, or some book or other in his hand, gets, at last, his head stuffed with such a jumble, that he knows not what to think about anything. An empty coxcomb, that wastes his time in dressing, strutting, or strolling about, and picking his teeth, is certainly a most despicable creature, but scarcely less so than a mere reader of books, who is, generally, conceited, thinks himself wiser than other men, in proportion to the number of leaves that he has turned over. In short, a young man should bestow his time upon no book, the contents of which he cannot apply to some useful purpose.

324. Books of travel, of biography, natural history, and particularly such as relate to agriculture and horticulture, are all proper, when leisure is afforded for them; and the two last are useful to a very great part of mankind; but, unless the subjects treated of are of some interest to us in our affairs, no time should be wasted upon them, when there are so many duties demanded at our hands by our families and our

country. A man may read books for ever, and be an ignorant creature at last, and even the more ignorant for his reading.

325. And, with regard to young women, everlasting book-reading is absolutely a vice. When they once get into the habit, they neglect all other matters, and, in some cases, even their very dress. Attending to the affairs of the house: to the washing, the baking, the brewing, the preservation and cooking of victuals, the management of the poultry and the garden; these are their proper occupations. It is said (with what truth I know not) of the present Queen (wife of William IV), that she was an active, excellent manager of her house. Impossible to bestow on her greater praise; and I trust that her example will have its due effect on the young women of the present day, who stand, but too generally, in need of that example.

326. The great fault of the present generation is, that, in all ranks, the notions of self-importance are too high. This has arisen from causes not visible to many, but the consequences are felt by all, and that, too, with great severity. There has been a general sublimating going on for many years. Not to put the word Esquire before the name of almost any man who is not a mere labourer or artisan, is almost an affront. Every merchant, every master manufacturer, every dealer, if at all rich, is an Esquire; squires' sons must be gentlemen, and squires' wives and daughters ladies. If this were all; if it were merely a ridiculous misapplication of words, the evil would not be great; but unhappily, words lead to acts and produce things;

and the " young gentleman " is not easily to be moulded into a tradesman or a working farmer. And yet the world is too small to hold so many gentlemen and ladies. How many thousands of young men have, at this moment, cause to lament that they are not carpenters, or masons, or tailors, or shoemakers; and how many thousands of those, that they have been bred up to wish to disguise their honest and useful, and therefore honourable, calling! Rousseau observes, that men are happy, first, in proportion to their virtue, and next, in proportion to their independence; and that, of all mankind, the artisan, or craftsman, is the most independent; because he carries about, in his own hands and person, the means of gaining his livelihood, and that the more common the use of the articles on which he works, the more perfect his independence. " Where," says he, " there is one man that stands in need of the talents of the dentist, there are a hundred thousand that want those of the people who supply the matter for the teeth to work on; and for one who wants a sonnet to regale his fancy, there are a million clamouring for men to make or mend their shoes." Aye, and this is the reason why shoemakers are proverbially the most independent part of the people, and why they, in general, show more public spirit than any other men. He who lives by a pursuit, be it what it may, which does not require a considerable degree of bodily labour, must, from the nature of things, be, more or less, a dependent; and this is, indeed, the price which he pays for his exemption from that bodily labour. He may arrive at riches or fame, or both; and this chance he sets against the certainty of independence in humbler life. There always have been, there always will be, and there always ought to be, some men to take this chance: but to do this has become the fashion, and a fashion it is the most fatal that ever seized upon a community.

327. With regard to young women, too, to sing, to play on instruments of music, to draw, to speak French, and the like, are very agreeable qualifications; but why should they all be musicians, and painters, and linguists? Why all of them? Who, then, is there left to take care of the houses of farmers and traders? But there is something in these " accomplishments " worse than this; namely, that they think themselves too high for farmers and traders: and this, in fact, they are; much too high; and, therefore, the servant-girls step in and supply their place. If they could see their own interest, surely they would drop this lofty tone, and these lofty airs. It is, however, the fault of the parents, and particularly of the father, whose duty it is to prevent them from imbibing such notions, and to show them, that the greatest honour they ought to aspire to is, thorough skill and care in the economy of a house. We are all apt to set too high a value on what we ourselves have done; and I may do this; but I do firmly believe, that to cure any young woman of this fatal sublimation, she has only patiently to read my " Cottage Economy," written with an anxious desire to promote domestic skill and ability in that sex, on whom so much of the happiness of man must always depend. A lady in

Worcestershire told me, that until she read " Cottage Economy " she had never baked in the house, and had seldom had good beer; that, ever since, she had looked after both herself; that the pleasure she had derived from it was equal to the profit, and that the latter was very great. She said, that the article " on baking bread," was the part that roused her to the undertaking; and, indeed, if the facts and arguments there made use of, failed to stir her up to action, she must have been stone dead to the power of words.

328. After the age that we have now been supposing, boys and girls become men and women; and, there now only remains for the father to act towards them with impartiality. If they be numerous, or, indeed, if they be only two in number, to expect perfect harmony to reign amongst, or between, them, is to be unreasonable; because experience shows us, that, even amongst the most sober, most virtuous, and most sensible, harmony so complete is very rare. By nature they are rivals for the affection and applause of the parents; in personal and mental endowments they become rivals; and, when pecuniary interests come to be well understood and to have their weight, here is a rivalship, to prevent which from ending in hostility, require more affection and greater disinterestedness than fall to the lot of one out of one hundred families. So many instances have I witnessed of good and amiable families living in harmony, till the hour arrived for dividing property amongst them, and then, all at once, becoming hostile to each other, that I have often thought that property, coming in such a way, was a curse, and that the parties would

have been far better off, had the parent had merely a blessing to bequeath them from his or her lips, instead of a will for them to dispute and wrangle over.

329. With regard to this matter, all that the father can do, is to be impartial; but, impartiality does not mean positive equality in the distribution, but equality in proportion to the different deserts of the parties, their different wants, their different pecuniary circumstances, and different prospects in life; and these vary so much, in different families, that it is impossible to lay down any general rule upon the subject. But there is one fatal error, against which every father ought to guard his heart; and the kinder that heart is, the more necessary such guardianship. I mean the fatal error of heaping upon one child, to the prejudice of the rest; or, upon a part of them. This partiality sometimes arises from mere caprice; sometimes from the circumstance of the favourite being more favoured by nature than the rest; sometimes from the nearer resemblance to himself, that the father sees in the favourite; and, sometimes, from the hope of preventing the favoured party from doing that which would disgrace the parent. All these motives are highly censurable, but the last is the most general, and by far the most mischievous in its effect. How many fathers have been ruined, how many mothers and families brought to beggary, how many industrious and virtuous groups have been pulled down from competence to penury, from the desire to prevent one from bringing shame on the parent! So that, contrary to every principle of justice, the bad is rewarded for the badness; and the good

punished for the goodness. Natural affection, remembrance of infantine endearments, reluctance to abandon long-cherished hopes, compassion for the sufferings of your own flesh and blood, the dread of fatal consequences from your adhering to justice; all these beat at your heart, and call on you to give way: but, you must resist them all; or, your ruin, and that of the rest of your family, are decreed. Suffering is the natural and just punishment of idleness, drunkenness, squandering, and an indulgence in the society of prostitutes; and, never did the world behold an instance of an offender, in this way, reclaimed but by the infliction of this punishment: particularly if the society of prostitutes made part of the offence; for, here is something that takes the heart from you. Nobody ever yet saw, and nobody ever will see, a young man linked to a prostitute, and retain, at the same time, any, even the smallest, degree of affection for parents or brethren. You may supplicate, you may implore, you may leave yourself penniless, and your virtuous children without bread; the invisible cormorant will still call for more; and, as we saw, only the other day, a wretch was convicted of having, at the instigation of his prostitute, beaten his aged mother, to get from her the small remains of the means necessary to provide her with food. In Heron's collection of God's judgments on wicked acts, it is related of an unnatural son, who fed his aged father upon orts and offal, lodged him in a filthy and crazy garret, and clothed him in sackcloth, while he and his wife and children lived in luxury; that, having bought sackcloth enough for two dresses

for his father, his children took away the part not
made up and hid it, and that, upon asking them what
they could do this for, they told him that they meant
to keep it for him, when he should become old and
walk with a stick! This, the author relates, pierced
his heart; and, indeed, if this failed, he must have
had the heart of a tiger; but even this would not
succeed with the associate of a prostitute. When this
vice, this love of the society of prostitutes; when this
vice has once got fast hold, vain are all your sacrifices, vain your prayers, vain your hopes, vain your
anxious desire to disguise the shame from the world;
and, if you have acted well your part, no part of that
shame falls on you, unless you have administered to
the cause of it. Your authority has ceased; the voice
of the prostitute, or the charms of the bottle, or the
rattle of the dice, has been more powerful than your
advice and example: you must lament this: but, it is
not to bow you down; and, above all things, it is
weak, and even criminally selfish to sacrifice the rest
of your family, in order to keep from the world the
knowledge of that, which, if known, would, in your
view of the matter, bring shame on yourself.

330. Let me hope, however, that this is a calamity
which will befall very few good fathers; and that, of
all such, the sober, industrious, and frugal habits of
their children, their dutiful demeanour, their truth
and their integrity, will come to smooth the path of
their downward days, and be the objects on which
their eyes will close. Those children must, in their
turn, travel the same path; and they may be assured,
that, " Honour thy father and thy mother, that thy

days may be long in the land," is a precept, a disregard of which never yet failed, either first or last, to bring its punishment. And, what can be more just than that signal punishment should follow such a crime; a crime directly against the voice of nature itself? Youth has its passions, and due allowance justice will make for these; but, are the delusions of the boozer, the gamester, or the harlot, to be pleaded in excuse for a disregard of the source of your existence? Are those to be pleaded in apology for giving pain to the father who has toiled half a lifetime in order to feed and clothe you, and to the mother whose breast has been to you the fountain of life? Go, you, and shake the hand of the boon-companion; take the greedy harlot to your arms; mock at the tears of your tender and anxious parents; and, when your purse is empty and your complexion faded, receive the poverty and the scorn due to your base ingratitude!

LETTER VI

ADVICE TO A CITIZEN

331. HAVING now given my advice to the Youth, the grown-up Man, the Lover, the Husband and the Father, I shall, in this concluding Letter, tender my advice to the Citizen, in which capacity every man has rights to enjoy and duties to perform, and these too of importance not inferior to those which belong to him, or are imposed upon him, as son, parent, husband or father. The word citizen is not, in its application, confined to the mere inhabitants of cities: it means, a member of a civil society, or community; and, in order to have a clear comprehension of man's rights and duties in this capacity, we must take a look at the origin of civil communities.

332. Time was when the inhabitants of this island, for instance, laid claim to all things in it, without the words owner or property being known. God had given to all the people all the land and all the trees, and everything else, just as He has given the burrows and the grass to the rabbits, and the bushes and the berries to the birds; and each man had the good things of this world in a greater or less degree in proportion to his skill, his strength and his valour. This is what is called living under the law of nature; that is to say, the law of self-preservation

and self-enjoyment, without any restraint imposed by a regard for the good of our neighbours.

333. In process of time, no matter from what cause, men made amongst themselves a compact, or an agreement, to divide the land and its products in such a manner that each should have a share to his own exclusive use, and that each man should be protected in the exclusive enjoyment of his share by the united power of the rest; and, in order to insure the due and certain application of this united power, the whole of the people agreed to be bound by regulations, called laws. Thus arose civil society; thus arose property; thus arose the words mine and thine. One man became possessed of more good things than another, because he was more industrious, more skilful, more careful, or more frugal: so that labour, of one sort or another, was the basis of all property.

334. In what manner civil societies proceeded in providing for the making of laws and for the enforcing of them; the various ways in which they took measures to protect the weak against the strong; how they have gone to work to secure wealth against the attacks of poverty; these are subjects that it would require volumes to detail: but these truths are written on the heart of man: that all men are, by nature, equal; that civil society can never have arisen from any motive other than that of the benefit of the whole; that, whenever civil society makes the greater part of the people worse off than they were under the law of nature, the civil compact is, in conscience, dissolved, and all the rights of nature return; that,

in civil society, the rights and the duties go hand in hand, and that, when the former are taken away, the latter cease to exist.

335. Now, then, in order to act well our part, as citizens, or members of the community, we ought clearly to understand what our rights are; for, on our enjoyment of these depend our duties, rights going before duties, as value received goes before payment. I know well, that just the contrary of this is taught in our political schools, where we are told that our first duty is to obey the laws; and it is not many years ago, that Horsley, Bishop of Rochester, told us, that the people had nothing to do with the laws but to obey them. The truth is, however, that the citizen's first duty is to maintain his rights, as it is the purchaser's first duty to receive the thing for which he has contracted.

336. Our rights in society are numerous; the right of enjoying life and property; the right of exerting our physical and mental powers in an innocent manner; but, the great right of all, and without which there is, in fact, no right, is, the right of taking a part in the making of the laws by which we are governed. This right is founded in that law of nature spoken of above; it springs out of the very principle of civil society; for what compact, what agreement, what common assent, can possibly be imagined by which men would give up all the rights of nature, all the free enjoyment of their bodies and their minds, in order to subject themselves to rules and laws, in the making of which they should have nothing to say, and which should be enforced upon them without

their assent? The great right, therefore, of every man, the right of rights, is the right of having a share in the making of the laws, to which the good of the whole makes it his duty to submit.

337. With regard to the means of enabling every man to enjoy this share, they have been different, in different countries, and, in the same countries, at different times. Generally it has been, and in great communities it must be, by the choosing of a few to speak and act in behalf of the many: and, as there will hardly ever be perfect unanimity amongst men assembled for any purpose whatever, where fact and argument are to decide the question, the decision is left to the majority, the compact being that the decision of the majority shall be that of the whole. Minors are excluded from this right, because the law considers them as infants, because it makes the parent answerable for civil damages committed by them, and because of their legal incapacity to make any compact. Women are excluded because husbands are answerable in law for their wives, as to their civil damages, and because the very nature of their sex makes the exercise of this right incompatible with the harmony and happiness of society. Men stained with indelible crimes are excluded, because they have forfeited their right by violating the laws, to which their assent has been given. Insane persons are excluded, because they are dead in the eye of the law, because the law demands no duty at their hands, because they cannot violate the law, because the law cannot affect them; and, therefore, they ought to have no hand in making it.

338. But, with these exceptions, where is the ground whereon to maintain that any man ought to be deprived of this right, which he derives directly from the law of nature, and which springs, as I said before, out of the same source with civil society itself? Am I told, that property ought to confer this right? Property sprang from labour, and not labour from property; so that if there were to be a distinction here, it ought to give the preference to labour. All men are equal by nature; nobody denies that they ought to be equal in the eye of the law; but, how are they to be thus equal if the law begin by suffering some to enjoy this right and refusing the enjoyment to others? It is the duty of every man to defend his country against an enemy, a duty imposed by the law of nature as well as by that of civil society, and without the recognition of this duty, there could exist no independent nation, and no civil society. Yet, how are you to maintain that this is the duty of every man, if you deny to some men the enjoyment of a share in making the laws? Upon what principle are you to contend for equality here, while you deny its existence as to the right of sharing in the making of the laws? The poor man has a body and a soul as well as the rich man; like the latter, he has parents, wife, and children; a bullet or a sword is as deadly to him as to the rich man; there are hearts to ache and tears to flow for him as well as for the squire or the lord or the loan-monger: yet, notwithstanding this equality, he is to risk all, and, if he escape, he is still to be denied an equality of rights! If, in such a state of things, the artisan, or labourer, when called

out to fight in defence of his country, were to answer:
" Why should I risk my life? I have no possession
but my labour; no enemy will take that from me;
you, the rich, possess all the land and all its products;
you make what laws you please without my partici-
pation or assent; you punish me at your pleasure;
you say that my want of property excludes me from
the right of having a share in the making of the laws;
you say that the property that I have in my labour
is nothing worth; on what ground, then, do you
call on me to risk my life?" If, in such a case, such
questions were put, the answer is very difficult to be
imagined.

339. In cases of civil commotion, the matter comes
still more home to us. On what ground is the rich
man to call the artisan from his shop, or the labourer
from the field, to join the sheriff's posse or the
militia, if he refuse to the labourer and artisan the
right of sharing in the making of the laws? Why are
they to risk their lives here? To uphold the laws, and
to protect property. What! laws, in the making of, or
assenting to, which they have been allowed to have
no share? Property, of which they are said to possess
none? What! compel men to come forth and risk
their lives for the protection of property; and then,
in the same breath, tell them, that they are not
allowed to share in the making of the laws, because,
and only because, they have no property! Not
because they have committed any crime; not
because they are idle or profligate; not because they
are vicious in any way; but solely because they have
no property; and yet, at the same time, compel them

to come forth and risk their lives for the protection of property!

340. But, the paupers? Ought they to share in the making of the laws? And why not? What is a pauper; what is one of the men to whom this degrading appellation is applied? A very poor man; a man who is, from some cause or other, unable to supply himself with food and raiment without aid from the parish-rates. And, is that circumstance alone to deprive him of his right, a right of which he stands more in need than any other man? Perhaps he has, for many years of his life, contributed directly to those rates; and ten thousand to one he has, by his labour, contributed to them indirectly. The aid which, under such circumstances, he receives, is his right; he receives it not as an alms: he is no mendicant; he begs not; he comes to receive that which the laws of the country award him in lieu of the larger portion assigned him by the law of nature. Pray mark that, and let it be deeply engraven on your memory. The audacious and merciless Malthus (a parson of the Church establishment) recommended, some years ago, the passing of a law to put an end to the giving of parish relief, though he recommended no law to put an end to the enormous taxes paid by poor people. In his book he said, that the poor should be left to the law of nature, which, in case of their having nothing to buy food with, doomed them to starve. They would ask nothing better than to be left to the law of nature; that law which knows nothing about buying food or anything else; that law which bids the hungry and the naked take food and raiment

wherever you find it best and nearest at hand; that law which awards all possessions to the strongest; that law the operations of which would clear out the London meat-markets and the drapers' and jewellers' shops in about half an hour: to this law the parson wished the Parliament to leave the poorest of the working-people; but, if the Parliament had done it, it would have been quickly seen that this law was far from " dooming them to be starved."

341. Trusting that it is unnecessary for me to express a hope, that barbarous thoughts like those of Malthus and his tribe will never be entertained by any young man who has read the previous Letters of this work, let me return to my very, very poor man, and ask, whether it be consistent with justice, with humanity, with reason, to deprive a man of the most precious of his political rights, because, and only because, he has been, in a pecuniary way, singularly unfortunate? The Scripture says, " Despise not the poor, because he is poor;" that is to say, despise him not on account of his poverty. Why, then, deprive him of his right; why put him out of the pale of the law, on account of his poverty? There are some men, to be sure, who are reduced to poverty by their vices, by idleness, by gaming, by drinking, by squandering; but, the far greater part by bodily ailments, by misfortunes to the effects of which all men may, without any fault and even without any folly, be exposed; and, is there a man on earth so cruelly unjust as to wish to add to the sufferings of such persons by stripping them of their political rights? How many thousands of industrious and virtuous men have, within these

few years, been brought down from a state of competence to that of pauperism! And, is it just to strip
such men of their rights, merely because they are
thus brought down? When I was at Ely, last spring,
there were, in that neighbourhood, three paupers
cracking stones on the roads, who had all three been,
not only ratepayers, but overseers of the poor within
seven years of the day when I was there. Is there any
man so barbarous as to say, that these men ought,
merely on account of their misfortunes, to be deprived
of their political rights? Their right to receive relief
is as perfect as any right of property; and, would you,
merely because they claim this right, strip them of
another right? To say no more of the injustice and
the cruelty, is there reason, is there common sense
in this? What! if a farmer or a tradesman be, by
flood or by fire, so totally ruined as to be compelled,
surrounded by his family, to resort to the parish-
book, would you break the last heart-string of such
a man by making him feel the degrading loss of his
political rights?

342. Here, young man of sense and of spirit; here is
the point on which you are to take your stand. There
are always men enough to plead the cause of the
rich; enough and enough to echo the woes of the
fallen great; but, be it your part to show compassion
for those who labour, and to maintain their rights.
Poverty is not a crime, and though it sometimes
arises from faults, it is not, even in that case, to be
visited by punishment beyond that which it brings
with itself. Remember, that poverty is decreed by the
very nature of man. The Scripture says, that " the

poor shall never cease from out of the land;" that is to say, that there shall always be some very poor people. This is inevitable from the very nature of things. It is necessary to the existence of mankind, that a very large portion of every people should live by manual labour; and, as such labour is pain, more or less, and as no living creature likes pain, it must be, that the far greater part of labouring people will endure only just as much of this pain as is absolutely necessary to the supply of their daily wants. Experience says that this has always been, and reason and nature tell us that this must always be. Therefore, when ailments, when losses, when untoward circumstances of any sort stop or diminish the daily supply, want comes; and every just government will provide, from the general stock, the means to satisfy this want.

343. Nor is the deepest poverty without its useful effects in society. To the practice of the virtues of abstinence, sobriety, care, frugality, industry, and even honesty and amiable manners and acquirement of talent, the two great motives are to get upwards in riches or fame, and to avoid going downwards to poverty, the last of which is the most powerful of the two. It is, therefore, not with contempt, but with compassion, that we should look on those, whose state is one of the decrees of nature, from whose sad example we profit, and to whom, in return, we ought to make compensation by every indulgent and kind act in our power, and particularly by a defence of their rights. To those who labour, we, who labour not with our hands, owe all that we eat, drink and wear; all that shades us by day, and that shelters us

by night; all the means of enjoying health and pleasure; and, therefore, if we possess talent for the task, we are ungrateful or cowardly, or both, if we omit any effort within our power to prevent them from being slaves; and, disguise the matter how we may, a slave, a real slave, every man is, who has no share in making the laws which he is compelled to obey.

344. What is a slave? For, let us not be amused by a name; but look well into the matter. A slave is, in the first place, a man who has no property; and property means something that he has, and that nobody can take from him without his leave, or consent. Whatever man, no matter what he may call himself or anybody else may call him, can have his money or his goods taken from him by force, by virtue of an order, or ordinance, or law, which he has had no hand in making, and to which he has not given his assent, has no property, and is merely a depository of the goods from his master. A slave has no property in his labour; and any man who is compelled to give up the fruit of his labour to another, at the arbitrary will of that other, has no property in his labour, and is, therefore, a slave, whether the fruit of his labour be taken from him directly or indirectly. If it be said, that he gives up this fruit of his labour by his own will, and that it is not forced from him, I answer, To be sure he may avoid eating and drinking and may go naked; but, then he must die; and on this condition, and this condition only, can he refuse to give up the fruit of his labour. " Die, wretch, or surrender as much of your income, or the

fruit of your labour, as your masters choose to take."
This is, in fact, the language of the rulers to every
man who is refused to have a share in the making of
the laws to which he is forced to submit.

345. But, some one may say, slaves are private
property, and may be bought and sold, out and out,
like cattle. And, what is it to the slave, whether he be
property of one or of many; or, what matters it to
him, whether he pass from master to master by a sale
for an indefinite term, or be let to hire by the year,
month, or week? It is, in no case, the flesh and blood
and bones that are sold, but the labour; and, if you
actually sell the labour of man, is not that man a slave,
though you sell it only for a short time at once?
And, as to the principle, so ostentatiously displayed
in the case of the black-slave trade, that " man ought
not to have a property in man;" it is even an advantage to the slave to be private property, because the
owner has then a clear and powerful interest in the
preservation of his life, health, and strength, and will,
therefore, furnish him amply with the food and raiment necessary for these ends. Every one knows, that
public property is never so well taken care of as
private property; and this, too, on the maxim, that
" that which is everybody's business is nobody's
business." Every one knows that a rented farm is not
so well kept in heart as a farm in the hands of the
owner. And, as to punishments and restraints, what
difference is there, whether these be inflicted and
imposed by a private owner, or his overseer, or by
the agents and overseers, of a body of proprietors?
In short, if you can cause a man to be imprisoned or

whipped if he do not work enough to please you; if you can sell him by auction for a time limited; if you can forcibly separate him from his wife to prevent their having children; if you can shut him up in his dwelling-place when you please, and for as long a time as you please; if you can force him to draw a cart or waggon like a beast of draught; if you can, when the humour seizes you, and at the suggestion of your mere fears or whim, cause him to be shut up in a dungeon during your pleasure: if you can, at your pleasure, do these things to him, is it not to be impudently hypocritical to affect to call him a free man? But, after all, these may all be wanting, and yet the man may be a slave, if he be allowed to have no property; and, as I have shown, no property he can have, not even in that labour, which is not only property, but the basis of all other property, unless he have a share in making the laws to which he is compelled to submit.

346. It is said, that he may have this share virtually, though not in form and name; for that his employers may have such share, and they will, as a matter of course, act for him. This doctrine, pushed home, would make the chief of the nation the sole maker of the laws; for if the rich can thus act for the poor, why should not the chief act for the rich? This matter is very completely explained by the practice in the United States of America. There the maxim is, that every free man, with the exception of men stained with crime and men insane, has a right to have a voice in choosing those who make the laws. The number of representatives sent to the Congress

is, in each State, proportioned to the number of free people. But, as there are slaves in some of the States, these States have a certain portion of additional members on account of those slaves! Thus the slaves are represented by their owners; and this is real, practical, open, and undisguised virtual representation! No doubt that white men may be represented in the same way; for the colour of the skin is nothing; but let them be called slaves, then; let it not be pretended that they are free men; let not the word liberty be polluted by being applied to their state; let it be openly and honestly avowed as in America, that they are slaves; and then will come the question whether men ought to exist in such a state, or whether they ought to do everything in their power to rescue themselves from it.

347. If the right to have a share in making the laws were merely a feather; if it were a fanciful thing; if it were only a speculative theory; if it were but an abstract principle; on any of these suppositions, it might be considered as of little importance. But it is none of these; it is a practical matter; the want of it not only is, but must of necessity be, felt by every man who lives under that want. If it were proposed to the shopkeepers in a town, that a rich man or two, living in the neighbourhood, should have power to send, whenever they pleased, and take away as much as they pleased of the money of the shop-keepers, and apply it to what uses they please: what an outcry the shopkeepers would make! And yet, what would this be more than taxes imposed on those who have no voice in choosing the persons who im-

pose them? Who lets another man put his hand into his purse when he pleases? Who, that has the power to help himself, surrenders his goods or his money to the will of another? Has it not always been, and must it not always be, true, that, if your property be at the absolute disposal of others, your ruin is certain? And if this be, of necessity, the case amongst individuals and parts of the community, it must be the case with regard to the whole community.

348. Aye, and experience shows us that it always has been the case. The natural and inevitable consequences of a want of this right in the people have, in all countries, been taxes pressing the industrious and laborious to the earth; severe laws and standing armies to compel the people to submit to those taxes; wealth, luxury, and splendour, amongst those who make the laws and receive the taxes; poverty, misery, immorality and crime, amongst those who bear the burdens; and at last commotion, revolt, revenge, and rivers of blood. Such have always been and such must always be, the consequences of a want of this right of all men to share in the making of the laws, a right, as I have before shown, derived immediately from the law of nature, springing up out of the same source with civil society, and cherished in the heart of man by reason and by experience.

349. Well, then, this right being that, without the enjoyment of which there is, in reality, no right at all, how manifestly it is the first duty of every man to do all in his power to maintain this right where it exists, and to restore it where it has been lost! For

observe, it must, at one time, have existed in every civil community, it being impossible that it could ever be excluded by any social compact; absolutely impossible, because it is contrary to the law of self-preservation to believe, that men would agree to give up the rights of nature without stipulating for some benefit. Before we can affect to believe that this right was not reserved, in such compact, as completely as the right to live was reserved, we must affect to believe that millions of men, under no control but that of their own passions and desires, and having all the earth and its products at the command of their strength and skill, consented to be for ever, they and their posterity, the slaves of a few.

350. We cannot believe this, and therefore, without going back into history and precedents, we must believe that, in whatever civil community this right does not exist, it has been lost, or rather unjustly taken away. And then, having seen the terrible evils which always have arisen and always must arise, from the want of it; being convinced that, where lost or taken away by force or fraud, it is our very first duty to do all in our power to restore it, the next consideration is, how ought one to act in the discharge of this most sacred duty; for sacred it is, even as the duties of husband and father. For, besides the baseness of the thought of quietly submitting to be a slave oneself, we have here, besides our duty to the community, a duty to perform towards our children and our children's children. We all acknowledge that it is our bounden duty to provide, as far as our power will go, for the competence, the health, and the good

character of our children; but, is this duty superior
to that of which I am now speaking? What is competence, what is health, if the possessor be a slave, and
hold his possessions at the will of another, or others;
as he must do if destitute of the right to a share in the
making of the laws? What is competence, what is
health, if both can, at any moment, be snatched away
by the grasp or the dungeon of a master; and his
master he is who makes the laws without his partici-
pation or assent? And, as to character, as to fair fame,
when the white slave puts forward pretensions to
those, let him no longer affect to commiserate the
state of his sleek and fat brethren in Barbadoes and
Jamaica; let him hasten to mix the hair with
the wool, to blend the white with the black, and
to lose the memory of his origin amidst a dingy
generation.

351. Such, then, being the nature of the duty, how
are we to go to work in the performance of it, and
what are our means? With regard to these, so various
are the circumstances, so endless the differences in
the states of society, and so many are the cases when
it would be madness to attempt that which it would
be prudence to attempt in others, that no general
rule can be given beyond this; that, the right and
the duty being clear to our minds, the means that
are surest and swiftest are the best. In every such
case, however, the great and predominant desire
ought to be not to employ any means beyond those of
reason and persuasion, as long as the employment of
these afford a ground for rational expectation of
success. Men are, in such a case, labouring, not for

the present day only, but for ages to come; and therefore they should not slacken in their exertions, because the grave may close upon them before the day of final triumph arrive. Amongst the virtues of the good citizen are those of fortitude and patience; and, when he has to carry on his struggle against corruptions deep and widely rooted, he is not to expect the baleful tree to come down at a single blow; he must patiently remove the earth that props and feeds it, and sever the accursed roots one by one.

352. Impatience here is a very bad sign. I do not like your patriots, who, because the tree does not give way at once, fall to blaming all about them, accuse their fellow-sufferers of cowardice, because they do not do that which they themselves dare not think of doing. Such conduct argues chagrin and disappointment; and these argue a selfish feeling: they argue, that there has been more of private ambition and gain at work than of public good. Such blamers, such general accusers, are always to be suspected. What does the real patriot want more than to feel conscious that he has done his duty towards his country; and that, if life should not allow him to see his endeavours crowned with success, his children will see it? The impatient patriots are like the young men (mentioned in the beautiful fable of La Fontaine) who ridiculed the man of fourscore, who was planting an avenue of very small trees, which, they told him, that he never could expect to see as high as his head. " Well," said he, " and what of that? If their shade afford me no

pleasure, it may afford pleasure to my children, and even to you; and, therefore, the planting of them gives me pleasure."

353. It is the want of the noble disinterestedness, so beautifully expressed in this fable, that produces the impatient patriots. They wish very well to their country, because they want some of the good for themselves. Very natural that all men should wish to see the good arrive, and wish to share in it too; but, we must look on the dark side of nature to find the disposition to cast blame on the whole community because our wishes are not instantly accomplished, and especially to cast blame on others for not doing that which we ourselves dare not attempt. There is, however, a sort of patriot a great deal worse than this; he who, having failed himself, would see his country enslaved for ever, rather than see its deliverance achieved by others. His failure, has perhaps, arisen solely from his want of talent, or discretion; yet his selfish heart would wish his country sunk in everlasting degradation, lest his inefficiency for the task should be established by the success of others. A very hateful character, certainly, but, I am sorry to say, by no means rare. Envy, always associated with meanness of soul, always detestable, is never so detestable as when it shows itself here.

354. Be it your care, my young friend (and I tender you this as my parting advice), if you find this base and baleful passion, which the poet calls " the eldest born of hell;" if you find it creeping into your heart, be it your care to banish it at once and for ever; for, if once it nestle there, farewell to all the

good which nature has enabled you to do, and to your peace into the bargain. It has pleased God to make an unequal distribution of talent, of industry, or perseverance, of a capacity to labour, of all the qualities that give men distinction. We have not been our own makers; it is no fault in you that nature has placed him above you, and, surely, it is no fault in him; and would you punish him on account, and only on account, of his pre-eminence! If you have read this book you will startle with horror at the thought: you will, as to public matters, act with zeal and with good-humour, though the place you occupy be far removed from the first; you will support with the best of your abilities others, who, from whatever circumstance, may happen to take the lead; you will not suffer from the consciousness and certainty of your own superior talents to urge you to do anything which might by possibility be injurious to your country's cause; you will be forbearing under the aggressions of ignorance, conceit, arrogance, and even the blackest of ingratitude superadded, if by resenting these you endanger the general good; and, above all things, you will have the justice to bear in mind, that that country which gave you birth, is, to the last hour of your capability, entitled to your exertions in her behalf, and that you ought not, by acts of commission or of omission, to visit upon her the wrongs which may have been inflicted on you by the envy and malice of individuals. Love of one's native soil is a feeling which nature has implanted in the human breast, and that has always been peculiarly strong in the breasts of Englishmen. God has given us a country of which to be proud, and that freedom, greatness, and renown, which were handed down to us by our wise and brave forefathers, bid us perish to the last man, rather than suffer the land of their graves to become a land of slavery, impotence, and dishonour.

355. In the words with which I concluded my English Grammar, which I addressed to my son James, I conclude my advice to you. " With English and French on your tongue and in your pen, you have a resource, not only greatly valuable in itself, but a resource that you can be deprived of by none of those changes and chances which deprive men of pecuniary possessions, and which, in some cases, make the purse-proud man of yesterday a crawling sycophant to-day. Health, without which life is not worth having, you will hardly fail to secure by early rising, exercise, sobriety, and abstemiousness as to food. Happiness, or misery, is in the mind. It is the mind that lives; and the length of life ought to be measured by the number and importance of our ideas, and not by the number of our days. Never, therefore, esteem men merely on account of their riches, or their station. Respect goodness, find it where you may. Honour talent wherever you behold it unassociated with vice; but honour it most when accompanied with exertion, and especially when exerted in the cause of truth and justice; and, above all things, hold it in honour, when it steps forward to protect defenceless innocence against the attacks of powerful guilt." These words, addressed to my own son, I now, in taking my leave, address to you. Be just, be

industrious, be sober, and be happy; and the hope
that these effects will, in some degree, have been
caused by this little work, will add to the happiness
of

Your Friend and humble Servant,

WM. COBBETT.

KENSINGTON, 25*th August* 1830.